the best of enemies

the best of enemies

England v. Germany,
a century of football rivalry

david downing

BLOOMSBURY

First published in Great Britain in 2000

Copyright © 2000 by David Downing

The moral right of the author has been asserted

Bloomsbury Publishing Plc, 38 Soho Square, London, W1V 5DF

A CIP catalogue record for this book
is available from the British Library

ISBN 0 7475 4978 8

10 9 8 7 6 5 4 3 2 1

Typeset by Hewer Text Ltd, Edinburgh
Printed in Great Britain by Clays Ltd, St Ives plc

contents

author's note

This book is about Anglo–German football rivalry. I have concentrated on the twenty-three international matches played by England against either Germany or West Germany, but important matches between the two nations' clubs are also featured. No matter how much we might wish it otherwise, football never exists in a social and political vacuum, and Anglo–German football relations have been given a particular edge by their twentieth-century contexts. These too I have examined, if only to make sense of chants like 'two World Wars, one World Cup'.

I am English and the book naturally reflects that fact, but I am also inclined to agree with Samuel Johnson's assertion that 'patriotism is the last refuge of the scoundrel'. Anyone seeking to bask in the triumphs and righteously rail at the misfortunes of England's football teams should probably look elsewhere for their inspiration. While there are English triumphs in this story there are also many failures, and the latter have tended to predominate in recent years. I would love to see an England team playing beautiful football, but my primary loyalty so far as writing this book was concerned was to football as it can and should be played.

I would like to thank David Platt for freely giving up some of his valuable time, a gesture which grew increasingly generous in the light of the extortionate interview fees demanded by other ex-England players. I would especially like to thank Ulrich Matheja of *Kicker* magazine, who spent two hours in their Nuremberg offices helping to fill many of the yawning gaps in my knowledge of German football history. Thanks also to David Reynolds and Mike Jones at Bloomsbury, and to everyone else I've talked football with over the last forty years.

David Downing, June 2000.

1: dribbling through no man's land

Only thirty-eight days remained of the nineteenth century when a party of youngish, fit-looking men could be seen assembling at the South-Eastern & Chatham Railway's Holborn Viaduct terminus for the departure of their Continental boat-train. These were the cream of England's footballers, selected by the Football Association from the ranks of both amateurs and professionals, and they were off to play against the Germans for the very first time.

While some of the players joked and chatted to the large farewell party, others scanned their newspapers for the latest news from the Boer War, now more than a month old and not going particularly well for the Empire. A few men doubtless walked down the platform to inspect the locomotive which would pull their train on the first leg of the day-long journey to Berlin. Trains, after all, were still the most glamorous form of public transport. The first few motor buses were only just appearing in the streets of London, and to reach Holborn Viaduct that morning the players would have relied on a combination of Underground trains, horse-drawn cabs and their own feet.

The squad of fourteen for the four-game tour had been announced a week earlier. It included C. Wreford-Brown (Corinthians, capt.), G.P. Wilson (Corinthians), H.R. Barrett (Corinthians), W.H. Waller (Richmond), E.D. Brown (Clapton), Stanley Briggs (Clapton), Bach (Sunderland), Needham (Sheffield United), Crabtree (Aston Villa), Cox (Derby County), Bassett (West Bromwich Albion), Chadwick (Burnley), Rogers (Newcastle United) and Fred Forman (Notts Forest). The strange mixture of surnames with and without accompanying initials was no accident. Professionals, as a lesser breed of human beings, were not granted the accolade of a Christian name unless there was a risk of confusing them with other players carrying the same surname.

In the event, C. Wreford-Brown, H.R. Barrett and Needham had not proved fit enough to travel and their places had been taken by O. Wreford-Brown (Old Carthusians), S.S. Taylor (Corinthians) and Holt (Everton). Of course, no one seriously entertained the possibility that this weakening of the team would make any difference to the results. The Germans had only recently taken up the game and could hardly be expected to offer more than token opposition for many years to come.

This optimism proved to be well founded. The first game between the two representative elevens – these were not official internationals – took place at the Berlin Athletic sports ground on Thursday 23 November 1899. Though the English party had been delighted by the warmth of their reception in Germany, on the pitch they showed no inclination to spare their hosts any embarrassment. *The Times* noted that 'a strong wind blowing across the ground hampered the scoring', but the English side were probably happy with the thirteen they scored. The Germans began well enough, 'rushing the ball dangerously near the visitors' goal', but some brilliant dribbling by Bassett soon showed them who the true masters were. The first goal was headed in from one of his centres, and although the Germans managed to equalise a few minutes later the English then scored five times in succession.

In the second half the Germans were 'seen to less advantage', scoring one goal to the Englishmen's eight. *The Times* noted that the hosts, though 'fairly fast', 'lacked combination and were quite outmatched'. The *Manchester Guardian* writer may have misread the same Reuter report – he substituted the more robust 'out-manned' for outmatched.

The English team were entertained at dinner after the game but showed no ill-effects the following morning, when the second fixture of the tour was played. This time they won 10–2. A dribble down the centre by Newcastle's Rogers set up the first goal after ten minutes, and by half-time the score was 6–1. Rogers went on to score five; Taylor, Wilson and Forman were also singled out for praise.

After lunch the party took the train south to Prague, then merely a provincial capital in the Austro-Hungarian Empire, and on the following afternoon played their third match in three days. This time the opposition eleven represented both Germany and Austria, and the English were restricted to eight goals without reply. According to the *Manchester Guardian* the Austro-German forwards were also let down by their lack of combination, but the defence and goalkeeper were both judged 'excellent'. Conceding eight goals to the English was obviously considered – in England at least – a quite respectable result.

The squad travelled back across southern Germany to the Rhine town of Karlsruhe for their final match. It was probably here (some claim it was in Berlin) that Bassett poked fun at the German man-to-man marking by leading his own shadow off the pitch, around the back of the goal and back on to it again. The English won by eight goals to nil for the second successive match and travelled back home by train and boat secure in the knowledge of their superiority. The Boers might be calling the British Army's credentials into question in distant South Africa, but no one could claim that the Continentals were mounting a comparable challenge on the football pitch.

More evidence was offered twenty-two months later, when a German party came to play two matches in England. The Boer War was still dragging on towards its inevitable conclusion, but Queen Victoria had died in the intervening period and relations between Germany and England, which had apparently been improving at the time of the English tour, were now decidedly edgy. This time the English had split up the amateurs and professionals; the Germans would play the former at Tottenham's new White Hart Lane home on Saturday 21 September 1901 and the latter at Manchester City's Hyde Road ground on the following Wednesday.

Only goalkeeper W.H. Waller survived from the amateurs who had visited Germany two years before, but there was little change in the margin of victory. On a wet day a sizable crowd of 6000 watched the English score twelve without reply. Inside-right Reginald Foster scored six, and his fellow forwards all scored at least once. The *Times* correspondent thought it might have been more, 'had not the Englishmen played a nice leisurely game that spelled no exertion'. It was a 'luxury' he added, 'in these days of leagues', to see a match 'played in such a splendid spirit of sportsmanship'.

The Times carried quite a full account of this game; the second, however, played in Manchester by those professionals who made up the down-market 'leagues', received much shorter shrift – a mere thirty-five words. The locally based *Manchester Guardian* was more fulsome but no kinder. After the match at Tottenham its correspondent had relayed the German list of excuses for their poor performance – the lingering effects of the sea voyage, the slippery ground, unsuitable boots – without sounding particularly convinced, and the visitors were now informed in best headmasterly fashion that an improvement was expected. 'At Manchester these troubles will not count,' he told the Germans. 'One hopes', he concluded imperiously, 'that the visitors will be able to take the field free from all such unfortunate handicaps.'

The state of the Hyde Road pitch – 'so dry that the top dressing rose like dust disturbed by sliding boots' – did not encourage any marked improvement in the German play, and after only five minutes it was clear that the two sides were hopelessly mismatched. Wolves' Woolridge scored four goals, Derby's Steve Bloomer a mere hat-trick, and the English team won 10–0.

The visitors, though welcomed by German music from the St Joseph's Industrial School band and treated to the sight of their imperial flag floating proudly above the grandstand, seemed less than enthusiastic in their approach, and quickly settled for 'swarming in front of the goal and making targets of their bodies' to keep down the number of goals conceded. They were neither busy nor skilful. 'If theirs is to be taken as representative German football,' the *Guardian* commented, 'one may safely conclude that abroad they have yet to learn what, in another connection, is here called "the rigour of the game".' As for skill, the Germans' 'crude efforts towards combination' had demonstrated all too obviously 'their inability to play what, for want of a better term, is called "the scientific game"'. Outfought and outplayed, their only hero was goalkeeper Lüdecke, who had saved them from an even more crushing defeat.

In footballing terms the Germans at this time were about twenty years behind the British. The game had only really taken hold in Bismarck's empire in the early 1880s, and much of its early encouragement had come from British members of the German academic and business communities. These missionaries of sport had also proselytised for cricket and rugby, but Germans from all sections of society took much more readily to the big round ball. According to FA Secretary Sir Frederick Wall the royal House of Hohenzollern thought it 'an admirable form of body culture'. Some of the young princes had taken up the game 'with the thoroughness that is characteristic of the German'.

The Kaiser's army liked it too. Writing in 1910, R.M. Berry noted that football was 'regarded by many of the younger generation of German officers as one of the best outdoor sports for cultivating the character and courage of men, teaching them to combine and sink personality, while at moments calling for the quickest decision and initiative'. The lower ranks were certainly happy to go along with their officers, and by the outbreak of the First World War football was as central to German military culture as gymnastics had been thirty years earlier. The same growth of en-thusiasm was reflected in civilian life; at the beginning of 1914 there were more than four hundred clubs in existence, with a combined membership approaching twenty-five thousand players.

The Germans had obviously taken to the game but for many Englishmen of the period that was only a beginning. Anyone could kick a ball around a pitch, could understand a set of rules, but football was like the British constitution – its most important rules were unwritten. In Britain football had grown up surrounded by the cult of 'the game', which had spread outwards from the public schools to infect the whole society. Rugby School's Thomas Arnold had hoped that sport would give young men the bodies of Greeks and the souls of Christian knights, and a fellow headmaster, who believed football would be 'productive of scarcely anything but good', expected it to provide 'an education in that spirit of chivalry, fairness and good temper'. Playing the game was supposed to be good for the body and the soul, to encourage self-reliance and team spirit, to prepare one, as *The Times* put it in 1899, for the 'battles of life'.

The previous year Sir Henry Newbolt had written the most famous poem of the era:

> There's a breathless hush in the Close tonight –
> Ten to make and the match to win –
> A bumping pitch and a blinding light,
> An hour to play and the last man in.

And it's not for the sake of the ribboned coat,
   Or the selfish hope of a season's fame,
But his Captain's hand on his shoulder smote –
   'Play up! play up! and play the game!'

Could any other nation be expected to understand something so breath-takingly English? Could the Continentals in general, or the Germans in particular? Many doubted it, but FA Secretary Sir Frederick Wall was inclined to think they could. He quoted Dr Robert Hefner, the German representative at the FA's jubilee banquet in 1913, as a case in point. 'He was an upholder of amateurism and even adopted the British definition of the amateur,' Sir Frederick wrote approvingly many years later. 'With fair hair and square head, he was a typical German, and at first had a passion to recast the laws of the game. Then he recognised that these laws were the fruits of long experience and was content . . . He admired England and English football and adopted the English phrase "play the game".'

In the years before the First World War deeply soured Anglo–German relations it was only to be expected that the Germans had a better chance than most of understanding the English notion of 'the game'. The English themselves were, after all, Germans in all but name. The first of them had arrived by boat in the fifth century – Angles, Saxons and Jutes from, respectively, Anglen, Saxony and Jutland. Their military successes en-couraged others, and over the next few centuries the various Saxon groups divided up what is now south-east England between them: Essex to the East Saxons, Sussex to the South Saxons, and so on. The Celtic peoples were pushed back into the fringe areas of Cornwall, Wales, Scotland and Ireland, but during the next and final wave of invasions – undertaken by the Vikings and their transplanted cousins, the Normans – the 'German' English preferred assimilation to retreat, and continued to consider themselves the backbone of their nation. The mythical Robin Hood was young, gifted and defiantly Saxon.

   Through most of the next seven hundred years the 'German' English and the 'German' Germans had little to argue or fight about. On the contrary, they shared a conversion to Protestantism (southern Germany excepted), numerous cultural and dynastic ties (including a 'German' German royal family for the 'German' English), and a distinctly north-

European temperament. Until the First World War they had never fought one another; their last meeting on a battlefield had been at Waterloo, where Blücher's Prussians had combined with Wellington's British to see off Napoleon's comeback.

The two nations not only shared ethnic backgrounds – in many ways they seemed destined to be friends. Many Germans admired the way the British organised their political life, their individualism, their global success. Many Britons admired German organisation, culture, education. There was nothing sloppy about the Germans – nothing, well, Mediterranean . . . or worse. Some Germans thought that the only real difference between the two nations was geographical. 'A nation with well-defined frontiers,' Hans Ziegler wrote in 1909, 'and protected all round by an insurmountable barrier, can afford to be liberal enough in her political institutions . . . If Norway had bordered on Scotland, or Spain and France on Ireland and Wales, England would have been obliged to keep a closer watch on events, to exercise a more categorical political grip, to organise huge land forces in order to make her position impregnable – she would, in short, have become a differently constituted nation, perhaps something like Germany herself.' As it was, the British had had an easier political existence, 'never having been called upon to fight for health and home'. As a result, though collectively prone to superficiality the Briton had developed into a 'good-natured, easy-going, comparatively well-to-do, broad-minded individual'.

The mutual admiration between sections of the two peoples was real enough, and could be glimpsed in action right up to the outbreak of hostilities. In June 1914 units of the two High Seas fleets shared an anchorage during Kiel Yachting Week. Germans were invited aboard the British ships to witness a boxing contest, and the Kaiser's brother Henry remarked that he had long hoped for such a display of friendship. The Kaiser himself appeared in the uniform of a British Admiral, and pronounced himself 'proud to wear the uniform of Lord Nelson'.

The vague feelings of shared ethnicity, culture and values which infused Anglo–German relations over the better half of a millennium ultimately proved no match for the more basic divergence of interests which dominated them in the late nineteenth and early twentieth centuries.

Since Bismarck's creation of the German Empire at the point of a sword in 1870, the two countries had finally had something to fight about – European and global mastery. The British had it, and were not willing to contemplate sharing it with their German cousins. The Germans wanted at least a portion, and if denied that were quite prepared to take it all. This conflict of interest between a declining 'have' power and a rising 'have not' power would precipitate two world wars, and would end with one nation on her economic knees, the other in ruins, not to mention sundered in two at the behest of the world's new masters, the United States and the Soviet Union. In the process, of course, the decades of conflict would deeply colour the way in which British and Germans reacted to each other, whether at war, during peace, or on a football pitch.

Like couples in mid-argument, nations in dispute tend to lose track of what they like about each other. Caught up in the emotions of the moment, they prefer dredging past, present and future for slights both real and imagined. The German middle classes might have admired much about the British, but as the new century advanced such admiration was soon buried under a rising tide of resentment. The German upper classes, grouped around the rural Junkers and the military, had never much liked the British and increasingly rationalised that dislike on the grounds that Britain's commercially obsessed democracy was destroying the old way of life they loved and undermining all the old Christian values. The conflict, according to Max Scheler, was between 'German heroism and the English tradesmen's mentality, between German society, with its devotion to idealistic values and preparedness to make personal sacrifices for the nation, and British society, dominated by a utilitarian philosophy which viewed everything in terms of personal gain and a comfortable material existence'.

The resentment of the German middle classes was more practical. Not only did the British stranglehold on world trade make it necessary for them to work twice as hard for the same rewards, but when they did work twice as hard they were accused of pushiness at best, underhand trading methods at worst. They had nothing against British commercialism as such – what they wanted was a level playing field. And slowly but surely they came to believe that this could only be achieved by freeing the world of its British master. 'There are but two alternatives in view of the incredible, fearful supremacy of Britain,' wrote Frederick Nauman. 'Either we submit or we fight. Our children will fight. If there is anything certain in world history it is that there will be a future world war, that is to say a war of those who will escape the British yoke.'

The British, of course, saw things very differently. If there was such a yoke, it was clearly a benign one. Democracy and free trade were obviously in everyone's interests, which was a lot more than could be said for Prussian authoritarianism. As early as 1872 one British prime minister's list of Prussia's contributions to human civilisation included military despotism, the rule of the sword, contempt for sentimental talk, indifference to human suffering, imprisonment of independent opinion and a total want of greatness or generosity. There were elements in the British elite who shared the Junkers' distaste for the merely commercial, but they wielded little influence. Generally speaking the British had the same unfocused disdain for the Germans which they had for all Continentals, but after the turn of the century there was growing agreement that the Kaiser's Germany was becoming more than a little uppity. The new German navy, growing as it was so prodigiously, could only be aimed at the Royal Navy. The Berlin to Baghdad railway which the Germans were so eager to build could only be aimed at the British position in India. Even the German population was growing at a faster rate than ever presumably with the army's needs in mind.

The British felt threatened; and just as German resentment had fuelled a rising tide of Anglophobia, so Britain now bore witness to a boom of Germanophobia. In both countries, press articles and patriotic groups stoked the fire. In 1909 the play *An Englishman's Home* broke all London's box-office records; it was about an English family's resistance in the aftermath of a successful German invasion.

The European War was eventually triggered by problems in the Balkans and the pressure of military timetables, but it soon came to be seen in both Britain and Germany as primarily a struggle between their two nations. Not surprisingly, their images of each other quickly reflected the new level of hostility.

French and Russians they matter not;
A blow for a blow, and a shot for a shot;
We love them not, we hate them not . . .
We have but one and only hate,
We love as one, we hate as one,
We have one foe and one alone.
He is known to you all, he is known to you all,
He crouches behind the dark grey flood,
Full of envy, of rage, of craft, of gall,
Cut off by waves that are thicker than blood . . .
We will never forgo our hate,
We have but a single hate,
We love as one, we hate as one.
We have one foe, and one alone – England!
Hate on water and hate on the land
Hate in the head and hate by the hand.
Hate for their people and hate for their kings
In the hearts of seventy million rings
United as one to strike every blow
At England, the hated, the only foe.

These are excerpts from Ernst Lissauer's 'Hymn of Hate', first published in September 1914 in a Munich newspaper and subsequently reprinted in leaflet-form by the million, taught to children in school and memorised by troops in the trenches. It caught the flavour of the times, in both Germany and England.

Down with the Germans, down with them all!
O Army and Navy, be sure of their fall!
Spare not one, the deceitful spies,
Cut out their tongues, pull out their eyes!
Down, down with them all.

This verse, printed in the *Daily Graphic* early in 1915, was fairly representative of British feelings. In the same month that Lissauer's 'Hymn' was published Lloyd George was portraying the Prussian Junker as 'the road-hog of Europe. Small nationalities in his way are flung to the roadside, bleeding and broken.' German behaviour in occupied Belgium and northern France – in particular the burning of Louvain and the military's habit of shooting large numbers of mostly innocent hostages – darkened their reputation with the English still further. The German was now irretrievably cast as 'the Hun', the new barbarian of Europe.

Such demonisation inevitably put an end to the prewar arguments over whether or not Germans could 'play the game'. In his *War Book*, Lord Northcliffe noted that 'our soldiers are individual. They embark on little individual enterprises. The German is not so clever at these devices. He was never taught them before the war, and his whole training from childhood upwards has been to obey, and to obey in numbers.' The reason for all this, Northcliffe realised, was that football, which develops individuality, had only been introduced into Germany in comparatively recent times. English tank crews, having been exposed to the game's benign influence from the cradle on, could become 'young daredevils who enter upon their task in a sporting spirit with the same cheery enthusiasm as they would show for football.' The Prussians, by contrast, didn't know how to 'play the game'.

The new hatred of all things English made some Germans wonder why they had ever wanted to 'play the game' anyway. When British officer prisoners were caught playing football with loaves of black bread the Germans punished them for their insolence and wondered whether they'd ever grow up. The French shared German despair at such attitudes. 'They consider the war a sport,' one Frenchman complained bitterly; and long after the war had ended Frenchmen could be heard angrily denouncing this particular expression of *l'egoisme anglais*.

Some Britons might have decided that 'the Hun' had proved himself unworthy of 'the game', and some Germans that such triviality was beneath them, but during the famous Christmas truce of 1914 soldiers from both nations seem to have been willing enough to play football with each other.

The truce, as spontaneous as it was sane, broke out at seemingly random spots along the lines of trenches separating the British and German armies in northern France and Belgium. After sharing songs and shouted messages from the safety of their trenches, soldiers from both sides walked out into no man's land where they shared cigarettes, jokes and souvenirs, and wryly remarked on the absurdity of it all. The higher-ups generally frowned on this widespread fraternisation – who knew where it might lead? – but had the sense not to interfere too obviously.

Just how many Anglo–German football 'internationals' took place in these few days remains a matter of conjecture. The state of the ground, a frozen wasteland pock-marked by artillery shell-holes and often littered with body-parts, would not have been encouraging, and footballs would have been hard to come by. But there is anecdotal evidence of several games being played with either a ball or a tin can between improvised goals. *The Times* reported that an unnamed British regiment had been beaten 3–2 by a Saxon unit; the official history of the Lancashire Fusiliers later revealed that one of its companies had triumphed by the same score over its German opponents.

Sometimes the organisation was minimal. 'The ball appeared from somewhere,' one Cheshire soldier remembered. 'I don't know where, but it came from their side . . . They made up some goals and one fellow went in goal and then it was just a general kickabout . . . Everybody seemed to be enjoying themselves. There was no ill-will between us . . . There was no referee, no score . . .'

The events of the truce made it hard for the soldiers of either side to sustain a demonised image of the enemy. One British soldier found the Saxons he encountered 'a very good class of fellows'; another found his new German acquaintances 'honourable', 'gentlemanly', 'not all so black as they are sometimes painted'. One officer wrote in the battalion diary that the fraternisation had induced both sides to 'play the game'.

There were exceptions, of course. Members of one Saxon unit of the German army warned their English opponents about the 'nasty Prussians' on their right: unlike Saxons and Anglo-Saxons, these people could not be expected to play fair or understand the word of a gentleman.

Other Germans – whether Prussian or not – were less impressed. 'The English are said to have told the 53rd Regiment they are exceedingly thankful for the truce because they simply have to play football again;' one German officer incredulously confided in his diary. 'The whole business is becoming ridiculous and must come to an end,' he added trenchantly.

If the Christmas truce of 1914 and the games of football which it spawned demonstrated how alike ordinary English and ordinary Germans were, the other famous footballing activity of the First World War offered proof of the gulf that still lay between them.

The practice of enlivening advances across no man's land by dribbling a football seems to have been introduced by the 1st Battalion of the 18th London Regiment at Loos in 1915. Perhaps the idea was to take the men's minds off the likelihood of sudden death or maiming, or perhaps some bright young officer thought the Germans might be momentarily unnerved by such an awesome display of the sporting spirit. Most probably it was just some idiot's idea of a good wheeze. Either way, body-swerving through dead and dying comrades with the ball meta-phorically tied to the bootlaces soon became extremely fashionable. The practice was even exported to Gallipoli. 'One of the men had a football', one soldier wrote home proudly. 'We kicked off and rushed the Turkish guns, dribbling the ball with us.'

The most famous such escapade occurred at the Battle of the Somme. Captain W.P. Nevill, a company commander in the 8th East Surreys, returned from leave in London with four footballs which he presented to the four platoons under his command. One bore an inscription which looked forward forty years to European football competition: 'The Great European Cup-tie Finals, East Surrey v. Bavarians'. Another simply said: 'No referee'. A prize was offered for the first platoon to dribble its way across the distant German line.

One soldier later described the kick-off: 'As the gunfire died away I saw an infantryman climb onto the parapet and into no man's land, beckoning others to follow. As he did so he kicked a football. A good kick. The ball rose and travelled well towards the German line.'

The long ball game proved no more efficacious for the Surreys than it would for later England teams. Sixty thousand Englishmen fell on that first day of the Somme offensive, Captain Nevill and many of his Surreys among them.

Such antics seemed ludicrous to some, but for others they offered further evidence, if such was needed, that only the English could really 'play the game'. Two of the footballs were recovered for future pre-servation in English museums, and Nevill's exploit was immediately immortalised in verse:

> On through the hail of slaughter,
> Where gallant comrades fall,
> Where blood is poured like water,
> They drive the trickling ball.
> The fear of death before them
> Is but an empty name.
> True to the land that bore them –
> The SURREYS play the game.

In his book *The English* Jeremy Paxman concludes that 'Captain Nevill was clearly mad'. What the game had taught such men, Paxman says, was the 'importance of "manliness" and self-control and obedience to orders'.

There are clues in this sentence to the whole development of English football in the century which followed the dribbling Surreys. On the credit side, the emphasis on self-control and obedience has made for good – if hardly inspired – soldiers, and has further reinforced an English tradition of fair play that is still, despite several notable lapses from grace, globally recognised. On the debit side, the importance of manliness – or at least a certain version thereof – has proved the most crippling of the legacies handed down to English football by the game's Victorian and Edwardian progenitors. On both hard grounds and soft, in the sun and the rain, this hangover of the imperial past has jealously guarded the primacy of courage and stamina over technique and invention.

Not much has changed, even to this day. The vocabulary of war can still be heard in any English TV or radio commentary; failed attempts at trickery still bring taunts of diminished manhood from the seated terraces. Roy Keane lunging into a tackle like Captain Nevill going over the top, is 'playing the game'; David Ginola going to ground for no better reason than that he has been fouled by a less gifted opponent, is palpably not.

Such an approach and attitude have arguably made English League football exciting to watch over the last few years, but it has now cost the English national team dear through many decades – and never more obviously than in games with its closest of enemies, the cousins from Germany.

2: FIFA and other foreigners

The Christmas truce of 1914 was not re-enacted in the years that followed, and there was little human contact between the two sides to counteract the increasingly deliberate efforts made by both governments to irrevocably smear the names of their adversaries. The enemy was now only seen *in extremis*, looming out of a gas-cloud with a mask on, white-faced behind a machine gun, spread-eagled in mud and death. His normal face remained hidden, whether just behind the tangled wire or far away in a foreign home.

After the war there was no occupation of Germany by the victorious Allies, no long period of mass human contact in which the enemy's human qualities could be rediscovered, the cartoon images of war propaganda eroded. Far from promoting peace the Versailles Treaty actually reinforced these images. The famous War Guilt clause, which attributed all blame to the Germans and their allies and laid the ground work for punitive reparations which would virtually destroy the German economy, was rightly seen as vindictive by the wiser heads of the day. These included the British Prime Minister Lloyd George, but he was unable to prevail against the righteous fury of the French and his own embittered public. Too many had been crippled and killed for common sense to prevail.

The popular view was that the Germans deserved everything they got. One British Empire Union poster from the twenties was headlined 'Once a German – Always a German' and contained four drawings: German soldiers bayonetting a baby and tying a wounded prisoner to an execution post; a German general with wine and an unwilling woman; a German soldier emerging from a corpse-strewn and burning city with a torch in one hand and a knife in the other; and – the *pièce de résistance* – this same soldier transmuted into a German businessman emerging from an industrial skyline with a hat in one hand and a suitcase full of samples in the other. 'Remember!' the writing at the bottom exhorted. 'Every German employed means a British worker idle. Every German article sold means a British article unsold.' The images of war were now good business.

The British football authorities were not about to travel boldly beyond the popular consensus. For one thing their patriotic credentials had been somewhat tarnished during the early years of the war by a reluctance to cease operations. The Home International Championship had only been suspended after a direct request from the War Office, and feelings had run high enough for a January 1915 edition of *Punch* to portray the football results as the 'Shirkers' War News'. When the war ended the FA was eager to prove itself every bit as eager to punish the Germans as any man in the street.

There was only one sanction available to the football authorities, and this they applied with exaggerated vigour. The FA refused to play either the former enemy nations or any of the former allies or neutrals who proved less choosy than themselves. This decision, though supported by Belgium, France and Luxembourg at a December 1919 conference, was opposed by many of European football's ruling bodies, including the Dutch, Italian, Spanish and Scandinavian associations. Having threatened to quit FIFA (Fédération Internationale de Football Associations) if it didn't back the veto, the FA duly announced in April 1920 that it was withdrawing from membership, and the Scottish, Welsh and Irish associations meekly followed suit.

This was not the FA's first brush with FIFA. The international body had been formed in 1904 at the behest of the French, and right from the beginning the British had regarded it as more of a threat than an opportunity. They were particularly worried that their existing monopoly of control of the game's laws might be jeopardised. But FIFA was there, like it or not, and eventually the FA, anticipating Lyndon Johnson's famous dictum that it was better to have your enemies inside the tent pissing out than outside the tent pissing in, decided they had no choice but to join and to graciously 'give all Continental associations the full benefits of [their] many years' experience'.

Once inside, the FA offered Europe a preview of Thatcherite Britain's later role in the European Union, alternating condescension with sulks and threats to quit if they didn't get their own way. The German FA's Dr Robert Hefner complained that all the European efforts to promote FIFA found themselves face to face with an English wall 'stopping every progress'. In such a light, it's not hard to believe that some of the Europeans felt distinctly ambivalent about the British withdrawal from FIFA in 1920. Britain might have been the home of football, the British game still unmatched by its Continental rivals, but the British themselves were so *difficult*.

The FA's 1920 withdrawal from FIFA proved short-lived. The policy of refusing to play games against friends of friends of ex-enemies was soon revealed as somewhat unworkable, not to say absurd. Norway scuppered an FA plan to arrange an amateur international with them by refusing not to arrange future games with the Swedes, who were guilty of playing ex-enemy nations. A Scottish club tour of Denmark was similarly hamstrung by the enquiries necessary to make sure that no Danish team had already played or planned to play against any other team which might one day choose to play Germany, Austria or the others.

The British bowed to common sense, dropping first the ban on those guilty by association and then, in 1922, the ban on the ex-enemy powers themselves. They were helped in these decisions by the changing mood towards the latter, as evidenced by the general *rapprochement* which followed the German economic crisis of 1923. The statesmen of Europe and North America had finally realised that they needed a prosperous Germany – if only to enable the payment of war reparations. These were needed by Britain and France to repay their war debts to the United States, which in turn were recycled as American loans to Germany, thus creating the virtuous economic spiral which assured world economic growth for the rest of the decade, until the Wall Street Crash jerked the whole process into reverse and plunged everyone into the Great Depression of the early thirties.

Once the ban on footballing contacts with ex-enemy nations was lifted club contacts swiftly multiplied: Arsenal, for example, undertook a close season tour of Germany in May 1924, playing matches in Düsseldorf, Berlin, Fürth, Stuttgart, Cologne and Hamburg. The British initially showed no sign of any desire to resume those contests between repre-

sentative elevens – at either the amateur or the professional level – which
had been suspended in 1914. The British FA's on-off relationship with
FIFA (they walked out again in 1926 over the issue of amateurism) was no
accident: British football, though occasionally prone to a missionary
vocation, remained fundamentally isolationist.

There were several mutually reinforcing reasons for this. One lay deep
in the island's long history and the imprint that had left on the national
psyche. Stanley Rous, Sir Frederick Wall's eventual successor as FA
Secretary, told the story of how the Belgian referee John Langenus
crossed the Channel to referee two home internationals in successive
years. On the second occasion, the FA Treasurer noticed a rise in the
expenses he was claiming and simply deducted the difference and paid
him the same as the previous year. When Langenus pointed out that the
fares had gone up the FA man simply shook his head and declared that
'the value of the English pound never changes'.

Secondly, along with the insularity went the arrogance borne of
being first on the football field, the game's inventors: if the FA had
had a theme tune in the 1920s it would have been Tina Turner's 'Simply
the Best'. What was the point of playing foreigners when the best
football was found at home? Also, with its long and gruelling League
programme and its legendary, all-encompassing Cup the domestic game
in Britain took up most of the FA's time and nearly all of its psychological space.

And last and probably least, travelling to the Continent was not the
simple matter it is today. Air travel, though available before the Second
World War, was considered too futuristic by the British football associations, and every British team travelling in the interwar period was
condemned to time-consuming combinations of motor coach, boat
and train.

Despite these major handicaps the British nations did manage to play a
few games against foreign opposition. The first official English internationals against non-British sides took place during a tour of Eastern
Europe in the summer of 1908. England played Austria twice and
Hungary and Bohemia once each, scoring twenty-eight goals and
conceding only two. This success was so gratifying that the tour was
repeated the following year, this time with two games played against

Hungary and one against Austria – with similar results. Apparently sated, the FA then confined the English team to the familiar round of Scotland, Wales and Ireland until the First World War put an end to all international football in Europe.

In the 1920s England played eighteen games against non-British opposition, sixteen of them away from home. The two home games, both against Belgium, were played at Highbury and The Hawthorns in March 1923 and December 1924 respectively (Scotland were the only team to be received at Wembley between the wars). These were the only mid-season internationals against foreign opposition. The sixteen away games, all played on post-season tours, were against Belgium (six times), France (six times), Sweden (twice), Luxemburg (once) and Spain (once). The FA were clearly anxious not to travel too far afield and the prewar jaunts to Eastern Europe were not repeated, despite invitations from the nations concerned.

The results were, at least initially, everything that the English expected they should be. The Belgians managed to draw one game in Antwerp in 1923, but the English won all but the last of the other fifteen. Suffering the first international defeat of their history in May 1929, they went down 4–3 to Spain in Madrid. 'I never thought I would live to see the day when eleven Spanish players humbled the might – more or less – of English soccer,' a *Daily Express* scribe cabled from the Spanish capital. Nonetheless the defeat was quickly explained away: it was the England team's third match in eight days of almost continuous rail travel, and only mad dogs could be expected to perform in such heat. In any case, the Spanish were coached by an Englishman, former Middlesbrough player Fred Pentland, so the game could hardly be counted as a genuinely foreign victory.

Uruguay's invitation to Britain to compete in the first World Cup competition provided an opportunity to learn just how far the rest of the world had travelled in England's footballing footsteps, but the offer was declined by the British associations. The most commonly cited explanations for non-participation were the amount of travel involved and Chelsea's unfortunate recent experiences in Argentina, and these were reinforced by the usual unconscious insularity.

The English did have one important fixture pencilled in for 1930. In November 1928 the FA had not only agreed to a first official international with Germany in Berlin but had also stated its willingness to host a return match in England. The two footballing cultures, precluded by events largely beyond their control from resuming the rivalry inaugurated in 1899, could now – almost thirty years later – finally resume hostilities.

According to the Foreign Office, more than footballing pride would be at stake. At the end of 1928 Thomas Preston, the British Consul in Turin, had responded to Italian press speculation about a forthcoming England – Italy match by writing a stiff warning to his bosses in London. The Italians could play, he said, and if England sent out a team it would have to be the best professional outfit available. 'It might be argued that sport is sport,' he wrote, 'and that it does not matter so much who wins; this is all very well with matches with our colonial teams, but not so with continental teams.' This would be more than a football match to the Italians; it would be 'an event of international importance'.

The Foreign Office pondered this missive, and decided that a semi-official word to the FA would not be out of place. 'Do you think that it would be possible to get a hint passed to the right quarters – the organisers of the England team – that it is worth their while to rend a really strong side?' the Foreign Office wrote to the FA.

The British press soon sniffed out this unprecedented political inter-ference in sport – the suspicion remains that Frederick Wall himself leaked the news – and for several weeks in late 1928 and early 1929 the matter was openly debated. The *Daily Express* took the lead in decrying such interference, while *The Times* took the opposite view. If English teams were regularly whipped by European opposition, the latter argued, then Europe (which of course excluded Britain) might decide that 'the race which produced them must be decadent'. And that would hardly be good for British interests, whether economic or diplomatic.

To complicate matters still further, the *Express* mistakenly assumed that it was the recently arranged Anglo–German match which had triggered the outbreak of anxiety at the Foreign Office. This fixture was already weighed down with more than enough emotional baggage, and it now seemed as if the English players selected for the game in Berlin would be expected to represent their country as ambassadors of more than football.

The England–Germany match was to be played on Saturday 10 May at the Grünewald Stadium, which had originally been built for the cancelled 1916 Olympics. German interest in the game was intense, and all available tickets had long been sold by the time the English party arrived on the Friday. After booking into their hotel, the fashionable Esplanade, the group dined and then trooped out to see a production of *The Merry Widow*. By 10.15 the players were safely tucked up in bed, leaving the accompanying trainer and officials free to to take a quick shufti at Berlin's notorious nightlife.

In England itself there was rather less interest in the game, and that Saturday morning's papers concentrated on the more important concerns of the day: Amy Johnson halfway through her solo flight to Australia; an American negro baked alive in his Texas prison cell; the government of India's ultimatum to the Haji of Turan Gzai. 'BARONET AND SCHOOLGIRL: HAZY ABOUT ORGY' ran one intriguing headline in the *Daily Mail*.

The Times and the *Manchester Guardian* didn't even mention that afternoon's game, and the more 'popular' papers only offered a few lines. The *Daily Worker*, true to form, used the occasion to make its own political points: the chosen German team, its writer announced, was 'the strongest eleven that bourgeois football could put into the field'. (Once the game was over he mysteriously drew the conclusion that 'boss sport has not the same hold over the workers in Germany as it has in Britain'.)

In far-off Berlin the match was scheduled to kick-off at 5.30 Central European Time, so there was time for both teams to be guests of honour at a lengthy lunch given by German sporting journalists. No alcoholic drinks were offered – the English had imbibed no alcohol since arriving in Berlin, a fact which, according to a Reuter reporter, had been 'particularly noted by the Germans'.

Outside in the city the streets were full of expectant spectators. Trains from the provinces had been disgorging fans at Berlin's principal termini since early morning, and the roads in and around the stadium became choked with walking fans and vehicles of all sizes. Long queues had formed at the box offices for those 5000 tickets reserved for latecomers; but many hopeful punters came away disappointed and ideal bait for the myriad touts, many of whom were said to be making a 400% profit on each ticket.

The England captain, Arsenal's David Jack, told reporters that he and his team were taking the match very seriously. 'I do not know the strength of the German side,' he said, 'but from what I have been told in England, I must be careful not to prophesy an English victory with such absolute certainty as I could do against any other European country.' England's confidence had been boosted by their winning of the 1929–30 Home International Championship, while their defeat by Spain twelve months earlier had been consigned to some limbo-land of the memory.

For their part the German players had reasons for hope. They had been unlucky to only draw with Scotland the previous year – and during the 1920s the Scots had won the Home International Championship outright on six occasions, the English not even once. Although there were no professional footballers in Germany and no national league of any kind, the selectors had been able to pick a team from 85,000 registered players. They had a national star in inside-left Richard Hofmann of Dresden, and the previous Sunday they had thrashed the Swiss 5–0. England had once been invincible, of course, but were they still?

There were heavy showers in the hours before kick-off, and the sky was still overcast when the two teams emerged on to the rain-softened pitch. A line of flagpoles marched behind the terraces, the Union Jack prominent in the centre. As the German band broke into 'God Save the King' the 50,000-plus spectators removed their hats and stood to attention.

The Germans began nervously, their passes going astray and their control letting them down. The English were more calm and collected, pushed forward and took the lead before ten minutes were up, Bradford hitting home from well inside the box after Watson had beaten several defenders to make room for a cross. German heads dropped momentarily, but within six minutes Richard Hofmann struck a fine shot past Harry Hibbs and brought the score level.

Soon after this (or perhaps even before – the newspapers of the time were not specific), England left-half Billy Marsden received a serious blow to the head in a clash with team-mate Blenkinsop. He was able to resume play after treatment; and although it soon became obvious that he was virtually a passenger the team as a whole didn't seem handicapped. They took the German equaliser in their stride and went on to dominate play for the next half-hour. Their crisp passing moves and good positioning emphasised a lack of sophistication in the German play, and it was only weak finishing which prevented them from reclaiming the lead until just before half-time, when a well-worked move put Bradford through to drive home a low shot from twenty yards.

The game was being played in good spirit, and English observers were quick to notice that the England forwards were refraining from shoulder-charging German goalkeeper Kress: someone had obviously done their homework and impressed on the team that such behaviour was frowned upon among the Continentals. The spectators were less happy with the Dutch referee, who seemed to be bending over backwards to please the tourists, and they responded – much to the interest of the watching English – with a chorus of whistles rather than the more familiar catcalls and boos.

Marsden didn't come out for the second half, and the Germans appeared to take immediate encouragement from that. Outside-left Rimmer had been helping out in Marsden's left-half position since the injury, and both he and the usually adventurous Webster found themselves almost exclusively occupied with defensive duties as the Germans pressed forward. Within five minutes of the re-start Germany had equalised, Richard Hofmann latching on to a centre from the right and crashing it home from close-range.

The Dresden inside-left, one of the smallest men on the pitch, was now giving England a torrid time. A few minutes after scoring his second goal he hit the post, with Hibbs comprehensively beaten, and around the hour-mark he completed his hat-trick. Centre-half Leinberger advanced deep into English territory like a proto-Beckenbauer and slipped the ball through for Hofmann to out-pace the English defenders and push it coolly past the advancing Hibbs: 3–2 to Germany. The crowd went wild, and with good reason. A goal ahead against ten men, their team would surely go on to win.

The English had other ideas. Falling behind seemed to galvanise the remaining men, who from that moment on left the Germans almost continually on the back foot. It is likely that the English professionals were fitter than their amateur opponents and that this made up in whole or part for their lack of numbers; that said, there was no doubting the sheer classiness of the onslaught they mounted on the German goal during the final twenty minutes.

Several good chances were thrown away. On one occasion Jack, one-on-one against Kress, rounded the goalkeeper only to run the ball out of play. A surging fifty-yard run from Crooks ended with a shot narrowly wide. Several efforts which on other days would have been rewarded with goals were saved by the brilliant Kress.

The German goalkeeper could do nothing about the equaliser seven minutes from time, though. Jack fed Crooks on the right and ran on into the penalty area to meet the inch-perfect return with as dramatic a diving header as anyone in the crowd had ever seen.

It was a very satisfying end for the English, and the German spectators were obviously not too disappointed. As the Dutch referee blew for time hundreds of them pushed aside the police, poured on to the pitch and shouldered off the German team in triumph.

It was not an unreasonable reaction – a draw was more than many Germans had expected and, in the context of the game, certainly no more than they deserved. The critical consensus was that England would have won the game had they not been reduced to ten men – and probably even then had they not been so profligate in front of goal. The Germans had produced some neat play, and Richard Hofmann's finishing had been first class, but overall the hosts had clearly been out-classed. Unsurprisingly, their own football writers were still in awe of the English. Such football, they claimed, had never before been seen in their country.

The English were happy to agree with them. 'The English team played like professionals,' Broadcaster wrote in the *Daily Express*, 'the Germans like amateurs, very clever amateurs, full of tricks and eagerness, but lacking the solidity of the English team.' That was from the narrow, footballing point of view. When it came to 'playing the game' Broadcaster was pleased to note that the Germans did it almost as well as their guests. 'There was no congratulating the goalscorers,' he wrote approvingly. 'On the English side everybody's feelings were under perfect control. The Germans allowed themselves to go a little more, but always in good taste.'

There was a celebratory dinner after the game; among those invited were three of the German players who had faced the English tourists in 1899. The next day the England party, minus the hospitalised Marsden, took the train south to Vienna. There, on the following Wednesday, they drew 0–0 in front of a 70,000 crowd, many of whom had travelled from as far afield as Prague, Budapest and Zagreb.

Billy Marsden was kept in the Berlin hospital for a fortnight. It had been assumed initially that he was simply suffering from concussion, but it was then reported that a precautionary X-ray had picked up a slight fracture, presumably of the skull. He never played again and, as was the habit of the times, received only a pittance in compensation.

3: entertaining the nazis

The promised return match did not take place for five and a half years, during which time the political and economic optimism of the late 1920s was comprehensively blown away. The Great Depression, which peaked in most industrial countries in 1932–3, wreaked havoc among the governments of the era; and in Germany, where unemployment reached more than forty per cent, the whole political system succumbed. By mid-1934 Hitler and his National Socialists had eliminated all meaningful opposition to their totalitarian state and were already making the first tentative moves towards dismantling the postwar European settlement imposed at Versailles. Internally, the Nazis were also beginning the systematic persecution of Germany's Jewish minority, promulgating in September 1935 the so-called Nuremberg Laws, which deprived German Jews of their German citizenship, forbade marriages between Jews and Germans, and prohibited Jews from employing German servants.

It was these sordid developments which provided the backcloth to England's second match against Germany and which fuelled a wave of protest in response that almost engulfed the football. The date and location – 4 December and an unintentionally ironic White Hart Lane – were agreed between the two FAs in summer 1935, but news of the fixture only reached the British government in late September and the press in the first weeks of October. Reaction was swift and intense. 'JEWS UP IN ARMS' ran a headline in the *Star* on 15 October. A protest organiser was quoted as saying that 'the Jews have been the best supporters of the Tottenham club since its formation, and we shall adopt every means in our power to stop the match. We regard the visit of the German team as an effrontery, not only to the Jewish race, but to all lovers of freedom.'

At the same time handbills were distributed in North London carrying details of a story which had recently appeared in the *Daily Worker* concerning a game between German and Polish teams in Ratisbon (now Regensburg), Silesia. One of the Polish players had been Jewish, a fact which had so incensed the German spectators that they first pelted the whole team with stones and then ran on to the pitch and assaulted the Pole in question. He had died on the way to hospital.

This story was now re-aired in many papers along with news that the FA had made enquiries of the German FA who had categorically denied that any such event had ever taken place. In the *Evening Standard* the matter was approached from several different angles. In one article Stanley Rous, the ex-referee who had taken over the FA Secretaryship from Frederick Wall the previous year, claimed that he had officiated in seven matches involving German players, and found them 'sporting footballers . . . thoroughly amenable to discipline', the clear implication being that these were not the sort of chaps who went around beating Jews to death on a football pitch.

Or perhaps they were. The *Evening Standard* also quoted the official Nazi *Voelkischer Beobachter*. 'Jews constitute the ringleaders of all the profiteers who carry on shady betting and financial operations in the world of sport,' this august publication announced. 'Jews are trying to wheedle the English football club Tottenham Hotspur into not giving up their ground for the international match . . . They are setting about it with unexampled insolence and are writing letters to the club, calculated to ruin all their games financially.'

These *did* sound like the sort of people who would beat Jews to death on a football pitch, but as long as they restricted such activities to their own country did that matter? In his regular weekly column Chelsea manager Leslie Knighton implied that it didn't. He wanted the match played. 'Football is a universal game,' he thought. 'Amateurs may play with or against professionals. There is no colour bar. All anyone asks is that the game shall be played in a sporting spirit and according to the rules.'

Regarding the events in Ratisbon, it had been the crowd, not the players, who had committed murder. Though even if the players had been involved Knighton would have remained opposed to cancellation of the forthcoming fixture. The British had a mission to spread their interpretation of sportsmanship. 'It may be pointed out,' he admitted, 'that some Continental nations have taken the rules of our game but have not absorbed its traditions.' These nations all wanted to 'play the game as we play it', but needed the guidance of British example. When all was said and done, 'the broad effect of the game' was to promote 'democracy, friendship and mutual understanding', and although it was clear that some people hadn't yet got the message, they would in time.

'In those countries to which football is relatively new,' Knighton concluded fatuously, 'the British idea of sportsmanship may yet have to spread from the players to the spectators.' He seemed to be suggesting that if only the Germans learned to play as sportingly as the English, it would be only a matter of time before their crowds stopped murdering people. The same bizarre logic was used to justify sporting contacts with South Africa forty years later.

The protests rumbled on. Plans were announced for 6000 Tottenham supporters to leave their places and march from the ground when a bugle sounded just before the kick-off of their match against Bradford on 19 October; this particular protest was apparently called off. A mass anti-Nazi rally called for the following weekend did take place, however, during which there were renewed calls for the German visit to be cancelled.

Various departments of the British government were still discussing the matter among themselves. The Home Office was increasingly worried about the prospect of 10,000 German fans invading London and the threat to law and order which their presence might provoke. The Foreign Office was eager for the match to proceed, partly so that England's footballers could demonstrate, in the Foreign Secretary's words, 'that we are not the effete and degenerate people we are misrepresented as being by our totalitarian rivals', and partly because they were busy appeasing those very same rivals. Earlier that year the British government had acquiesced in Hitler's illegal re-introduction of military conscription, and it had no desire to see the resultant fund of goodwill dissipated by having to issue an insulting withdrawal to a football invitation. It was therefore decided, on balance, that politics should not be brought into sport.

The German government had been party to the arrangements from the outset and was only too pleased that the British government took this view. Hitler was anxious for closer links with Britain, which at that time he saw as a possible partner. There was also the small matter of the 1936 Olympics, which were scheduled to take place in Berlin the following summer. It was assumed that the many campaigners in the United States for an American withdrawal would have their case significantly weakened by an English willingness to play football against Germany.

On 9 November the *Daily Worker* re-printed a report in the *Frankfurter Zeitung* of another player's murder. The story wasn't picked up by other papers; and generally speaking the campaign against the match remained in abeyance throughout the first three weeks of November. On the eighteenth the TUC reminded the Home Office that it was still in favour of a ban. They argued that if the government allowed the match to go ahead they would be conferring respectability on the Nazis' abhorrent racial policies and enabling the Germans to make use of the occasion itself for propaganda purposes. The TUC reminded the British government that it had itself set a clear precedent for intervention in 1930, when it refused to allow a Soviet team to tour the country.

While the government did not intend to cancel the match, it was quite willing to pursue a policy of damage limitation. The German Ambassador was summoned to a meeting by Home Secretary Sir John Simon and informed how essential it was that 'no risks should be taken'. He responded with a guaranty that there would be no provocation from the German fans – no singing, no shouted slogans, no swastika badges. A few days later Hitler himself – perhaps anxious at the prospect of embarrassing protests on the day of the game – meekly offered to accept a British cancellation of the fixture; but the British government had made up its mind.

By this time the controversy was returning to the boil in the public domain. 'NAZI FOOTBALLERS FEAR PROTESTS OF ANTI-FASCISTS' ran the *Daily Worker* front-page headline on 26 November above a story claiming that the Germans were running scared, demanding segregation for their supporters and making grovelling appeals to British sportsmanship.

On the twenty-seventh the TUC formally requested that the game be called off; two days later the government formally refused. Armed with the German Ambassador's promises that the occasion would not be used for propaganda purposes, the Home Secretary wrote to tell TUC General Secretary Sir Walter Citrine that 'government approval was neither sought nor required' for the match, which had 'no political significance whatsoever' and did not imply 'any view of either government as to the policy and institutions of the other'. He hoped that all concerned would 'do their utmost to discourage the idea that a sporting fixture in this country had any political implication'.

The press were now on the whole hostile to the protesters. Most papers trotted out the usual homilies about keeping politics out of sport, but the *Star* argued that this particular sporting occasion would probably be politically beneficial: the German visitors would be given the privilege of twenty-four hours 'in a country without wholesale spying, racial antag-onism, private vengeance masquerading as public duty, and hands shooting up in the air because their owners will suffer if they don't *Heil Hitler*'.

The football authorities were represented by Herbert Dunnico, Chairman of the Counties Association of Football Clubs and an ex-Speaker of the House of Commons. In a widely reported speech on Saturday 30 November he praised the FA's 'dignified refusal to take the slightest notice of that small but noisy section of people in this country who were incapable of living up to the high traditions of British sportsmanship'. He hoped that the Germans would receive 'a cordial welcome from every section of British sport'. FA Secretary Rous, commenting on Dunnico's views, thought that they reflected 'the sentiments of the FA exactly'.

The match was now only a few days away. The TUC made one last effort, demanding and receiving a personal audience with the Home Secretary on Monday 2 December, to no avail. Sir Walter Citrine accepted defeat but continued stating the TUC's case to the nation. 'Sportsmen in this country,' he said, 'should understand that the Nazi government has destroyed everything in the nature of independent facilities for sport in Germany.' It had 'not only compulsorily disbanded all sports organisations which were attached to the Christian churches, youth movements and athletics bodies, and confiscated their funds, but has imposed a political and racial test on athletes'.

The German party arrived at Croydon Airport that morning, the first European team to travel to an away match by air. The event was reported in the *Daily Worker* under the extraordinary banner headline 'HITLER FOOTBALL GANG LANDS'. There were three planes full of them, according to the *Worker*, 'swastikas flying from every window'. The players emerged in 'full military style' and duly *heiled* their waiting ambassador. Questioned by more sympathetic newspapers, one German player insisted, 'We are nothing to do with the Government'. Another claimed that 'Hitler has sent us no message. We are here as sportsmen to play football against the best footballers in the world. That is all.'

On the following morning a *Times* editorial announced that 'a sporting fixture in this country has no political implications. So says everyone.'

First impressions of the Germans were predictable enough. They weren't big, according to the *News Chronicle*, but they looked fit and young and their average age was twenty-five. The *Daily Express*, which pronounced them 'a fine, upstanding, whistling crowd of youngsters', knocked two years off the average age and revealed that their average hair colour was blond. Like all German footballers they were amateurs; away from the pitch six were clerks, the other five a technician, an architect, a butcher, a buyer and a shoemaker.

According to one report they had done a week's hard training; according to another, two weeks. In *Football Pictorial* W. Schmid-Parker settled for eight days of the following regime: 7.00 reveille; 7.30 cross-country run, physical exercises; 9.30 breakfast; 10.30 tactical instruction; 12.00 lunch, then rest; 3.00 ball practice; 5.30 baths and massage; 7.00 dinner; 8.30 walk; 9.30 lights out. Goalkeeper Hans Jakob recalled many years later that the team had done no special training before the match 'other than on our own at home', but this seems unlikely given the importance which the authorities in Germany attached to the game.

The Germans' potential tactics were also discussed. The *Daily Telegraph* confidently predicted that the Germans would play 'the third back game' which had been the norm in England since shortly after the offside law was changed in 1925. Schmid-Parker confirmed that the Germans, unlike other Continentals – the pretty–pretty Austrians or the Italians, whose control of the ball was only matched by their inability to control themselves – played 'the English style'. They would 'fight them with their own weapons: tactics, speed, robustness and endurance'.

But how good were they? In a manner which was to become increasingly familiar over the years, the Germans were happy to down-play their own potential. Manager Otto Nerz confided that his team didn't have much of a chance, and the accompanying GFA representative gave them none at all in his cheerful acknowledgement of 'the superiority of English football with all the world'. The visitors expressed their anxieties about the slippery English pitches, and even about the local ball – 'don't you blow your footballs hard?' Nerz remarked.

Neutral observers were not so certain of an English walk-over. According to Schmid-Parker the German team, which had been progressively selected from squads of sixty and twenty-two, was 'undoubtedly the strongest' on the Continent. They had already played five internationals that season – against Luxembourg, Finland, Poland, Romania and Yugoslavia – and within the team there was a good understanding. Inside-right Fritz Stepan, who played for German champions Schalke, was a very dangerous forward, and his twenty-three-year-old right-wing partner Lehner had already won twenty-one caps. The centre-forward Hohmann had scored eighteen goals in seventeen internationals. The defence was not as not good as the forward line, but the 6'4" goalkeeper Jakob was an excellent shot-stopper. The *Express* concluded that this was a stronger side than the one which had drawn 3–3 with England five years earlier.

While the papers tried to weigh them up, the German players were busy being tourists. They had reportedly been supplied with two shillings pocket money a day, but chances to spend it proved thin on the ground. On the evening of their arrival they visited the Windmill Theatre but left halfway through the performance to ensure a good night's sleep at their hotel, the Metropole on Northumberland Avenue. The following morning they were driven round central London in a bus to visit Westminster Abbey and other attractions, but had to abandon an earlier plan to watch King George VI drive down the Mall on his way to open parliament. In the afternoon they arrived, kitted out, at White Hart Lane only to be told that the turf was too soft for use, so instead went through a light work-out on a nearby training pitch. 'We did all our serious training in Germany,' Nerz told the press.

That evening they went to the Palladium by Tube and were forced by the lack of available seats to 'strap-hang'. They were accompanied by their two German-speaking Special Branch minders, who had instructions to keep a keen look-out for agitators.

The English players' first sight of each other seems to have been on the eve of the match. Ten days earlier the team had been announced, and the selection was generally welcomed by the press as suitably adventurous. Derby's Barker was more attack-minded than most centre-backs of the time; Crayston and Bray were wing-halves who liked to push forward; and the forward line was full of goalscorers. On the Saturday before the game outside-right Birkett pulled a muscle playing for Middlesbrough, and the young Stoke winger Stanley Matthews was brought in to win his third cap as his replacement.

England's national team had had a rather chequered career since the last meeting with Germany five years before. They had played eleven games against non-British opposition in that time, winning six, drawing two and losing three. But the statistics presented rather a false story: England may have had won all three home games, beginning with a 7–1 revenge thrashing of Spain, but their two subsequent victories, over Austria (4–3) and Italy (3–2) had both been a lot closer than the one-goal difference suggested. Indeed, most observers thought the Austrians had deserved to win the match at Stamford Bridge in 1932.

On the Continent England had suffered a 5–2 defeat at the hands of the French, gained a creditable draw in Italy, and beaten weak Swiss and Belgian sides before calamitously losing both matches of their 1934 post-season tour in Prague and Budapest. The easy superiority of the 1920s was gone: as Leslie Knighton wrote, somewhat pathetically, on the eve of the German match – 'England ought to win, but no longer can we take it for granted that we *shall* win.'

The reasons for this fall from grace were already being debated, and the schizophrenia which has afflicted British football ever since was becoming increasingly apparent. A few weeks before the 1930 match the then-manager of Sunderland stated that to succeed in English football a team required seventy-five per cent enthusiasm and twenty-five per cent skill, but the same percentage breakdown was already proving inadequate in the wider world. The Austrians had been coached by Jimmy Hogan, the Englishman who later helped to inspire one of the world's greatest ever teams in Hungary, and he had no doubts as to what was going wrong. He told a coaching course in 1935 that his fellow countrymen, were falling behind in technique, tactical skills and pre-match preparations. Overall, the English game was much too static.

The same dissociation was on display at Upton Park two days before the Germany game. West Ham were playing a friendly against FC Austria, and it was the visitors who attracted the eye of *Express* correspondent Stanley Halsey. 'Here was classic soccer,' he wrote. 'These Austrian lads judged the run of the ball to a fraction. They clicked into position like cogs in a wheel. Their passes were unorthodox and puzzling, polished to a high glitter.' But they also lacked 'punch', and Halsey's epiphany proved less than complete. 'West Ham's methods are best suited to the struggle for points of the English game,' he decided. 'But for soccer entertainment, watch the Austrians!'

Doubts were beginning to grow despite determined efforts to look the other way, and there seemed more than a trace of anxiety in the *Daily Mirror* writer's demand that 'England must beat Germany this afternoon by a margin of five or six goals to avoid any chance of another blow at our prestige being struck'. As if to squelch such rampant pessimism, Trevor Wignall in the *Daily Express* gaily predicted an 8–2 win for the home side.

4: you only sing
when it's permitted

Match-day arrived and with it, according to whose figures you believe, ten or twelve thousand German fans. Sixteen hundred of them travelled aboard the specially chartered liner *Columbus* from Bremerhaven, having gathered from all over Germany. The GFA flag fluttered from a mast, and there were a lot more women on the passenger list − many of them travelling alone − than there would be in similar circumstances today. Though none of the passengers appeared to be toting flags or swastika badges, a speech was made by the tour manager and broadcast throughout the ship during the voyage reminding the fans of their responsibilities, just to be on the safe side.

The crossing was calm enough, and at five a.m. on the morning of the match the ship docked at Southampton. The German fans were welcomed by representatives of the Southampton FC Supporters Club and treated to a few tunes by Dell regulars the Albion Silver Band before being herded into waiting trains for the trip to Waterloo.

Most of the rest of the travelling Germans took the shorter sea journey to Dover in seven special boats, then transferred to sixteen special trains for the trip to Victoria. Each party of fans had been assigned a colour in advance − grey, yellow, blue, pink, green, red, brown or mauve − and each member of the party a rosette badge of that colour. These allowed them to identify the similarly marked boats and trains they should travel on. Once they reached London and their colour-coded motor coaches, they would first be given a meal and then taken on a short tour of the capital's highlights. The exact itinerary was supposedly unknown even to the coach drivers, who were not permitted to open their sealed orders until the passengers were on board. The whole plan had been worked out by the German 'Strength Through Joy' organisation in collaboration with the British authorities, and was pursued with almost stereotypical rigour by the Germans. One married couple happened to be issued with different colours at the outset and travelled from Bremerhaven to White Hart Lane and back without ever seeing each other.

Moving this many guests round London required a fair degree of organisation, and this the British were determined to do as efficiently, and as unmilitaristically, as they could. It would be, one *Daily Mirror* writer trumpeted in advance, 'the greatest achievement in the history of tourist traffic'. He proceeded to detail the operation with boyish enthusiasm: the trains arriving at twenty-minute intervals, the radio messages from the trains to a police car at the station, from that car to another one waiting with the 350 motor coaches, from that second car to the leading coach of the colour-coded fleet. German-speaking police were ready to help the arrivals find their coaches at Victoria. From there they would be driven to Leicester Square where a large restaurant was waiting to serve lunch in shifts. While the fans gorged themselves on English cuisine the coaches would be stationed in pre-arranged parking places where the drivers would await the next radio message, the announcement that the meal was over and the fans were ready for collection. And just in case any of the latter went walkabout, a police car with German-speaking officers and loudspeaker equipment was patrolling up and down Piccadilly ready to shoo them back in the general direction of their Leicester Square enclosure.

It was supposed to go like clockwork and generally it did. Despite all the fears of confrontations the overall mood in London was mostly benign. A *Guardian* reporter described one German visitor at Liverpool Street as being 'strangely arrayed in riding-breeches, riding-boots, spurs, a leather jacket, and a shiny black cap like a postman's', and remarked on the 'indulgent smiles' which followed his progress. The *Star* noted that 'headgear ranged from Tyrolean hats with feathers to the black, peaked cap which is so favoured in Germany. There were Homburgs by the thousand'. Most of the visitors had no more than sixteen shillings in their pockets – the amount suggested by the German authorities – but looked a good deal more prosperous. 'All wore heavy overcoats, many of which had fur collars, and they were smartly dressed. Almost every third man carried a camera and a pair of binoculars.'

One group of Germans made their way to the Cenotaph in Whitehall, and there laid a large wreath inscribed: 'In memory of the British dead, from fifteen hundred German football supporters who have travelled to attend the England–Germany game.' The British government was clearly not alone in trying to make a good impression.

As for the anti-match protests, they proved something of a damp squib. True, the enormous number of police on duty showed scant regard for basic civil liberties, arresting protesters for shouting slogans and tearing up the leaflets they were trying to hand out. However, there were not that many protesters in attendance – larger numbers may have been deterred by a sense that the battle had already been lost, or even by the unexpected ordinariness of the visiting hordes.

The *Daily Worker* certainly continued its campaign against the fixture up to and beyond the day of the match. On the morning of 4 December, under the by-line 'Where to Meet Nazis Today', the paper gave a detailed breakdown of one particular group's supposedly secret itinerary. The Dusseldorf Yellow Group was tracked through its morning sightseeing tour to luncheon near Leicester Square and then, street by street, all the way from the Coventry Street Lyon's Corner House to White Hart Lane. The 'Method of Approach' and 'Method of Picking Up' were both detailed, along with the final setting down in St George's Road near Victoria in time for departures at eight-thirty and eight-forty p.m. If thousands of angry trade unionists wanted to harangue the visitors they now knew exactly where to find them.

The only activist to really make his mark that day was thirty-four-year-old Ernest Wooley, who cut through the guy-rope holding the Nazi flag above the White Hart Lane grandstand. The flag fluttered down onto the roof but was quickly re-hoisted. Wooley was arrested and charged with doing three shillings and sixpence' worth of damage. He pleaded not guilty on the grounds that he was trying to unfurl the flag, not cut the rope, and the case was dismissed.

Queues several hundred yards in length were still shuffling towards the White Hart Lane turnstiles when the teams walked out onto the sunlit pitch, Germany in their traditional white shirts and black shorts, England – for the first time – wearing blue shirts and white shorts. Once the players were in line the band struck up the German national anthem and the whole crowd rose. The massed Germans in the East Stand looked at each other with surprise – hadn't they been warned against patriotic singing? – but duly sang their hearts out. An equally tumultuous 'God Save the King' ensued, following which the band trooped off the pitch, revealing a darkened area where boots had cut into the heavy ground. Glancing around at his fellow spectators in the West Stand, *Express* football correspondent Trevor Wignall noticed 'an astonishing number of Jews', and concluded that the much-publicised Jewish boycott of the game was 'an almost laughable fizzle'.

Straight from the kick-off it was apparent that the Germans had an enormous and probably self-defeating respect for their opponents. Their half-backs played like backs and their inside-forwards like half-backs, leaving only centre-forward Hohmann and the two wingers to threaten the English defence. The result was almost continuous English pressure and the creation of enough chances to finish the game in the first five minutes.

Every chance was missed. Matthews headed a Bastin centre wide, Raich Carter shot over, Camsell touched one cross straight into Jakob's hands and headed another over. The England supporters assumed it was only a matter of time before their team began running up the expected cricket score and seemed, at this juncture, more amused than annoyed by the forwards' profligacy.

As the minutes went by, though, it became clear that a pattern had been set. The England forwards – particularly Matthews – were having a bad day, and the German defence was gaining confidence with each muffed effort. The young Stoke winger received wonderful service from Carter in the first twenty minutes, but could do absolutely nothing with it. The German left-back Münzenberg was as fast as Matthews himself ('Never in my short career had I come up against a full-back of his class,' Matthews wrote later) and on those rare occasions when he managed to get a cross in he was unable to get the heavy ball off the ground. After about ten minutes his confidence was given a near-fatal dose by a bad miss. Several yards inside the area, with time to take aim and the goal gaping in front of him, he took a mighty swing at the ball . . . and completely scuffed his shot. The ball only travelled five yards; the crowd groaned with 'one gigantic voice'.

Matthews' poor game apparently affected Carter, who faded just as thoroughly after that first twenty minutes. One magical thrust into the penalty area excepted, Westwood, the Bolton inside-left, had an inconsequential game, which left only Camsell and Bastin to capitalise on the brilliant work of Crayston, who proved the game's outstanding wing-half on his England debut. The Germans spent most of the game in their own half, but in their rare attacks Hohmann, Fath and Lehner combined impressively at speed. Ex-Arsenal star Charles Buchan went so far as to award them the honours of the game and thought that it was solely a tendency to over-elaborate in front of goal which prevented a German score. As it was, their only two efforts in the first half came when Hohmann headed their one corner over the bar and shot wide from distance after bursting between static English defenders.

The England team had most of the possession and did most of the pressing, yet after that first frantic five minutes rarely looked like scoring. The reason for this, as explained by Frank Coles in the *Telegraph*, was that England 'were playing down-the-middle football, and Germany, just as orthodox, were bolting the door by using Goldbrunner, their centre-half, as a stopper'. Jakob, though inclined to punch in the continental fashion, was obviously a competent goalkeeper, and the German defenders were quick and strong enough on the ground to make up for England's superiority in the air. Imagination was needed but was in short supply, and as half-time approached the teams looked set to go in still level.

It was Middlesbrough's Camsell who broke the deadlock. With three minutes of the first half remaining he drifted left to receive an ordinary enough long-ball from Bray, cut in, and unleashed a vicious ground-shot from an almost impossibly acute angle. Jakob later blamed himself for not getting down to the ball quickly enough, but it was one for the feet rather than the hands and in those days goalkeepers were less inclined to improvise in such a manner. The ball was inside his near post and billowing the far-side netting before he hit the ground.

The teams went off for their half-time refreshments, England no doubt relieved and Germany somewhat disappointed. In the German dressing room Nerz told his team to continue playing in the same way; in the stands above someone was relaying news of the match to the Chancellery and Air Ministry in Berlin, where Hitler and Goring were respectively working, if not actively chewing their pencils. All over Britain football fans were tuning in for the second half commentary by Charles Eade on BBC Regional Radio.

Presumably, they were not unsurprised to find England ahead but the first ten minutes of the second half must have left a few hearts in mouths. A crisp attacking move by the Germans broke open England's defence, and a hard shot at close-range from Rasselnberg hit goalkeeper Hibbs in the chest and rebounded away to safety. At the other end Westwood put the ball in the net, but play had already been halted for a foul and the Germans were soon on the attack again. Fritz Szepan had impressed throughout and suddenly seemed ubiquitous; the two wingers were even sharper than in the first half. Ten minutes into the second Lehner was put clean through by Hohmann and slipped the ball past Hibbs, only to be called back for an offside which Charles Buchan, for one, thought dubious.

At this point a German equaliser might have swung the game. Instead, their threat slowly waned and the English gradually reasserted their superiority. A thirty-yard cannonball from centre-back Barker came back off a post with Jakob motionless, and ten minutes later a string of passes down the English left ended with Bastin's centre being glanced home by Camsell. The second goal had evidently disheartened the Germans, and three minutes later Camsell's deft flick gave Bastin the time and space to beat Jakob with a well-placed shot.

The final twenty-two minutes passed with little excitement. The game continued to be played in a spirit of almost excessive goodwill. There were few fouls of any kind and none that seemed cynical or deliberate. The English, with the occasional exception of Westwood, left Jakob well alone when he had the ball, and the Germans showed less inclination than most Continentals to use their arms when tackling. When a player went down, whether as a result of accident or foul play, there was much rueful smiling and shaking of hands. Like their governments – perhaps at the behest of their governments – these teams appeared determined to get on.

When the final whistle blew both had reason for mixed feelings. England had won but not played well; Germany, though defeated, had proved impressive in defence and dangerous on the counter.

Following the game there was no gauntlet of protesters for the German fans to run. In fact, no one was running anywhere – the streets around

White Hart Lane were jammed with barely moving vehicles and pedestrians for at least an hour after the final whistle, and many of the visitors had a hard time reaching their colour-coded coaches. The German and other Continental journalists experienced equal difficulty reaching the telephones near the ground which they had booked in relays for dispatching their copy. Some were in pubs, some in shops; the *Frankfurter Zeitung* correspondent was calling home from the local undertaker's office.

Back in town the travelling fans were being deposited close to Victoria, where they happily discovered that the local restaurants had scented an opportunity and laid on copious quantities of lager and sausages. Germans crowded the cafes and pavements, cheerfully telling pressmen that they were in no hurry to leave, until the time came for their colour-coded trains to depart.

Midway through the evening contingents of British blackshirts and communists arrived at Victoria and raised the tension-level somewhat. The only real trouble, though, came as the last two trains were about to leave. The *News Chronicle* reporter merely mentioned 'a skirmish in front of the Continental platform'; the *Telegraph* man gave the story a bit more flesh, describing how 'two men and a woman in the crowd suddenly began to shout, "Down with Germany! Down with Germany!"'. They were immediately seized by a number of policemen, who hurried them out of the station at the double.'

They were not seen by Herr Gier of Mönchengladbach, who rushed up to the barrier just as the last train was steaming out of the station. Far from being upset at the prospect of confronting the protesting hordes alone, his face was wreathed in smiles. 'You see, I have a friend in London and I like your city,' he told a lingering reporter from the *Daily Mail* who then proceeded to question him like a B-movie Nazi. 'On this, his first visit to London, Herr Gier was forced to confess that what impressed him most was railway punctuality.'

Sir Charles Clegg, president of the Football Association, was probably impressed by Mussolini's efforts in that direction. He chose the post-match banquet at the Hotel Victoria to express his organisation's 'regret at the annoyance to which our visitors have been subjected'. This was, he said, 'the first time the TUC [Trades Union Congress] had interfered in football', and he hoped it would be the last. 'Before the TUC tells a

sporting organisation what to do it should see that its own members, who
are responsible for rowdyism, are kept under proper control.' Warming
to his theme, he added that 'these TUC people seem to forget that
football is a sport. It is a great sport, free of all political influences, and, as
far as I know, they will never succeed in dragging politics into the great
game of football.'

A toast to the King was followed by the national anthem, during which
the German team, all dressed completely in brown, stood to attention.
When it was over they gave the Nazi salute, which perhaps encouraged
the FA's vice-president, Mr W. Pickford, to propose a toast to Herr
Hitler. More Nazi salutes were followed by the singing of the 'Horst
Wessel' song and, eventually, an exchange of gifts: a silver rose bowl for
the GFA, a porcelain cup for the FA, and silver souvenirs for the players of
both sides.

The leader of the German party went out of his way to dispel any
impression that its members had been annoyed or upset by the controversy surrounding their visit – and with good reason. From everything
but a footballing point of view the match had been an unqualified success,
and reports in the German papers over the next few days reflected as
much. Given the 'obvious superiority of the English footballers', defeat
on the field had been 'regarded as inevitable from the beginning',
according to one. More importantly it had been a fair game, 'as
honourable for the losers as for the winners', and once again sport
had provided 'a bridge between two peoples who stood on opposite
sides in the rain of bullets during the World War'.

The two peoples had much to thank the English TUC for, the German
paper *Angriff* noted sarcastically. In trying to stoke up resentment the
English unions had merely succeeded in demonstrating how well-
disposed the English people were towards Germany. Apparently unaware
that his sense of priorities would prove the TUC's point, the writer added
enthusiastically that for Germany the fixture had proved 'an unrestricted
political, psychological, and also sporting success'.

In purely footballing terms, the Germans seemed to have learned
something from the game. The GFA's Dr Bauwens disclosed that before
kick-off his team had decided to concentrate on defence for the first
twenty minutes, on the grounds that most sides who came to England lost
their matches in that period. They had, he admitted, probably persevered

with those tactics for too long, but had been hampered by the loss of their best centre-forward Kohner before the match and the injury sustained by Lehner during play.

The GFA's Dr Erbach thought speed was the key: the English were simply faster at everything. Captain Fritz Szepan believed fitness was the crucial element; as professionals the English were bound to be superior in this regard. Unlike the English press, Szepan also had praise for England's forwards, all of whom could both dribble and combine well in contrast to the German forwards, who were all better at one than the other.

For their part the English remained content to argue over the individual merits and failings of those who had represented English football, not about English football itself. Stanley Matthews, one paper decided, obviously lacked the big match temperament. As to the Germans, they liked Szepan for his stamina, Jakob for his reliability, Hohmann for his trickery and the defence as a whole for their resilience. Although the team was a good advert for Germany's 'physical culture' it was, when all was said and done, only a Continental team — and, as *Football Pictorial* smugly pointed out in its pre-Christmas edition, the whole Continent was now raving about the English style of play.

5: craven salutes, wonderful goals

During the two and a half years that passed before England took the field against Germany in Berlin's Olympic Stadium, the world moved inexorably towards a general conflagration. Three months after the match at Tottenham German troops re-occupied the Rhineland, and later that year Italy and Germany began giving military aid to Franco's fascists in the Spanish Civil War. In 1937 the Japanese, who had already taken over Manchuria in 1931, invaded the rest of China. On 11 March 1938, two months before England's scheduled game in Berlin, Germany forcibly incorporated Austria into the Third Reich; only a few weeks later the German nationals living within Czechoslovakia began clamouring for a change in their status. Inside Germany the persecution of racial and other minorities was reaching towards its barbaric apogee.

Those in charge of British football may have noticed most if not all of these events, but they certainly did not consider them relevant to their relationships with the nations in question. The FA's most meaningful contact with Germany in this period followed a visit from a Universities side in 1936 which cabled ahead that its party 'numbered thirteen'. The British misread this as 'numbered to thirteen' and assumed it was a request to number to this effect the kit they were supplying. Numbering was rare in those days, primarily because of its association with supposedly lower-class activities like greyhound- and horse-racing, but the International Committee watching the subsequent tour match found the numbers useful in identifying players, and were more inclined thereafter to promote the practice.

The FA's only other major contact with Germany concerned the arrangement of two international fixtures, one in Germany scheduled for

14 May 1938 and the intended return in England, which was to be played at an unspecified date during the 1939–40 season. The England party for the first match left Harwich for the Hook of Holland at ten p.m. on Wednesday 11 May. It was led by C. Wreford-Brown, the originally chosen captain of the 1899 tour party, and FA secretary Stanley Rous. Trainer Tom Whittaker was on loan from Arsenal and several members of the International Selection Committee were along for the ride. Of the fourteen players chosen for the tour – which also included later matches against Switzerland and France – only captain Eddie Hapgood, Stanley Matthews and Cliff Bastin remained from the team which had played the Germans at White Hart Lane.

Most survived the night sea-crossing without ill effects and after a brief flurry of panic at the Hook (goalkeeper Vic Woodley thought he had left his luggage behind) the party climbed aboard the train for their twelve-hour journey to Berlin. At lunch somewhere in Belgium left-back Alf Young broke a tooth on a radish.

At the time of the tour overseas travel was hardly routine, particularly for the working-class men who formed the vast majority of professional footballers. Not surprisingly, those who embraced the experience found it both daunting and inspiring. Raich Carter, who had been on the tour of Hungary and Czechoslovakia earlier in the decade, found the train fare 'particularly Continental – queer-looking *hors-d'œuvres* and unrecognisable dishes laden with garlic'. Most of the players, he said, could 'do no more than peck at the food'. But once they reached their destination such insularity became almost a blessing. Budapest was 'a fairyland'; Carter had 'never known anywhere so wonderful'. It was 'so completely removed and superior to poor, smoky old Sunderland'.

It was not the sort of place a professional footballer could have afforded to visit off his own bat. The players on this trip were on £8 a game, whether they played or not, and ten shillings a day pocket money. On top of this they would probably as international players be receiving the top-club summer wages of £6 a week which would, all in all, make for a grand return of £52 for the three weeks they were away. It was hardly the sort of sum to encourage globetrotting.

Certainly none of the players had been in Germany before, and they were not at all sure what to expect. Hitler was far from a popular figure back home, but he probably had his good points – who didn't? Many

years later England manager Joe Mercer remembered being 'very impressed with the depth of [the Germans'] interest in sport and fitness, and
the organisation they were prepared to put into it'. What he hadn't
realised until after the war was that 'the political side of it wasn't so
healthy'. These were a footballer's sentiments and were probably shared
by many in the 1938 tour party, whose first, eagerly awaited view of
Hitler's Reich came at the Dutch-German frontier. Stanley Matthews
had expected to see some would-be Aryan superman in shining boots and
was 'disappointed by the frightened little official who seemed so anxious
to show he was doing all he could to help us'.

They reached Berlin late in the afternoon and were met at the station
by only a few officials, photographers and the German captain, Fritz
Szepan. They were then driven to the Hotel Esplanade, where their
predecessors had stayed in 1930. As there were still a couple of hours of
daylight remaining, several players left their unpacking for later and set
out to explore, Stanley Matthews and Leeds full-back Bert Sproston
among them. After stopping for a cup of tea at a cafe on one of the main
thoroughfares they were suddenly surprised to see their fellow diners all
rushing for the door. Probably some local big cheese, Matthews remarked
to Sproston, only to be politely informed by an English-speaking German
nearby that the *Führer* himself had just motored past.

Eddie Hapgood didn't find Berlin quite so exciting. 'I think the
majority of the party were a little disappointed there was no fighting
or lorry-loads of Stormwehr rushing hither and thither,' he wrote
tongue-in-cheek in his autobiography. Cliff Bastin, on the other hand,
was shocked by the lack of uniforms in evidence. He had expected a
'purgatory of militarisation', but claimed to have seen hardly any during
the England party's stay. He was obviously not looking in the same
direction as tour journalist Clifford Webb, who felt 'conspicuous' without one. 'Everybody then had one,' he wrote. 'Black, brown, grey; top
boots, shining belts; student-scarred cheeks beneath rigid hat-peaks.'

All these accounts were written long after the war and were probably
coloured, consciously or not, by that event. When, in the last of his three
autobiographies, Matthews claims to have detected 'an air of menace and
foreboding about the place', there is a suspicion of hindsight at work, and
when he quotes Sproston in the aftermath of Hitler's drive-past – 'All I
know is football. But the way I see it, yon 'Itler fella is an evil little twat' –

one can only wonder at the omission of such a treasure from the two earlier memoirs. Memories of this tour, as became apparent in later accounts of the Nazi salute controversy, have proved less than completely reliable.

There was no argument about the Olympic Stadium, which the team inspected on the Friday morning. The consensus view was that the turf was better than Wembley's, and everyone was bowled over by the sheer size of the place with its 75,000 seats and room for another 35,000 standing. The one complaint was the location of their allocated dressing room, which was at the very top of the huge stand, up an endless flight of stairs. The England players suspected that these arrangements had been designed to both tire and anger them and decided to treat each fresh ascent as an opportunity for jokes.

They trained under Tom Whittaker's supervision at a nearby training ground that morning, then later in the day attended an official get-together with their opponents. Hapgood thought the Germans looked like 'a bunch of arrogant, sun-bronzed giants', while Matthews qualified a similar assessment with the observation that Münzenberg, his tormentor at White Hart Lane, looked considerably older. Both players thought the Germans seemed highly confident, and Hapgood remembered that the England players 'were a thoughtful bunch when we returned to our hotel that evening'.

The Germans had indeed taken some care with their preparations for this match. The players had been released by their employers on Hitler's orders a fortnight prior to the match, and had spent the time at a training camp in the Black Forest, utilising the services of the newly absorbed Austrians as practice opposition and benefitting from the best diet and physical-culture doctors which Nazi Germany could provide. They also had a relatively new manager, Sepp Herberger, who had been installed at Nerz's expense after Hitler had witnessed Norway's defeat of Germany in the 1936 Olympics.

The team was said to be in good form, but recent results didn't support that claim – they had been lucky to escape with a 2–0 defeat at Austria's hands in April, and had recently shared three 1–1 draws with Switzerland, Hungary and Portugal, all on home territory. According to the *Daily Herald* they were now playing an 'M formation', with the centre-forward lying deep behind the two inside-forwards. The team chosen for the coming Saturday contained five veterans of the 1935 match against England: captain Szepan, goalkeeper Jakob, centre-half Goldbrunner, left-back Münzenberg and outside-right Lehner.

This time, it seems, expectations were higher. The German press were certainly stoking them up. Aston Villa's Frank Broome, who was to play the Germans twice in two days, once for England and once for his club as part of their summer tour, remembered club manager Jimmy Hogan translating the German papers, 'which were full of how the Germans were going to stuff it right up us. They were the master race. No one could beat the Reich.' Goebbels' Ministry was working overtime to convince the German people that this was the most important match ever played in Germany, and the Strength Through Joy organisation had invited twenty thousand deserving workers to attend it. Special trains were pulling into Berlin's termini from all over the country throughout Friday. It was confidently assumed that several of the Nazi luminaries, if not Hitler himself, would be gracing the occasion.

If the German political authorities were taking the match seriously, so – at rather less notice – were the mandarins of the British Foreign Office. News of the game apparently reached Whitehall only ten days before it was due to be played, a fact which both strains credulity (did nobody in government read the sports pages?) and raised more than a few questions about communications between the Foreign Office and its representatives in Berlin. It was clearly too late to call the visit off, but in any case there was little inclination in that direction. The Foreign Office was now firmly committed to that policy of appeasement which later generations would find so craven and which would reach its own dismal climax six months later with the Anglo–French betrayal of Czechoslovakia at Munich. The question, therefore, was not how to distance the England football team from the Nazi regime, but how to ingratiate it and, by implication, the rest of Great Britain, with that regime. The chosen answer was the team's performance of a Nazi salute.

At the 1936 Olympics the British players had given the customary 'eyes right' salute as they passed in front of Hitler, whereas the French had performed the old Olympic salute, holding their arms out sideways from the body. The former had been considered disrespectful, while the latter's similarity to the Nazi salute had pleased the Germans. The French had ended up with the best dressing room in the stadium, the English with the worst. While the Foreign Office didn't much care where the England players changed in 1938, they were determined that no disrespect should be offered at such a delicate moment in the affairs of Europe.

The first intimation that the politicians would ask the England players to *Heil Hitler* came from the *Daily Worker*. 'If the FA have not done so already,' G.W. Sinfield wrote in the Wednesday edition, 'we strongly advise them to agree at once not to have anything to do with efforts to embrace them in a political stunt designed especially for the consumption of the German masses, thus kidding them that we in this country are in support of Hitler.' Why should the players be asked to do such a thing? Sinfield asked his readers. They were all working-class lads and many were probably Labour supporters; he knew of at least one who had strong socialist sympathies.

The *Daily Express* weighed in on the Friday, claiming that the England players would probably give the Nazi salute. According to tour leader C. Wreford-Brown the matter was considered so vital that a conference had been arranged for that morning to decide the issue. A list of those invited to this conference was not offered, but was unlikely to include the players. On the Saturday morning both the *Mail* and the *News Chronicle* attempted to muddy the waters with erroneous claims to the effect that English teams had always followed their guests' customs when travelling abroad. Henry Rose in the *Express* had already pointed out that the England team would be creating a precedent in this respect, not following one.

Wreford-Brown's morning conference seems to have involved himself, Rous and the British ambassador Sir Neville Henderson. 'When I go in to see Herr Hitler,' Henderson told the two FA men, 'I give him the Nazi salute because that is the normal courtesy expected. It carries no hint of approval of anything Hitler and his regime may do. And if I do it, why should you or your team object?'

Whether the players had any idea of the controversy now swirling towards them is hard to say. It is hard to believe that they received no warnings from the pressmen who were unofficially attached to the party, yet both Matthews and Bastin later maintained that the news broke over them in the dressing room just before the match. According to Hapgood he, as captain, was called in by Rous and Wreford-Brown after they had returned from their meeting with Henderson, and was told 'what they thought the team should do'. Hapgood said he disagreed with them and the Germans 'should understand that we always stand to attention for every national anthem'. He claims he then went out and told the players 'what was in the offing', and that there was 'much muttering in the ranks'.

They were still in the hotel at this stage, and there remained several hours to go before the kick-off when Wreford-Brown officially told the rest of the players that they should give the salute, adding that 'there were undercurrents of which we knew nothing' and that it was the politicians who had taken the decision. 'Well, that was that,' Hapgood concluded, 'and we were all pretty miserable about it.'

Rous' version is rather different. According to him, he put the choice to the players but pointed out that their choice might well affect the atmosphere surrounding the game. 'All agreed that they had no objection, and no doubt saw it as a bit of fun rather than of any political significance.' Bastin's account supports Rous to some extent: he says they were requested to give the salute by the British Ambassador, and that he himself 'did not feel very strongly about the incident'.

Matthews places the whole drama in the dressing room and claims that opposition was universal. An unnamed FA official gave the team the news, and 'immediately he said it, the dressing room erupted. All the England players were livid and totally opposed to this, myself included.' Captain Hapgood, 'in language richer than a Dundee cake', told the official 'what he could do with the Nazi salute'. Hapgood eventually suggested a compromise – that the team would simply stand respectfully to attention – which the official took away with him, only to return with a 'direct order' from Henderson and Rous. The political situation was now so sensitive, they said, that it needed 'only a spark to set Europe alight', and faced with this sudden responsibility for keeping the world at peace the players caved in.

Who was telling the truth? If Rous' account is to be believed, one can only assume that the players, shamed by the act itself and the subsequent criticism they received, later decided to exaggerate both the pressures applied and their own instinctive opposition. This sounds improbable, but if Matthews' account is to be accepted in its entirety then both Rous and, to a lesser extent, Bastin were being decidedly economical with the truth. It seems most likely that the players held a variety of views, that some objected to giving the salute because they despised the Nazis, that others demurred because they hated the idea of being involved in any political act, and that others again had no strong feelings one way or the other. They were pressured, they capitulated, and some at least came to regret the fact. Sixty years later Matthews was still referring to his 'shameful salute'.

What was not in doubt was that the government had put pressure on the FA, and that the FA had proved unwilling to stand and fight, either for its own independence or the integrity of the players. Those very same people who had three years earlier been so outraged by the notion of introducing politics into sport had now demonstrated that they were quite prepared to do exactly that themselves – and for a cause moreover which had precious little to recommend it.

While this drama was being played out in the English dressing room high above the pitch, the Germans had worries of their own. Only an hour before the kick-off Hans Jakob learned that his four-year-old daughter had been taken seriously ill at his family home in Bavaria. His request for permission to leave at once was turned down by manager Herberger on the grounds that it was too late to change the team, and yet it was clear to all Jakob's team-mates that he would be hard put to maintain his concentration in such circumstances.

At about five past five the two teams emerged into the huge bowl of the Olympic Stadium. There they received a thunderous welcome from 110,000 almost exclusively German spectators. Huge swastikas floated above the stands; and for the younger English players – such as nineteen year-old debutante Jackie Robinson – it might have been not a little daunting. However, the dispute in the dressing room had stiffened a few sinews and made the England players even more determined to stuff the opposition. One of them was probably still smiling to himself about an incident which had occurred in the tunnel. A member of the FA selection committee had breezily said, 'Have a good game, Goulden' to Frank Broome as he went by, and then, 'Have a good game, Broome' to Len Goulden. Broome had turned to Goulden and told him he'd 'better make bloody sure you have a good game or I'll be out for the next one'.

They lined up for the anthems, and when the time came the English arms went up. 'They are not happy about it,' Henry Rose later wrote in the *Express*. 'Hapgood, the captain, looks along the line. There is a shuffle and, orders being orders, hands are raised. They are lowered again as one anthem finishes (I detect relief) and raised again with some diffidence.' There was no doubting the German crowd's approval, though: the English gesture was greeted with a deafening roar. In the *Führer's* box high above the pitch Sir Neville Henderson was able to give his German hosts – Hess, Goebbels, Göring, von Ribbentrop, *et al.* – a suitably ingratiating smile.

Hapgood won the toss and decided that England would play with the setting sun behind them, a not inconsiderable advantage. The referee was John Langenus, the Belgian who had encountered such difficulty in trying to reclaim his legitimate expenses from the FA. As far as was known he hadn't held a grudge.

The English played well from the outset; the game was hardly a minute old when Jakob was forced to make his first save from Frank Broome. This set the pattern for the first fifteen minutes, which were played almost exclusively in Germany's half. Willingham put a free kick just over the bar, a corner was cleared with difficulty by the German defence, Bastin shot just wide. Broome, who usually played on the wing for Villa, was looking assured as a mobile centre-forward, and the two inside-forwards – Robinson and Goulden – were finding their wingers with a stream of accurate passes. These last two – Matthews and Bastin – posed a constant problem for the German side as they out-paced, out-dribbled and out-thought them. Matthews was up against his 1935 nemesis Münzenberg and was delighted to find that the German ('built like a Coca-Cola machine and with a neck that looked like it could dent an axe') was no longer the player he'd once been. Time and again Matthews simply took the ball past him.

One such occasion led to the first goal. Mathews combined with Welsh, then opened up space for Goulden to hit a powerful shot which Jakob could only block-punch away; Bastin volleyed the loose ball home. The crowd were already subdued by England's dominance and greeted the goal with chilly silence, but four minutes later were given reason to cheer when a Pesser corner was touched on by Szepan for Gellesch to find the corner with a low drive. Within a few moments England were saved by an astute lineman's flag from going 2–1 down, and then went on to dominate the rest of the first half.

Two corners were given in succession, the second of which found Bastin in possession on the left. His dribble left Janes dizzy and his cross was headed in by Robinson, the ball powering between Jakob's outstretched arms and under the bar. Three minutes later Broome reacted first to a long upfield pass from Goulden, took the ball past Goldbrunner – 'like a trout slipping round a rock', in the wonderful words of the *Sunday Dispatch* correspondent – and slammed it past Jakob.

England were now in full cry, the crowd mostly silent. Robinson shot fractionally wide from outside the penalty area; Willingham sent another free kick just past the post after Kitzinger handled. The Germans when in possession tended to over-elaborate and with Szepan well-shackled by Willingham their few attacks lacked coherence. Matthews and Bastin continued to torment the German full-backs, although Bastin was considerably slowed by an injury after thirty-five minutes.

Six minutes after that Matthews found the ball near the touch-line just inside his own half and went at the German defenders, several of whom were left spinning in his wake before he shot past the advancing Jakob. It was a brilliant goal, and recognised as such by the crowd. It was probably at this point that Sir Neville Henderson offered Göring his binoculars with the words: 'What wonderful goals. You really ought to get a closer look at them.'

The Germans were apparently out-classed and well-beaten, yet managed to climax a brief flurry of pressure with a goal on the stroke of half-time. Szepan was on the point of shooting but was robbed by Bastin; one corner was headed narrowly over the England bar, another headed home by Gauchel after Woodley missed the ball. He claimed he had been impeded but the goal stood.

The half-time whistle blew and the England players, though doubtless drained by their efforts in the heat, tackled the long climb to their dressing room with a spring in their steps. They knew they were better than their two-goal lead suggested and that they were very much the superior team. 'Master race, my arse!' they probably told each other over cups of tea.

Perhaps they came out for the second half a little too confidently: within less than a minute Pesser and Szepan had combined beautifully to put the latter in an excellent scoring position. Fortunately for England he missed – another goal for the Germans at that point might have made all the difference. Instead, the English restored their three-goal advantage as Robinson rifled home a distinctly harder chance from twenty yards after another dazzling run down the right by Matthews.

England now seemed to sit on their lead – perhaps by choice, perhaps forced back by German determination – and the game became more even. Though not crippling, Bastin's injury had taken the edge off his play, and the forwards were not combining as fluently as they had. The Germans were now making chances but were missing as many as they made. Both Lehner and Szepan shot wide when well-placed before an injury to Pesser upset their rhythm. At the other end Jakob saved from Broome with an outstretched leg and Bastin hit the post from just inside the area. Kitzinger then had a long shot acrobatically saved by Woodley.

With only fifteen minutes to go the Germans were gifted with a goal. Gauchel drew one defender before passing to Lehner, who switched the ball in the direction of Pesser on the far side. Willingham's intended interception only helped the ball on, and the Austrian nipped in between a static Sproston and Woodley to fire home.

The Germans now threw everything into attacking, and with Szepan playing as a second centre-forward they gave the English defence a few bad moments. Nonetheless with six minutes remaining the final goal – the best of the match – went to England. Yet another brilliant run and cross by Matthews was met with stunning power on the half-volley by Len Goulden some twenty-five yards from goal. Jakob got his hand to it and probably wished he hadn't: Hapgood thought it one of the hardest hit goals he had ever seen; one journalist thought the ball would have gone on to Cologne if the net hadn't stopped it. It was one of those cathartic, game-ending goals that are scored so much less often than they ought to be – one glorious blast to sum up all that had gone before.

Once the applause had died down the *Führer*'s box was seen to be empty of Nazi dignitaries; they had all stormed off to sulk in private. Later, at the ceremonial banquet for the two teams four of the Germans – those 'sun-bronzed giants' – collapsed from heat exhaustion. It had not been the best of days for Hitler's master race.

It had been a good day for English football, and the next proved just as satisfying when Aston Villa beat a German representative side largely comprising ex-Austrian internationals 3–2. Villa had only recently been promoted from the Second Division but were managed by Jimmy Hogan, who had spent several years coaching in Austria and Hungary and knew a thing or two about Continental football. They also had the speeding Frank Broome, who played even better in his usual position for Villa than he had on the previous day for England.

This excellent result was slightly marred by accompanying controversy. After the match most of the Villa team hurried off the pitch, but attempts were then made to get them back in order to join the Germans in the Nazi salute as the FA had 'requested'. Motivated less by politics than by the bad feeling engendered during the match, some of the Villa players refused to return and adhere to instructions, whereby the rest trudged off to join them. The German crowd whistled and booed, their anger at Villa's offside tactics and an appalling foul by Massie now compounded by the implied disrespect to their beloved *Führer*. The Foreign Office was furious with the FA, and the FA was furious with the Villa players. Arms were twisted, and after the second and third matches of their tour – in Düsseldorf and Stuttgart – the Villa players obediently performed the dreaded salute.

Their refusal to do so on the first occasion had been praised in some quarters and condemned in others, and much the same was true of the England players' compliance. *The Times* noted that giving the salute had 'made a good impression', and L.V. Manning in the *Sunday Graphic* thought that the match was 'set off on the right note'. Several other Sunday papers mentioned the gesture with approval, but Henry Rose in Monday's *Express* and Paul Irwin in the following week's *Reynolds News* were critical. 'The FA have blundered badly,' Irwin wrote; things were 'getting to a sorry pitch when the game's rulers can begin to tamper with a man's political feelings, professional hoofer of the wee ba' though he may be'.

Rather more interestingly, Charles Buchan wrote that there was nothing wrong with saluting the fact that Hitler and his cronies were in power; the mistake – if mistake there was – lay in arranging such a visit in the first place. Hitler's press were understandably happy to maximise the significance of the gesture. 'When one knows the disinclination of

English footballers for every kind of formality,' the *Voelkischer Beobachter* commented, 'this proof of esteem and comradely feeling should be particularly emphasised.'

At least England had won, and won well. First the national team then Aston Villa had proved 'the supremacy of England in the football world', Charles Buchan wrote in the *News Chronicle*. 'The greatest display on the Continent since British supremacy was first seriously challenged,' Frank Carruthers echoed in the *Daily Mail*. And the Germans agreed. The standard of English professional football was 'unattainable' according to the *Hamburger Fremdenblatt*; Fritz Szepan thought 'they showed everything good football should embody'. Once the England–Germany game was over the public reaction was rueful rather than harsh. 'It was realised that England was so much better,' Jakob admitted. Even during the game one German spectator was heard to mutter that the difference between the two teams was like day and night.

Armed with such accolades England went on to Zürich, where they lost a bad-tempered match to the Swiss by two goals to one. Bastin typically blamed the pitch and the Swiss; more objective observers noted how poor England's passing was. A more satisfying 4–2 victory against France in Paris completed the tour, and the England players retired across the channel for their extended summer break.

Hans Jakob's daughter died soon after the Berlin game, and he withdrew from the German squad for the 1938 World Cup in France. Germany were knocked out in the first round by Switzerland – a result which should have put England's recent results in a more accurate perspective, but British interest in the tournament was negligible, and even those who witnessed it seemed inclined to substitute wishful thinking for realistic assessment. 'Some of the matches produced football of an elegance never seen in Britain,' a *Guardian* correspondent reported home, 'and the impartial observer had the impression that many of these foreign exponents have speedier reflexes than those of our players. But none of the teams displayed the majestic power of our great side . . . or gave to the spectacle that touch of clean unsparing virility that must surely belong to the Association code.'

With the outbreak of the Second World War only a year away, the Continentals still hadn't quite learned how to 'play the game'.

6: the german boy
from manchester

In the autumn of 1940 a pamphlet entitled 'Black Record' was published in London; its author was Lord Vansittart, a distinguished British diplomat and former permanent undersecretary for Foreign Affairs. Repulsed in the Battle of Britain, the *Luftwaffe* was mounting heavy bombing-raids against London and other big cities, and the views expressed by Vansittart reflected this nadir of Anglo–German relations. In proto-Orwellian fashion he recast the whole of German history in the image of the present.

The Germans had always been dirty fighters incapable of keeping a treaty – Gibbon had said as much in *The History of the Decline and Fall of the Roman Empire*. 'German barbarism' had first crushed Latin civilisation at the battle of Adrianople in AD 378 and had been keeping up the bad work ever since. Frederick Barbarossa, Bismarck's Prussians, the current despicable crew – they were all simply links in a chain, according to Vansittart. The 'lust for world domination' persisted through the generations, fuelled by the unholy trinity of 'envy, self-pity and cruelty'. The moral to be drawn, Vansittart concluded, was to beware another 'sham reformation'. The German was both trapped in his history and doomed to recreate it.

This was an extreme view but hardly an unusual one in the early years of the war. British newsreels in the 1930s had generally shown Germany as a nation happily, sometimes hysterically united behind its elected *Führer*; and, although informed opinion was aware of domestic opposition to the Nazi regime, to most people the words German and Nazi had become virtually synonymous. In Vansittart's view, of course, this made absolute sense – Nazism was simply the latest expression of the real German character. It fitted the nation like the proverbial glove.

Familiar archetypes were taken out and dusted off. J.B. Priestley, usually a perceptive writer, wrote that Dunkirk would have been impossible for the Germans: 'That vast machine of theirs can't create a glimmer of that poetry in action which distinguishes war from mass murder.' Similar criticism, minus the war and mass murder, would be applied to German football teams throughout the postwar years – and winning teams at that.

In his book *The Myth of the Blitz*, Angus Calder provides lists of English and German 'qualities' as perceived by him during the Second World War. On the English side are 'freedom, improvisation, volunteer spirit, friendliness, tolerance, timeless landscape, patience, calm and a thousand years of peace'. On the German side are 'tyranny, calculation, drilling, brutality, persecution, mechanisation, aggression, frenzy and the Thousand Year Reich'. When measured against the real world such lists are patently laughable – it would be interesting to hear an Irish nationalist's views, for example, on the qualities of the English – but as long as they reflect widely held beliefs they remain important. And what is really interesting about the Second World War and its aftermath is how insubstantial such images proved to be. In the public mind the German was not demonised to the same extent as he had been in the First World War – as evidenced at the most trivial level, the substitution of the almost affectionate 'Jerry' for 'the Hun'.

One man had a key role in moulding British perceptions. The army's longest land-campaign of the war took place in the North African desert, where their chief adversary was a force commanded by General Erwin Rommel, a man who fitted few if any of the stereotypes listed above. Rommel had first come to British attention during the Battle of France and following his transfer to command of the Afrika Korps in 1941 he continued to behave more like a *Boy's Own* war-hero than a Nazi. He fought a chivalrous war (admittedly an easier accomplishment in an almost unpopulated desert) and ran rings around his opponents. He received a virtual accolade from Churchill in the House of Commons, and the phrase 'do a Rommel' became Eighth Army slang for doing something well. When he was eventually defeated everyone knew it had been sheer force of numbers and equipment that had worked the trick. His involvement in the 1944 plot against Hitler, and his subsequent death – he was offered the choice of suicide and immunity for his family or a

State Trial – added a noble lustre to his reputation. Rommel became an authentic hero for both the British and the Germans – the first of modern times – and as such drove as deep a wedge between Nazism and the Germans in the public mind as the later Nuremberg trials.

He admired the English. He would be happy to lead such men into battle, he announced on one occasion after seeing a number of them as prisoners. However, he was also conscious of both virtues and faults: 'tremendous courage and tenacity' on the one hand; a 'rigid lack of mobility' on the other. Rommell, like J.B. Priestley, could have been describing future football teams – in his case those representing England.

Rommel's admiration for the English was not unusual on the German side in the Second World War. Hitler himself said that he didn't wish 'the crown of the British Empire to lose any of its pearls, for that would be a catastrophe for mankind'. He often claimed he would be happy to give Britain a free hand outside Europe if he was given similar latitude on the Continent, and frequently expressed his disappointment at the British failure to realise that their own interests would have been best served by such an arrangement. The real war, so far as he and many of his countrymen were increasingly concerned, was against the Jew, the Slav and the Communist, against those primeval hordes from the East who had been knocking at Germany's door for centuries. The conflict in the West was a regrettable sideshow, and the exaggerated hatred of England which had convulsed a previous generation of Germans had mostly faded away.

This time the war ended with the occupation of Germany; and the discovery of the death camps produced a highly understandable surge of hatred towards the German race as a whole. It didn't last. The distinction between Nazis and Germans was clearly established at Nuremberg, allowing the former to be punished and the latter to be given, at worst, the benefit of the doubt. The Soviet occupation of Eastern Europe and the gradual breakdown of relations between East and West which that helped to precipitate also changed German status in Western government eyes, transforming the nation from defeated outcast to much-needed ally within a few short years.

Nevertheless, there was more to German reclamation than sheer Western self-interest. The Second World War had involved more than armies: both Britain and Germany had suffered intensive bombing from the air, and could therefore identify with each other over the experience. In addition, the occupation of Germany had not only revealed the horrors of the death camps but also the ruin of a country and the degradation of its people in a cause now utterly discredited. Ordinary people knew more about the world beyond their country in 1945 than they had in 1918, and knowledge, as they say, is the key to forgiveness.

In England there were many thousands of German prisoners, and in the years immediately after the war as they awaited repatriation to their country many of these men were treated with a kindness which would have been hard to imagine after the previous war. One such man chose not to return home and went on to become as famous and respected as Rommel had been.

The great Russian keeper Lev Yashin once said that there had only been two world-class goalkeepers, himself and 'the German boy who played in Manchester'.

Berndt Trautmann was born in 1923 in the north-German city of Bremen, where his father worked on the docks for Kalle Chemicals. Berndt was not a gifted student and left school at fourteen to work as an agricultural labourer on a state programme in eastern Germany. A little over a year later, in March 1939, he returned to Bremen and signed on as an apprentice with a large diesel-truck manufacturer. Six months after that war broke out, and in March 1941, at the age of eighteen, he volunteered for the *Luftwaffe*.

He was taken on as a wireless operator but soon transferred to a parachute regiment. He had an eventful war, serving three months in a military prison for a glorified prank during the early months of the Russian campaign, and then surviving two years of action on the Eastern Front. When he was transferred to France late in 1943 only nine per cent of his original unit remained, a figure which presumably dropped further as the Germans conducted their fighting retreat through France and the Low Countries. Trautmann was involved at Arnhem and in the Battle of the Bulge, and was captured by the Americans in March 1945. He was allowed to escape and was almost immediately recaptured by the British, who shipped him off to the first of several prisoner-of-war (POW) camps in England.

By June he was ensconced in the camp at Garswood Park in South Lancashire, where he stayed until his release from POW status in February 1948. Now the war was over German prisoners were not allowed to sit around plotting escapes or digging tunnels under vaulting horses, but were instead given the postwar equivalent of community service and put to work at whatever jobs the national and local governments wanted doing at any given time. Trautmann mostly worked as a driver and like his fellow prisoners soon got to know many of the locals, through both work and social activity. Berndt proved hard for Lancastrians to pronounce, so he became Bert.

His camp had a football team and were soon playing host to local English teams. The big blond Trautmann was their centre-half until an injury forced him to take a convalescent spell in goal. He proved so effective between the posts that he never came out again.

As the months went by the regulations concerning POWs were relaxed and the camp team began to play away games. They were a good side – up to Third Division standard, according to some who watched them – and there was no doubting who their star player was. Wherever he went Trautmann received rave notices, and soon after his official release in 1948 he was invited to join the Liverpool Combination League team St Helens Town. By this time he had sired a child by an English woman, made several good English friends and grown to like the country which had taken him prisoner. He was in no hurry to get home so took up the offer from St Helens. When he eventually went back to Germany for a visit in January 1949, the Supporters' Club presented him with a trunk packed with food for his relations in Bremen. 'They had gone without their own food-ration allocations in order to give me these things,' he later recalled. 'Then they handed me an envelope containing fifty one-pound notes. I was completely overcome.'

On the pitch he had become the local hero. He was mercilessly taunted by opposition supporters and revered by his own, especially the girls. Trautmann's team-mate Bill Twist remembered him being buried in an avalanche of young females at the end of one match, and emerging 'with his hair all over the place, lipstick marks all over his face, and a twenty-one-inch smile'. In Twist's opinion Trautmann was football's first pin-up, pre-dating George Best by fifteen years.

He was also obviously the best young goalkeeper in Lancashire.

Manchester City were seeking a replacement for the ageing Frank Swift and soon expressed an interest. Early in October 1949 Trautmann signed up with the First Division club and suddenly found himself a figure of enormous controversy. It was one thing for an ex-German POW to play for a small club like St Helens, but quite another for him to play for one of the biggest clubs in the country.

The letters came pouring in. 'City must be mad,' three servicemen wrote; 'I have followed City up and down the country and will cease to follow my club if they sign this man,' read one supporter's letter. Boycotts were threatened, season tickets returned, and a new reason created – if one were needed – for fights between City and United fans. The fact that City had a large number of Jewish supporters added fuel to the fire.

All that aside, Trautmann had his supporters. These ranged from some who refused to condemn a man for his nationality ('One would think that the player was the Belsen camp commandant') to those more interested in the season's fight to avoid relegation ('I don't give a fuck what you are or where you come from as long as you can play football, and can put some life into this fucking City team'). Manchester's Chief Rabbi, himself a refugee from Hitler's Germany, entered the fray on Trautmann's side. 'We would not try to punish an individual German who is unconnected with these crimes,' he said. 'If this footballer is a decent fellow, I would say there is no harm in it.'

One letter-writer suggested that if the Manchester City players were 'proper men they will refuse to turn out with such a man', but Trautmann's new team-mates were persuaded into letting sleeping enemies lie. 'There's no war in this dressing room,' captain Eric West-wood said upon greeting the new goalie. 'We welcome you as any other member of the staff. Just make yourself at home – and good luck.' What Westwood didn't say was that this little speech had been privately scripted by the club authorities, and that he – a veteran of the Normandy beaches – had suppressed his own misgivings in the service of the team as a whole.

In doing so he gave Trautmann the opportunity to win over the others with his personality and through his brilliance on the pitch. The latter was soon in evidence, as was the campaign of hate which followed him up and down the country. Chants of '*Heil Hitler*' and 'Nazi' were common currency during his first season, though occasionally he played so well that his critics were stunned into silence. One match at Fulham in January

1950 began with relentless yells of 'Nazi' and 'Kraut' and ended with a standing ovation from both crowd and opposing team. Not long after that Trautmann saved a penalty at Sunderland only for the referee to order a re-take because he had moved too soon. Trautmann angrily kicked the ball into the terraces and the crowd started chanting '*Sieg Heil*' . . . He still saved the re-take.

Trautmann's team-mates also found endearing his peculiar grasp of English, a legacy of sharing a house with his fiancee's grandmother, a latterday Mrs Malaprop – she once remarked of a prism that 'you can see all t'colours of t'rectum'. Bert showed himself an apt pupil. 'It's like Bethlehem in here,' he once said of the City dressing room, mistaking the biblical location for bedlam. His peculiar accent, like that of a Lancastrian playing a German in an English war movie, added to the effect.

He no longer considered the possibility of going home to Germany to live. Manchester City were relegated in his first season, came straight back up again the following year, and then struggled to survive in the First Division for three consecutive seasons. It was Trautmann's brilliance more than anything else which kept them up, and when an improving team twice reached the FA Cup final in the mid-fifties he was the jewel in their crown.

Though anti-German feeling still followed him around the grounds and hate-mail still popped through the letterbox, Trautmann slowly but surely won the affections of the vast majority. He worked hard at this in every way possible, escorting visiting German trade delegations, acting as an interpreter for German football visitors and helping out youth teams – particularly those associated with the Jewish community. His felling, with impunity, of Tottenham's George Robb in the 1956 FA Cup semi-final produced an avalanche of hate-mail, but his publicising of the fact induced another torrent of letters, this time in his favour. A few weeks later he was named Footballer of the Year by the Football Writers' Association, and shortly thereafter occurred the event which turned him into a legend.

Playing for City against Birmingham in the Cup final that year, Trautmann broke his neck in a collision with Peter Murphy, yet played on in obvious agony until the final whistle. He might have been a German, but he had played the game – both on the pitch and off – in the way the English liked to see it played: with courage and dignity. In his biographer Alan Rowlands' words, he helped 'restore respect and civility back to the minds of the English towards his country. Many men could have hidden behind a curtain of apologetic excuses about Germany's past, but Trautmann was proud of his nationality and never flinched publicly when the wrath of the anti-German feeling descended on him, despite the fact that inside it hurt him and his family deeply. He was determined to prove that as an individual and a sportsman his ability and his qualities as a human being would transcend the prejudice and hate.'

It didn't hurt that he was also the best on offer. Bert Trautmann had all the qualities of a great traditional keeper – spellbinding reflexes and athleticism, bravery, sure positioning, authority and reliability – and he virtually introduced the swift long-throw out to a waiting team-mate. Decades later Bobby Charlton wrote that he had 'never seen a goalkeeper to compare with Trautmann in the form he was in for two or three seasons before he broke his neck in the Cup final of 1956. The man was inhuman.' Charlton had seen the likes of Gordon Banks, Lev Yashin and Bill Brown make great saves, but not as frequently as Trautmann – 'they were a normal part of his game'. During his professional career Traut-mann saved sixty per cent of the penalties he faced, a record which, to the best of my knowledge, has never been approached let alone equalled.

I saw one of the saves myself, at White Hart Lane in the spring of 1960. The usually reliable Cliff Jones was given the ball, but to a home supporter Trautmann looked huge on his goal-line. It wasn't a bad kick, low and close to the corner, yet Trautmann acrobatically sprawled to keep it out and although Jones put the rebound in, the referee had blown for half-time and it didn't count. Tottenham went on to lose 1–0, a defeat that probably cost them the title that year, but there were few if any anti-German insults from the terraces. By that time Bert Trautmann was greeted mostly with awe by home and away supporters alike.

7: the road not taken

On his visits home during the early 1950s Trautmann found that his country and its football were recovering from the war and its aftermath. Sport was still organised along prewar lines; in Germany, as well as in most Spanish-speaking and Communist countries, huge clubs catered for a wide variety of different sports and all age-ranges. Footballers were still part-timers, most of them working for companies owned by club directors or their friends. There was no national league but there was a national sense of purpose, as evidenced by the German FA's new coaching course at Cologne University which offered a deeper and more comprehensive approach than anything the British FAs had yet dreamed up. In 1952 Trautmann heard that Sepp Herberger, who had survived the war as national-team coach, was in the process of assembling an excellent team for West Germany's first postwar crack at the World Cup, in two years time.

The English FA had played a significant role in drawing the Germans back into international football after the Second World War, partly through behind-the-scenes persuasion and partly by their encouragement of youth fixtures between the two nations in the late 1940s. FA secretary Stanley Rous was actually given the West German Grand Cross of the Order of Merit for his services to German football, particularly those provided in this period.

The FA's work at home offered fewer reasons for congratulation. The first shock of the postwar world to English complacency arrived with the touring Moscow Dynamos in November 1945. However, the good results and even better performances achieved by the tourists against four British Leagues sides were explained away by any number of feeble excuses; and the lessons which might have been learned through a simple admission that the Russians had played better football were lost. As soon as the Soviet party returned home British football settled comfortably back into its now customary rut, happily cushioned by the enormous popularity of the game through the years of austerity that followed the war.

England's post-season trips continued and fixtures against foreign opposition were now being arranged in mid-season on a regular basis. Between the beginning of the first postwar season in summer 1946 and their departure for the World Cup in Brazil in the spring of 1950, England played seventeen internationals against non-UK sides of which they won thirteen, drew one and lost three. One of the defeats was at home – the first to foreign opposition on English soil – but the Irish were not considered foreign enough and their 2–0 win at Goodison in autumn 1949 was not allowed to count.

Still, all in all England's record was better than respectable, and there seemed little incentive for the FA to make radical changes in the way it organised the team. They had re-joined FIFA in 1946 and even appointed a national-team manager for the first time in that same year. How progressive could they be? Admittedly the manager, Walter Winterbottom, had been given powers which any club manager would have considered derisory, but so far the system – in which he coached the team selected by an FA committee – was apparently working well. The England party set off for Rio with high hopes, and arrived to find that the bookmakers had made them joint-favourites with their hosts.

Disaster followed. Only one member of the international selection committee – fish-processing millionaire Arthur Drewry from Grimsby – was on hand to select the team. They rather fortunately beat a skilful Chile side 2–0 in the first game so, ignoring the pleas of Winterbottom and Rous to bring in Stanley Matthews against a no-hope United States team in the second game, Drewry persevered with the same eleven. The Americans took to the pitch exhausted from a night of partying and won 1–0. England then needed to win their third game to stay in the tournament but went down to the Spanish by the same score in Rio's Maracana Stadium. Ninety thousand Brazilians waved white handker-chiefs in derision, a gesture the England party mistakenly interpreted as a gallant farewell. Their flight home had been booked for the day after the final but they neither waited nor took the opportunity to watch the final pool matches. What could they have learned, after all?

More excuses followed. The Spanish had time-wasted, the refereeing had been inadequate, and the USA had fielded three ineligible players (a Scot from the English Third Division, a Haitian and a Belgian emigrant who had never played professionally). No wonder England had been eliminated. At home League football continued to pull in the customers and the England team, as if determined to prove that its failure in Rio had been nothing more than a regrettable lapse, lost only one of its next twenty-five games – against Scotland.

In the penultimate match of this run – staged to celebrate the FA's ninetieth anniversary in October 1953 – England managed a 4–4 draw with a star-studded Rest of Europe side, although they required a last-minute penalty from Alf Ramsey to do so. To mark the same occasion FIFA's general secretary Kurt Gassmann paid tribute to England's con-tribution to the game: 'They not only taught us their methods of play but they made known to us these true English traditions, the famous English sporting attitude, sportsmanship and fair play as well.'

And if the pride was well-earned, then so was the fall.

There have since been other occasions at Wembley when a foreign side has played well enough to humiliate their English hosts – the Germans in 1972 and the Dutch in 1977 spring to mind – but there has never been a shock to the English system as great as that administered by the Hungarians in 1953. It was England's twenty-sixth home game against foreign opposition (including the one against Eire) and though the Hungarians' reputation had preceded them no one seriously foresaw defeat, let alone on such a cataclysmic scale.

It was a turning point in English football in more ways than one. Many Englishmen who watched the game though naturally upset by the fact that their country was being disgraced, nevertheless found themselves entranced by the manner of the Hungarian victory. This was football as it was meant to be played, with grace and skill and strength and speed, with goals that made spectators gasp in wonder. When Ferenc Puskas scored his famous goal – dragged the ball back as if it were a cape for Billy Wright's charging bull and in almost the same movement smashed it exultantly past Gil Merrick's left shoulder – no true football-lover's heart could help but leap.

Future West Ham and England manager Ron Greenwood, then a Chelsea player, was at Wembley that day. 'It struck me shortly after the start that I was watching something very precious. The game was so near to what I'd always had in mind that I almost purred.' The Hungarians had great players – Hidegkuti and Boszik were attacking midfielders of astonishing virtuosity; Koscis was one of the best headers of a ball in football history; and Puskas perhaps the game's deadliest ever finisher – but there was more to them than individual quality: in Greenwood's words, they 'simply played football differently'.

They played the short-passing game which Moscow Dynamo had brought to Britain in 1945, but they played it better and with more variety, occasionally throwing in a long ball, always moving. Their technique was tremendous, and 'they understood the value of space, how to make it and how to use it'. They were precursors of 'Total Football' in the sense that no player was limited to a particular job or area of the pitch. They were happy to play the ball to marked men and let them either lay it off or try to turn the marker, something rarely seen in British football at that time. They played in moving triangles 'so the size, angles and direction of their triangles were constantly changing. Their style was all about understanding, rhythm and intuition'.

Greenwood was inspired by the Hungarians – and much of what he witnessed was later reflected in West Ham's attractive teams of the 1960s and 1970s – but other, less poetic souls wanted none of it. Alf Ramsey made his last international appearance on the fateful day and refused to believe that there was anything to be learned from the defeat. 'Four of their goals came from outside the penalty area,' he said. 'We should never have lost.'

Six months later England travelled to Budapest for a World Cup warm-up game and went down 7–1. There were eight changes to the team which had played at Wembley – only Gil Merrick, Billy Wright and Jimmy Dickinson survived – but the manner and margin of defeat was even more emphatic. The two teams went into the World Cup in very different frames of mind, England hoping for a 'decent showing', Hungary virtually assuming the championship was already theirs.

The latter enjoyed a tempestuous World Cup, hitting nine past the

South Koreans and eight past a deliberately weakened West German side in the group matches, out-scrapping the Brazilians in the notorious 'Battle of Berne' and shading the brilliant Uruguayans in a wonderful semi-final. Puskas had been badly injured (intentionally, he claimed) by a Liebrich tackle in the group game against West Germany; and when the two teams met again in the final his insistence on playing proved ultimately fatal to his team. Though two up in eight minutes the Hungarians eventually succumbed to a West German side which combined prodigious levels of fitness with those attributes most often associated with the better British teams: speed, strength, simplicity and an adamant refusal to be beaten.

The Hungarians went home bitterly disappointed, one of several best teams in a World Cup not to win it. England, meanwhile, having been eliminated by the talented Uruguayans in a hard-fought quarter-final, probably travelled back across the Channel in a better frame of mind than they might have expected. This latest failure had been far from a disgrace, and with changes already planned in the way the national team was selected and organised there seemed, particularly to those congenitally incapable of imagining any lasting English inferiority on the football pitch, plentiful reasons for optimism.

Walter Winterbottom had learned several lessons from the debacles against Hungary and England's less than overwhelming performances in Switzerland. Firstly, he needed greater control over the team that was selected. Secondly, it was time to stop selecting the team for each international on an ad *hoc* basis and to start treating the England team as a long-term proposition – to build a team over a period of years, gradually introducing products of the Under-23 side which had played its first game against Italy the preceding January. Thirdly, he needed more time with the team or party that was selected, for tactical instruction and the building up of understanding between the disparate players.

He put these points to a meeting of the FA technical sub-committee in August 1954 and in theory at least they were broadly accepted. The FA *did* have control over how the team was selected and this was immediately changed, the former eight- or nine-man committee giving way to a streamlined three-man junta comprising the chairman of the old committee, one other member and the team manager. So far, so good. However, the FA's other recommendations – which included better training facilities, more individualised training, more work with young players and more floodlighting – were beyond its power to implement. The clubs owned the facilities and paid the players' wages, and they had no vested interest in a successful national side. On the contrary, their interests, particularly when it came to releasing players, were often diametrically opposed. There were few if any chairmen or managers who didn't offer patriotic lip service to the needs of the national team, but words were never going to be enough. As Johnny Haynes wrote seven years later, it was all very well Winterbottom being aware of the need for a shake-up, 'but until this fact had dawned on all the other football authorities our England coach was powerless to put his modern methods into operation'.

Of course some people simply distrusted the new plans – and not all of these people were to be found in club offices. Stanley Matthews thought that the England team's will to win had been sapped by too much tactical instruction from Winterbottom. 'You just cannot tell star players how they must play and what they must do when they are on the field in an international match,' he said. 'You must let them play their natural game, which has paid big dividends in the past.'

The key words here were 'in the past', and Matthews was certainly not the only man living there. Over the weeks and months which followed the August 1954 meeting some efforts were made to introduce those wider changes which would help England's international prospects, but more often than not excuses were found for blocking or postponing them. As Tom Finney would wryly observe of these efforts four years and another World Cup failure later, 'it all soon fizzled out'.

8: the glittering past

On 17 November 1954, a fortnight before England were due to resume their rivalry with the Germans after a sixteen-year hiatus, Wolves beat the much-touted Spartak Moscow 4–0 in a friendly at Molyneux. Perhaps the memories of British humiliation at Hungarian hands were still rankling, because this victory was quickly blown out of all proportion. Bob Ferrier in the *Mirror* waxed as lyrical as anyone. 'They did what we all secretly hoped they would do, hammered and hammered and hammered at them until Spartak were shattered,' he wrote, sounding more like a war correspondent than a football writer. 'And Wolves spoke for England under the lights and through the mists of Molyneux last night. Make no mistake, they gave us a result that will reverberate around the soccer world.'

It was a certainly a memorable night, and not only for those crammed into the Wolves' ground. The second half was shown live on TV – one of the earliest, if not the very first, night games to be so shown – and the BBC, forced to place their single camera behind one of the goals, were lucky to find themselves with the best possible view of Wolves' four-goal storming of the Spartak net. The swirling mist which all but obscured the unimportant events taking place at the other end added further drama to the occasion.

Amid all the excitement it was easy to forget that Wolves had only been 1–0 up with five minutes to go and that the true quality of Soviet football in 1954, though hard to judge with any accuracy, was clearly a long way short of the Hungarian standard of 1953. One journalist immediately suggested that the entire Wolves team should represent England in the forthcoming international at Wembley, where they would presumably hammer and hammer and hammer at the World Champions until they were shattered. This was a point of view which in essence if not in detail would haunt England for most of the next forty years. The desire to play eleven Wolves players in England shirts has long since vanished, but the impulse to keep hammering has been harder to quell.

Even in 1954 some saw the danger in this attitude. In a very thoughtful piece on the eve of the West Germany game *The Times*'s football correspondent neatly divided footballers into 'ball players' and 'runners'. He admitted that the Wolves' victory had given English football a 'distinct fillip', but pointed out that they were 'a team of "runners" – adherents to a style of headlong speed, long first-time passing, and hard tackling.' These qualities might work in the British Leagues and one-off glory nights against foreign opposition, but 'one doubts very much if the salvation of English football, in the long run and in the international comparison, lies in that direction. One has only to look at the list of "runners" who have lately proved failures in English colours against imaginative Continental opposition . . .'

In the event there was an unusual preponderance of 'ball players' chosen for the West German match on 1 December, and the casual observer might well have been forgiven for assuming that Walter Winterbottom and at least one of his fellow selectors shared the views of *The Times*' correspondent. He would, however, have been only half right, as one player's account of his own selection later made clear. Ball player *par excellence* Len Shackleton had recently been recalled to the national team after five years of involuntary exile: his long exclusion had been explained to the Sunderland inside-forward, off the record by one FA selector, as part of a deliberate policy of not picking individualists. The selectors wanted men who would get rid of the ball quickly; and one of them had made it clear to Shackleton, in the latter's own words, that 'it was an unforgivable sin for a player like Stanley Matthews or myself to beat an opponent by employing any skill we might possess'.

When Shackleton was picked for the game against Wales in November it was not for his skills on the ball: his pre-match instructions were once again to get rid of the ball as quickly as possible. Because he wanted to play in the match against West Germany ('To try and prove in my own small way that it was not the prerogative of every footballing nation to rub the Englishman's nose in the dirt') Shackleton obeyed orders. England ground out a 3–2 win against the Welsh and, though acutely aware that he had let his own fans down, the Sunderland man was pleased to find that he had not disappointed the selectors. 'Shack played just as we wanted him to,' one said. 'Why can't he always play that way?' It was obviously all right to be a ball player as long as you didn't play with the ball.

If picking ball players to play like runners seemed a rather strange policy, opening a new chapter in the national team's history by selecting eleven players with an average age of almost thirty was equally perverse. Only five of those chosen had been to Switzerland in the summer, so it was hardly a case of maintaining continuity. It appears that on this occasion the selection committee's main aim was simply to put out the side best capable of beating the West Germans – contrary to Winter-bottom's notion of gradually building a good England team. Perhaps it was felt that a good win over the World Champions would give the new England set-up the kick-start it needed, though one more glorious hurrah for this group of ageing legends – 'Any country in the world would be proud to present these players,' West German manager Sepp Herberger eulogised – promised little for the future. Indeed, a comprehensive England win would merely encourage the belief in those concerned that there was nothing to learn from the Continent. The West Germans had beaten the Hungarians, so if we beat the West Germans . . .

The significance of such a victory also depended on how strong a side West Germany turned out on their first ever visit to Wembley. In the event the Germans were in disarray, having lost the services of more than half their World Cup-winning team. Wing-half Horst Eckel broke a leg in late summer, and then player after player came down with what was claimed to be jaundice. The reserve goalkeeper was the first to succumb, and was eventually followed into the Bad Mergentheim convalescent clinic by four of the forwards who had played in the 1954 World Cup final: Helmut Rahn, Max Morlock, and brothers Fritz and Otto Walter. Finally, only a week or so before the England game, the fifth forward, Hans Schäfer, broke his ankle playing for Cologne.

According to the *Daily Herald* – and only the *Daily Herald* – there was more to this malady than met the eye: the Continent was said to be 'seething with rumours' that the players' jaundice was a consequence of their drug-taking during the summer's World Cup. One European paper had even named the drug and the *Herald*, though coyly refusing to reprint the name, had asked the Pharmaceutical Society of Great Britain about it. This learned body had never heard of the drug in question but had gone on to claim, somewhat confusingly, that jaundice could not be brought on by the use of stamina-enhancing drugs. There the *Herald* case for the prosecution rested, or perhaps simply collapsed.

Whatever precisely the cause, the loss of so many first-choice players was a crippling blow to the West German team and their recent record showed as much. In late September they had lost 2–0 to an average Belgian side in Brussels, and three weeks later had been soundly beaten by the French in Hannover. When the squad gathered once more in late November at their Gruening training camp near Frankfurt the mood was far from optimistic. Herberger, adopting an approach which his successors would make all too familiar, played up the opposition and his own side's difficulties and played down any chances of a German victory. He was worried by West Brom's Ronnie Allen, he said, and by the sort of tackling Wolves had shown the Russians; he was also worried about using the heavier English ball, and about the prospect of having to play with one of the new white balls. He was even being forced to introduce a mere eighteen-year-old at centre-forward, one Uwe Seeler. And the English journalists on the spot, though bowled over by the facilities at the German state-of-the-art training camp, thought he was probably right to be worried. The West Germans looked decidedly ordinary in practice.

Only John Camkin in the *News Chronicle* was looking beyond the coming match. The facilities at Gruening might not produce a German win at Wembley, but setting up such establishments, he thought, would 'pay big dividends in the years to come'.

The German party arrived at Liverpool Street early on the morning of Monday 29 November. They had found match programmes for sale on the boat which brought them over and had been unimpressed by their typicality – Eckel, who had broken a leg in August, was down to play at right-half. That afternoon they trained in the rain at Barnes and found the white ball less problematic than they had feared. They had brought their own cobbler with them, one Adolf Dassler who made the team's boots in his shop in Erlangen, and were soon joined by Bert Trautmann, who was to act as the party's interpreter. He would doubtless have dearly loved to be joining the party as its goalkeeper but in those days the idea of foreign-based players in national teams was inconceivable.

Interest in the game was high in both countries. All Wembley tickets had been sold and the BBC were to offer live television and radio broadcasts. In addition, eight London cinemas were showing large-screen relays of the match for the inflated sum of 7/6 (seven shillings and sixpence), – thus undercutting the Wembley touts, some of whom were sadly reduced to selling 3/6 seats for 3/6. 'You can't even make a decent profit,' one lamented to an unsympathetic journalist from the *Daily Worker*.

In Germany those few lucky souls who owned TV sets were being showered with offers of a visit, while beer-hall proprietors were planning to levy an extra charge for customers to watch as they drank. Upward of ten thousand Germans were making the trip to Wembley, this visit organised by British and German travel agents rather than Strength Through Joy. Seven thousand people were coming just for the day, which made it the most populous cross-channel away-day on record. The price of a day-return from Frankfurt to Wembley was around £8.

This time there were no fears of political protests, or indeed of trouble of any kind. It was less than ten years since VE Day (Victory in Europe, 8 May 1945), and yet anyone from another galaxy either attending the match or reading the publicity which surrounded it would have had a hard job realising that a war had ever taken place. There were a few offhand references in the press – one reporter at Gruening mentioned that these were the same roads he had covered as a war correspondent; another revealed that the German trainer had once been a Messerschmitt pilot – but the really critical comments came only from the now marginal *Daily Worker*, which complained rather weakly about German triumphalism in the aftermath of the World Cup final. If anyone asked any of the players about their feelings towards the enemies of not so long ago, their replies were not printed. The German ambassador, diplomatic to a fault, said that of course his nation hoped for a victory but that he had learned from his time in England that it was 'probably more important for us to be good losers if the game goes that way'.

The English press certainly thought it would. *The Times* and *Daily*

Express both confidently predicted a comfortable England win; the *Daily Herald* suggested a two- to three-goal margin; the *Daily Mail* 'at least 5–1'. In the *News Chronicle* Charles Buchan pointed out that the Germans were fielding only 'a shadow team', but then went on to claim that England would have won comfortably against even their strongest eleven. In the white heat of expectation the two nations' relative performances in the World Cup seemed to have been swallowed up by a footballing variant of amnesia.

In contrast to the Germans' first two days in England, which had been all gloomy clouds and rain, the sun was shining out of a cloudless blue sky, when the teams emerged from the Wembley tunnel at a quarter to three on Wednesday afternoon. England were in red shirts, white shorts, and red socks with white tops; Germany wore white shirts trimmed with black, black shorts, and black socks with white tops. The players trooped across the still-sodden turf and lined up for the national anthems, both of which were received in respectful silence. It was 'a sight that did much to obliterate memories,' Frank Coles wrote in the *Telegraph*.

The game itself began with a deceptive flourish from the West Germans. In the first minute right-back and captain Josef Posipal began the move which left Gerhard Kaufhold with only Bert Williams to beat, but the chance came too soon for the Offenbach winger who was winning his first and last cap that day. His shot was too straight, Williams blocked it and England took the game by the scruff of the neck. In the first twenty minutes they could have been four up had the forwards finished better and had Fritz Herkenrath not proved himself as adept at blocking shots as his English counterpart. Matthews and to a lesser extent Finney were keeping the German full-backs at full stretch, and the chances kept coming. Twice Herkenrath denied Ronnie Allen and twice Tom Finney as the West Germans were forced deeper and deeper into their own half. It was fortunate for them that right-half Herbert Erhardt and inside-right Michael Pfeiffer played at right-back and right-half for their clubs, for they were now virtually playing in these positions.

The eighteen-year-old Seeler was left with both Billy Wright and Bill Slater to deal with, but in a rare German attack he showed his potential, cutting in from the wing and unleashing a fierce shot from a narrow angle which Williams did well to save. The West Germans were obviously full of spirit, and in midfield Gerhard Harpers, Erhardt, Pfeiffer and future national team manager Jupp Derwall were moving the ball about in neat triangles. Still, there was little real penetration and no player of Fritz Walter's stature to impose his presence on the pattern of play.

The only surprise about England's first goal was how long it took to arrive. A free kick was awarded about five yards outside the penalty area, Allen ran over the ball and Shackleton chipped it towards him. The West Brom man's first-time shot was sliced off the line by Posipal but fell obligingly for Matthews, who hit a perfect far-post cross on the half-volley for Roy Bentley to head home from an acute angle.

This was in the twenty-seventh minute, and for the rest of the first half the ball hardly left the German half. Matthews seemed to be almost playing with the experienced Werner Kohlmeyer, and Len Shackleton had finally decided to free himself from the expectations of the selection committee. He had started the game, he said, playing 'straightforward stuff, refusing to let myself go', but after half an hour 'I was fed up, and decided the pretence had gone on long enough'. Now the tricks started to flow, delighting the crowd but irritating the selectors, who wanted England's superiority translated into goals, not glory.

At only 1–0 up they had a point, and one which Alfred Beck's miss from point-blank range – only the third real chance the West Germans had made – probably reinforced. At the other end the German defence continued to hold out, with centre-half Liebrich playing a commanding role and Herkenrath's wonderful positioning denying those forwards who did break through. Ronnie Allen volleyed over following another superb run and cross from Matthews and half-time arrived, leaving the crowd to listen to the massed bands and wonder if the home team's wastefulness might cost them dear in the second half.

After the interval English anxieties were swiftly assuaged by a second goal. In the forty-eighth minute Shackleton turned and hit a perfect reverse chip over the German back line for the surging Finney and, though Herkenrath once more managed to parry the shot, this time the ball ran obligingly into the charging Allen's path; the West Brom centre-forward had the simplest of tasks to steer it home.

For the next fifteen minutes or so England were at their most dominant. Finney had finally got the measure of Posipal and both he and Matthews were now running riot down the flanks and continually setting up shooting opportunities for the other forwards to spurn. Kohlmeyer tried everything he knew to stop Matthews but this proved, in *The Times* correspondent's memorable phrase, 'like trying to imprison a shaft of light in a matchbox'. One minute the ball was there, the next it wasn't. Kohlmeyer 'lunged, he slid into the tackle, he employed the defensive retreat. But always there was that aggravating outside flick that takes Matthews past a defender's left side after once having anchored – by suggestion of body swerve – the opponent on the other foot.'

The moment of the match, though, came from Shackleton. Picking up the ball just inside the German half he ran at goal, dribbling past one man, dummying a second, jinking past a third and finally taking the ball round the advancing Herkenrath only to run it out for a goal-kick. The crowd were on their feet, scenting glory, and the groans as the ball ran out soon swelled into an enormous cheer. This was the moment to remember, the memory that would bring a smile of pleasure in years to come.

The game was too one-sided now, an exhibition of dominance marred only by poor finishing. The crowd got restless as the passing became sloppy and then suddenly, with just fifteen minutes to go, the Germans were back in it. Seeler twisted away from Billy Wright, found Beck with a quick pass and the West German left-winger took the ball past Staniforth before driving a low shot past Williams. The travelling German fans went wild with joy, the English muttered 'I told you so' to each other, and for several minutes what had once seemed inconceivable seemed anything but. For the only time in the game the Germans pushed forward as a team, and the English spectators, in the words of the on-form *Times* correspondent, could only gnaw at the handles of their umbrellas and bite the brims of their hats.

Fortunately for England no chances were made, and five minutes after Beck's goal Shackleton made it safe for his team. A brilliant reverse pass from Allen sent him arrowing through a gap in the German lines and he elegantly chipped the ball over the advancing Herkenrath. He said afterwards that what pleased him most about the goal was that it had been planned in advance. The German goalkeeper was obviously an outstanding shot-stopper, particularly at close range, and during the match Shackleton had come to the conclusion that the best ways of beating him were by dribbling around or chipping him. He had tried the first and failed, so when a second chance came his way he attempted the second. 'True to type, he ran out to meet me but just as he was about to pounce I produced my right-foot "mashie niblick", and was relieved to see the ball float over his head into the untenanted goal.'

The last ten minutes saw a couple more chances wasted by England but no further threat from the West Germans. The World Champions – in name at least – had been comprehensively beaten. In the West German dressing room after the match Jupp Derwall remembers that the Matthews-tormented Kohlmeyer didn't say a word. 'He just sat on the floor with his head in his hands and he was still there after the rest of us had dressed, and we had to wait for him in the bus before we could leave.'

The most widespread emotion in the following morning's English papers was relief. The terrible defeats by Hungary and the less than sparkling performances in the World Cup had been consigned to the past. England was 'on the way back to the top' according to the *Mail*; her victory over West Germany 'bore further evidence of the gradual restoration of our national football standards,' claimed the *Telegraph*; 'signs of England football recovery confirmed,' trumpeted *The Times*. Most of the visiting Germans seemed to agree. Manager Sepp Herberger said he was well satisfied, having expected a much heavier defeat. Like everyone else he paid glowing tribute to Matthews, who had been 'a menace' in 1938 and who in sixteen years had 'forgotten nothing'. One Herr Zimmerman, said by the *Telegraph* to be the doyen of German football commentators, insisted that no one in Germany had expected any other result, and praised the sportsmanlike character of the match in 'England, the motherland of sport'.

There were a few divergent voices. In the *Mirror* Peter Wilson thought the Germans the worst team seen at Wembley since the war and soundly castigated the England players for being 'too gentlemanly – too damn swollen-headed, pig-headed, complacent, smug – what you will – to bury the opposition as completely as they deserved.' Not surprisingly, Wilson disagreed with the assessment of the *Die Welt* football correspondent who considered that the match had been won by the weaker of two weak teams. In his opinion England had ceased to be a football power, was far too reliant on Stanley Matthews and had a thoroughly average defence. Had Rahn and Schäfer been fit England would have lost.

This far from outlandish conclusion sent Wilson into a xenophobic rage. Under the headline 'STAB IN THE BACK FROM GERMANY' he gratuitously quoted Winston Churchill's dictum that the Germans are 'always either at our feet or our throats' and wondered out loud why the West German papers, 'instead of consigning the recollection of this match to the "rejected memory" section', were being 'downright impertinent'. The description of England's defence as 'average' was deemed an 'unjustifiable insult'.

This gem of small-minded English journalism looked even more ridiculous when placed alongside Charles Buchan's considered piece in the *News Chronicle*. In some positions, he thought, England were worse off than they had been in the immediate postwar period – Allen and Bentley, for example, were not in the same class as their postwar predecessors Lawton and Mortensen – but this was not the central problem. It would be hard, Buchan surmised, to find better players than Matthews and Shackleton; but even they, for all their skill on the ball, appeared to lack the positioning skills, the tactical fluidity, which the Hungarians had shown. The attack still did not function as a complete unit and the team as a whole 'looked little better than the side beaten 6–3 by Hungary at Wembley last year. The same faults and weaknesses were there'.

If this was one obvious problem for the England manager and selectors, the other was the age of the team. Matthews was now thirty-nine, and could not be expected to continue bamboozling foreign defences for very much longer. Four of the team that beat West Germany in this match – Staniforth, Phillips, Shackleton and Allen – never played for England again, and only Wright and Finney would still be around for the next World Cup in 1958.

The West German team were younger and yet proved no longer-lasting. Seeler came back to haunt England sixteen years later but the other four forwards only won one more cap between them, and of the defenders only Herkenrath and Erhardt enjoyed extended international careers.

In retrospect the 1954 game marked the passing of an age, not the dawning of a new era. When the time came a mere eighteen months later for the return fixture, only three of the twenty-two players – Byrne, Wright and Herkenrath – were still wearing their national shirts.

9: panzer edwards

England played six internationals before that next meeting with the West Germans. The 1955 post-season summer tour of south-western Europe accounted for three of them, with defeats in France and Portugal sandwiching a draw in Spain. Things improved in 1955–6: a 5–1 autumn victory in Copenhagen was followed by a 4–1 thrashing of Spain at Wembley in November, and the home season ended with a hard-fought draw at Hampden and a sparkling Matthews-inspired 4–2 victory over Brazil. Manchester City's victory in the FA Cup final made good the promise of their Hungarian-style 'Revie plan' and also cast a progressive glow over the nation's football. The England party set off for their 1956 post-season tour in confident mood despite the defection of Matthews, who had decided he would rather spend the summer coaching in Kenya.

The first match, against Sweden in Stockholm, proved a deflationary experience. Press forecasts had averaged out at a three-goal win for England but, as most match-observers agreed, a three-goal win to Sweden would have been a much fairer result than the actual goalless draw. The English moved on to Helsinki, where a 5–1 trouncing of the hapless Finns put them in rather better heart for the tour's last game in Berlin.

They left for Germany immediately after the match, enduring bumpy flights from Helsinki to Hamburg via Copenhagen and a three-hour coach trip down the autobahn to Hannover. The *Times* correspondent who travelled with the party waxed lyrically about Hamburg's great docks, the huge tracks of heath, the fields full of tulips. The world was 'a small place these days, especially for the footballer.' One wonders what he would have made of Moldovan away-days.

The England players, most of whom were probably too busy playing cards to look out of the window, eventually arrived at their destination, the sports complex at Barsinghausen which had so impressed Walter Winterbottom on an earlier fact-finding tour. It was one of nine such centres in Germany – all built by the German FA with pools money – and its facilities took the English players' collective breath away.

There was a full-size pitch, an open-air swimming pool and a running track. There was even an indoor pitch with full-size goals and a wooden floor. A microphone-fitted gallery behind one goal allowed coaches to share their thoughts with the players; and a huge unbreakable glass window ran down one touch-line, offering a panoramic view of the German countryside. In the club house, according to captain Billy Wright, there were 'beautiful bedrooms, tiled bathrooms, a lecture room equipped with microphone and blackboard . . .' The players' first reaction on arriving was to arrange an eight-a-side game for straight after dinner, and in keeping with the excellence of the surroundings they invited Winterbottom and trainer Jimmy Trotter to inspect and meet the teams before the match.

The England party were at Barsinghausen for two whole days, and their only complaint seems to have been the late arrival of their morning tea. 'The slick service of the staff was also appreciated by us,' Wright wrote diplomatically, 'and as a gesture to them, and to make sure that we had our morning tea on time, it was agreed among us that we would take over this stint . . .'

In this wonderfully appointed rural idyll it was hard to gain any sense of the new West Germany, other than to wonder at how far it had come in such a short time. The enmity between the two nations seemed a thing of the past: one German youngster asked Wright where Wolverhampton was and on being told it was near Birmingham cheerfully replied that his uncle had been shot down there during the war.

On Thursday morning the party took a plane from Hannover across Communist East Germany to the island city of West Berlin, which only seven years earlier had been under virtual siege from the Soviets, and yet now, in the words of the *Mirror* correspondent, 'breathed prosperity and well-being'. They stayed at the Gurhas Hotel and over the next day and a half visited various sights, including the old Reichstag building, the ruins of the Führerbunker and the Russian war-memorial. Wright enjoyed the trips but thought that 'a feeling of depression' hung over the whole Eastern Sector.

On the Friday they trained at the Olympic Stadium where England had triumphed eighteen years before. Both the Birmingham full-back Jeff Hall and the Manchester United centre-forward Tommy Taylor were struggling to recover from injuries, but with substitutions possible it was eventually decided to risk them both. Taylor, now twenty-four and one of the older 'Busby Babes', had finally established himself in the England team, as had his precocious team-mate, the nineteen-year-old wing-half Duncan Edwards. Other up-and-coming youngsters, like Blackburn's Ronnie Clayton, Fulham's Johnny Haynes and Sheffield United's Colin Grainger, were also in the chosen eleven: Winterbottom was at last achieving his ambition of building a team.

By contrast the West Germans seemed to be going backwards. They had played eight internationals since their last encounter with England, winning only three (against Portugal, Ireland and Norway) and losing the other five (against Italy twice, the Soviet Union, Yugoslavia and Holland) – all this despite the return of many first-choice players and Fritz Walter's decision to rescind his retirement. There was still no national league and the players remained part-timers, earning a flat rate of £25 a month for their football services and nothing for international appearances.

The eleven named for the coming match included four of the World Cup-winning team forwards – Max Morlock, Hans Schäfer and the Walter brothers – but not the in-form Rahn, who had been injured again recently. The three World Cup-winning defenders who had played at Wembley – Posipal, Liebrich and Kohlmeyer – were either injured or out of favour. The West Germans had simultaneously regained their experienced attack and lost their experienced defence, and the age advantage they had enjoyed at Wembley had been reversed.

Somewhat surprisingly, the player who caused most concern in the English camp was Robert Schlienz, the right-half from Stuttgart. They weren't frightened of his skill or his stamina – they were merely embarrassed by the fact that he had only one arm. How would they tackle him, and how would the crowd react if he was injured, the players wondered out loud. Writing in the *Express*, Desmond Hackett supported them. Schlienz's selection, he thought, was 'an unhappy choice'.

Saturday 26 May in Berlin was one of a series of very hot days. The England team was given the same dressing room in the clouds that their forbears had enjoyed in 1938, and they clattered down the same four long flights of steps to the Olympic Stadium pitch. The two teams were in the same colours they had worn at Wembley, the English having agreed to anticipate an imminent FIFA rule-change: in future only away sides in international matches would be allowed to change their strip.

The match was being shown live on Eurovision – it could be seen 'at British firesides', *The Times* noted happily – but on this particular occasion the English team were well supported in the Olympic Stadium. Around ten thousand fans had managed to get hold of tickets, most of them soldiers stationed in West Germany. The Cheshire Regiment in particular was out in force and making itself heard. As Billy Wright chatted in the centre-circle with opposite number Fritz Walter and referee Istvan Zsolt (a Shakespearian producer from Budapest) he could hear the shouts and friendly accents. 'I've known us to play abroad with only a handful of Englishmen to give us vocal support,' he wrote later. 'In Berlin we had quite easily the largest fan-following I can ever remember anywhere outside of England.'

The match began explosively, with Wolves' Dennis Wilshaw latching on to a Johnny Haynes through-ball and shooting only inches wide with just twenty seconds on the clock. A minute or so later German goal-keeper Fritz Herkenrath knew little about a Colin Grainger volley which rebounded off his body for a corner. Stung by this opening and roared on by the huge crowd, the West Germans responded and for the next twenty minutes England were mostly on the receiving end. Fritz Walter and Karl Mai looked the part in midfield, but England's defence held firm and no clear-cut chances were made.

In the twenty-fifth minute one piece of brilliance turned the game. A lofted German clearance from a Grainger corner came back to earth some thirty yards from Herkenrath's goal; Ronnie Clayton and Max Morlock locked legs and took each other down and the ball ran loose for Duncan Edwards. He surged forward, powered his way through three defenders – the word 'tank' was much used in newspaper descriptions of this goal – and from the edge of the area sent a blistering right-foot drive past the despairing Herkenrath's flailing right hand. It was a goal of astonishing power and assurance, especially coming from a nineteen-year-old, which left England feeling suitably inspired.

Now they were firing on all cylinders, stroking the ball around with great confidence and biting into the tackle. Anyone who had seen England play against West Germany eighteen months previously would have been astonished at the difference: this eleven was not necessarily better – indeed, the players as individuals were probably less skilled – but they played as a *team*, and a young one at that. One wonderful move involving six players ended with a Taylor shot brilliantly parried and Grainger firing the rebound straight into the fallen goalkeeper.

No second goal arrived, though, and slowly the Germans recovered from the shock of the first. Reg Matthews was forced to arch his back to tip over a glancing header from Ottmar Walter, and minutes before half-time the stretching Morlock couldn't get quite enough of his foot on a cross to keep the intended deflection under the bar. He hurt himself in the process and gave way to a substitute, Eintracht Frankfurt's Alfred Pfaff.

The first fifteen minutes of the second half saw the visitors still on the back foot, but for all Fritz Walter's skills the West Germans could not find a way through the England rearguard. Byrne and Hall (the latter playing with an injured arm tucked into his side) had the mastery of Waldner and Schäfer, and Billy Wright, in the process of winning his seventy-seventh cap, strode the centre like the proverbial colossus.

It was from defence that the second goal came. Byrne dribbled the ball down the left and slipped it inside to Haynes. The Fulham inside-forward, who up until this moment had been rather less prominent than many of his colleagues, hit a fine through-ball to Gordon Astall, who immediately switched it inside to the fast-moving Grainger. The winger took the ball in his stride, swept past Wewers into the area and hit an unstoppable ground-shot past Herkenrath.

This was in the sixty-second minute. Four minutes later an Astall throw-in found Tommy Taylor near the by-line. He switched it inside for Wilshaw, who intelligently slipped it between two German defenders and into the path of the advancing Haynes. He went for accuracy rather than power, almost caressing his shot past the helpless German keeper. Three–nil to England and for the next few minutes a few thousand Cheshires made a lot more noise than 90,000 Germans.

The home team was playing only for pride now, which appeared to be motivation enough. During the last twenty minutes they once more extended the England defence. A Pfaff header was well saved by Matthews, but it was not until five minutes from the end that the Germans got the goal they deserved when Fritz Walter finished off a beautiful move involving himself, Karl Mai and Hans Schäfer. By the time the final whistle blew the English players must have been feeling the effects of the heat and their all-out performance, but they didn't let it show. They insisted on doing a lap of honour before bounding up all four flights of stairs to their dressing room, antics which prompted the president of the German FA to venture the opinion that they must be 'supermen'.

After the match the press-response to the rather startling victory was mixed. Some refused to celebrate, partly in the belief that anything short of perfection was unworthy of England and partly, one suspects, because there was something vaguely unpatriotic about not taking English superiority for granted. The *Daily Herald* was unhappy about the forwards, of whom only Taylor and Grainger escaped censure, while the *Express* was more interested in lauding English fair play than English good football. Wright, the paper claimed, had provided 'an example of scrupulously fair play', and in doing so had provided 'a lesson to the Germans, who indulged in jersey-tugging, arm-grabbing and savage tackles after England players had parted with the ball'. At first sight this view seemed to be at odds with that of the *Daily Mirror* correspondent, who claimed that 'England simply crash-tackled Germany out of a grim game without frills'. But of course both papers were stuck in the same past. Rough play the English way was 'playing the game'; rough play the German way most definitely was not.

Most of the other papers were happily gazing into the future. *The Times* thought there had been immense progress made over the previous year, and that England now had the 'nucleus of a good young team'. The *News Chronicle* believed that the future of English football was 'as bright as it had ever been'; while the *Mail* thought that England's hopes were 'at the highest point since the war' and quoted admiring tributes from half a dozen German newspapers to support this opinion. Winterbottom's modernising of the team and set-up were roundly praised in many quarters and the youth of his current players repeatedly pointed out. The *News of the World* proudly repeated the German manager's assertion that 'England are a world football force again'. Less widely quoted but even more astonishing was Herberger's prophecy that England would win the 1958 World Cup. 'They are a team of hard fighters,' he said, 'and pure football teams do not win the World Cup.'

Five months later on 18 October, a Manchester United team containing Byrne, Edwards and Taylor played the first leg of a first-round European Cup-tie against Borussia Dortmund at Moss Side. This was the first Anglo–German meeting in European club competition (there have since been more than eighty), and it more than met the expectations of the 75,000-plus crowd, then the highest ever for a floodlit game in England.

There were nine internationals and future internationals in the United side that night, and seven in the Dortmund eleven, but the home team were much the younger outfit. This was just the second European tie for both teams: United had disposed of Anderlecht on a 12–0 aggregate in the preliminary round, while Borussia had needed a play-off to get past Spora Luxembourg. Away goals counting double were still a thing of the future so United surged forward from the off, creating chances for themselves but also leaving their defence dangerously exposed. A break down the middle by Kelbassa almost brought a goal for the Germans, but United looked more consistently threatening. They weren't playing Continental-style football but nor were they relying on high balls forward and non-stop hustle in the manner of their First Division rivals, Wolves. United were prepared to use the long ball when it suited, but they could also play a fast short-passing game and this mix of tactics soon had Borussia undone. Dennis Viollet scored twice, in the eleventh and twenty-seventh minutes; a David Pegg shot was deflected past his own keeper by Burgsmuller in the thirty-fifth. The crowd settled down to watch a repeat of the ten goals hit past Anderlecht.

It wasn't to be. The Germans kept playing neat, technically adept football without looking really threatening while United were now apparently content to rest on their laurels. Taylor brought two fine saves out of Kwiatkowski, but it was Borussia who surprisingly scored, twenty minutes from the end, when Byrne found Kapitulski rather than Wood with a chested back-pass. Too late, United tried to raise their game and

Borussia managed a second, Preissler shooting in after Wood had palmed away an effort from Schmidt.

Three–two might have seemed an inadequate score to take to Germany, but in this instance it proved enough – for the simple reason that Borussia failed to take their chances in the second leg. Cheered on by a large contingent of British servicemen, United defended well, if often desperately, for most of the match, while Kelbassa and Preissler appeared to be competing with each other for the most glaring miss of the night.

It was an apt beginning for the long struggle between English and German clubs in European competition, a struggle which would be in the majority dominated by the English clubs. It also hinted at being another good omen for the national team: this Manchester United team – unlike almost all of the great Football League teams which came later – was built around a backbone of great English players.

10: meet the new boss

European competition was a more relaxed affair in the 1950s, and five weeks elapsed between the two legs of Manchester United's tie with Borussia Dortmund. In the interim a revolution in Hungary was crushed by Soviet troops and British pretensions to world power were finally laid to rest in the fiasco of Suez. The world was moving beyond the mental patterns of the war era, and that in itself was bound to have an impact on Anglo–German relations.

The Federal German Republic's President Heuss paid a state visit to Britain in 1958. In her welcoming speech the Queen generously pointed out that both she and her husband were descended from the union of Queen Victoria and her highly popular German husband, Prince Albert. Though Heuss was not exactly greeted with open arms by the British public, the emotional thrust of the visit was clearly to focus on the positive aspects of the relationship rather than the darker hours of the past. These days, went the clear suggestion, we often have more in common than we realise.

Four years later in a series of specials on Britain's European neighbours the *Daily Mirror* painted Germany and the Germans in a highly positive light, stressing how hard they worked, how rarely they went on strike and how prosperous they were. Despite lacking the design-sense of Italians or the sophistication of the French, they produced sturdy, reliable merchandise. They took music and beer seriously, kept their homes 'spotless, shining, and not a thing out of place', and wore wedding rings on their left hands until the wedding. They were mad about sport and their facilities were incredible. Their women were more likely to be bosses – one in five German businesses was run by a woman – and had the biggest bosoms in Europe. In schools German children were taught about the shameful crimes of the Nazis and how they had damaged their country's name abroad. 'Everywhere I go I can see what they can tell US,' the *Mirror* man lamented, 'but I keep wondering what we can tell THEM.'

The Germans had become not so distant relations who were perhaps a bit unimaginative and a bit obsessive about cleanliness and order, but who were also doing very nicely thank you. As the photographs of lovely girls, happy families and musicians showed, they were certainly no threat.

This was one picture, in many ways the real one, but the British public was persistently being presented with another, less attractive set of images. On the cinema screens, in books and comics, with plastic or metal figures on tabletops, the war was being re-fought. In my probably exaggerated memories of the 1950s, films like *Reach for the Sky*, *The Dam Busters*, *The Wooden Horse* and *The Cockleshell Heroes* were almost constantly on television. Germans clicked their heels and said '*Jawohl, Herr Leutnant*' or ran around like headless chickens shouting '*Achtung!*' or '*Schnell! Schnell!*', They were not only unimaginative, they were also evil and it was OK to kill them.

Films that presented a more complex picture of the war, like *The Young Lions* (1958), were few and far between and it would be the mid-1960s before mainstream films began to explore the German side with any depth or sympathy. *Cross of Iron* (1977) was probably the first Hollywood film to centre on a German platoon, and then only because it was fighting on the Eastern Front. In the late 1950s and early 1960s it was still all *Boy's Own* stuff, and the enduring images were of Steve McQueen on his motorbike with half the German Army in pursuit or of fellow Great Escapees mowed down in cold blood by the Gestapo.

This simple identification of Germans with the war, which came as second nature to many Britons in the 1950s (and to a lesser extent still does to this day), uneasily co-existed with the growing understanding that the two nations were not really so different from each other. And of course whenever there was a dispute between them the old stereotypes reasserted themselves with a vengeance. In the 1950s and early 1960s there were continuing arguments about who should be paying for the British Army on the Rhine – was it defending West Germany or Great Britain? – and how its soldiers were being treated by German civilians. There was also much British discomfort about both West Germany's growing economic strength and that country's *rapprochement* with France. Having originally encouraged the latter, the British were now feeling excluded.

In addition the tabloids were occasionally beginning to make themselves heard in a way that became distressingly familiar later in the century: new events and incidents were treated as excuses for re-hashing and in some cases even re-inventing the past. One paper, for example, used the visit of President Heuss to raise the figure of those murdered by the Germans in the war to a round ten million.

For all this, any existing bad feelings between the two nations seemed to be waning as the years went by. As far as the British were concerned the Germans were becoming just one more set of foreigners they had to deal with, like it or not. The ever tactful Prince Philip told a Russian journalist in 1961 that Soviet success in space was down to their Germans being better than our Germans – as if Germany was a household of servants which had been divided up between its victors. On a Royal Visit to Germany in 1965 the Queen was more diplomatic in her reminder to her hosts that their two nations had combined to defeat Napoleon. The French were insulted, of course, but by 1965 their ranking on the list of Britain's enemies was pretty close to that previously enjoyed by the Germans.

In terms of football, nine years passed before England and West Germany resumed their rivalry and, as years go, these were eventful ones. The developed West fully emerged from postwar austerity into a period of unprecedented growth and all that implied for communications, politics, culture, and indeed sport. Most of Africa gained a form of independence; humans went into space. In 1956 Eisenhower was in the White House and Elvis was at his pre-Army peak; by 1965 Kennedy was dead, the Vietcong was rampant and Bob Dylan was going electric.

It was an equally revolutionary period for football which saw the rapid internationalisation of the game. At club level one European competition quickly became three, at national level the European Nations Cup (which later became the European Championship) was slotted in between World Cups to provide an international tournament every two years. As the number of involved nations grew so the qualifying competitions rapidly expanded to fill most of the slots previously reserved for so-called friendly internationals. The few such games which survived increasingly lost any intrinsic meaning; they became opportunities to try out players and tactics, an essential part of the process of building teams for the games that really mattered.

Neither English nor German clubs took very well to European club competition in its early years, and won only one trophy between them before 1965. The Busby Babes were beaten by eventual winners Real Madrid in the 1956–7 semi-final; the following season they were on their way home from winning a quarter-final tie when their plane crashed during take-off from Munich airport, killing many important members of the team. Hardly surprisingly, they again went out in the semi-final – this time to A.C. Milan.

This set the pattern for both English and German teams, who were knocked out at the semi-final stage of the European Cup by south European teams in four of the next seven years. During this time the Spanish, Portuguese and Italian clubs dominated all three competitions, and with good reason. Their technique was clearly superior, their tactics more imaginative; they simply had better players. No impartial observer of Real Madrid's 7–3 demolition of Eintracht Frankfurt in the 1960 European Cup final could have missed the gulf which existed at this time. Eintracht had hit twelve goals past Glasgow Rangers in the two-leg semi-final and were a fine, hard-working team of considerable skill, but the Real Madrid of Di Stefano and Puskas reduced them to the footballing equivalent of straight men. A large British TV audience was given another lesson in how the game should be played, and once again it was Ferenc Puskas doing the teaching.

The only English or German team to win a trophy in this period was Tottenham Hotspur, who owed much of their style to former manager Arthur Rowe, once a coach in Hungary. Tottenham followed their narrow loss to Benfica in the 1961–2 European Cup semi-final with a victory over holders Athletico Madrid in the succeeding year's Cup-Winners' Cup final. This Tottenham team included six world-class players – Bill Brown, Danny Blanchflower, Dave Mackay, John White, Cliff Jones and Jimmy Greaves – but only Greaves was English.

The extravagant hopes inspired by England's 3–1 win in Berlin in 1956 were soon dissipated. The national team went through the 1956–7 season undefeated, winning the Home Championship and qualifying for the

1958 World Cup in the process, but in February of that year the Munich air crash tore the heart out of the England team. Byrne, Edwards, Taylor and Pegg were all killed.

Their loss was undoubtedly one reason for England's failure in Sweden that summer, but it was far from the only one. Just as the shock of the Hungarian humiliations had worn off, so the resolution required to make the necessary changes to the English game had slowly ebbed away. In a book written after the 1958 World Cup Tom Finney found it 'hard to be optimistic' about English football. Continentals and South America valued ball skills above all else – Finney remembered watching with fellow England players, their mouths agape, as Brazilian urchins juggled oranges with their feet on Copacabana Beach – and these had to be placed at the heart of future training programmes, along with more intelligent use of the ball. 'Watch a Brazilian pass the ball,' he wrote. 'No lofted centre from the wing for him, no forty-yard long-balls that need only to be a yard out to be wasted.' The English were also far too stereotyped in their positional play, as if the numbers on their backs only allowed them to use a certain portion of the pitch. These were all symptoms of a fundamentally skewed approach to the British game, an approach more-over which reflected pretty basic British values. 'Coaches think directness, speed and fight are the three great virtues,' Finney wrote, 'but they emphasise them at the expense of skill with the ball.'

The British teams were not alone in being stuck in this rut, but some were making an attempt to lift themselves out. It was Sepp Herberger who had said that 'a team of hard fighters' had a better chance of winning the 1958 World Cup than a 'pure football team'; but the style of his West German team which, according to Finney, tried to marry 'north-European soccer with the more artistic Latin style of play' reflected an awareness that something more was needed on the international stage. While the Germans had very similar values to the English and were not about to give up on directness, speed and fight, they were beginning to realise that they needed to more closely match the Latin teams in terms of technique. Significantly, they reached the semi-finals, only to be beaten in highly controversial circumstances by the host nation. England mean-while failed to get past the opening round and in the process of overall defeat were upstaged by Wales and Northern Ireland, both of whom reached the quarters.

Nineteen fifty-eight was the first World Cup to receive extensive coverage on British TV; and demands that something be done about the England team probably lasted slightly longer than usual. Nevertheless the demands of the new League season soon relegated the national team's woes to the periphery of the average fan's consciousness. Traditionally, supporting one's club in League and Cup was emotionally involving; and supporting one's nation in friendly internationals much less so – it would take the combined effects of more TV, European club competitions and the anticipation of a major international competition in England to bring them even vaguely into line. When England undertook a disastrous post-season tour of Latin America in the summer of 1959 – losing 2–0 to Brazil, 4–1 to Peru and 2–1 to Mexico – most fans hardly noticed, nor cared.

English insularity was alive and well despite participation in three World Cups. The FA, like their counterparts in West Germany, Italy and Sweden, had decided against entering the first European Nations Cup in 1958–60, and their preparations for the 1962 World Cup in Chile were not particularly thorough. The party did at least arrive in South America two weeks ahead of the first match (in Sweden only three days had been allowed for acclimatisation). After beating Peru 4–0 in a warm-up game they continued south to their Chilean base camp, which turned out to be a rest camp for copper-company executives high in the Andes. The facilities were wholly inadequate and surrounded by grinding poverty. When Ray Wilson and Jimmy Wilson were persuaded to hire a weak-looking local child to caddie for them, they ended up having to carry the boy home.

On another occasion centre-half Peter Swan nearly died because the FA had not arranged for the party to be accompanied by a doctor. The players didn't complain about the authority's ignorance of those health, diet and training regimes which other national set-ups took for granted – they shared it. According to Ray Wilson, the players 'used to laugh at the entourage of the Brazilian team. They always used to have a squad of specialists with their international party and we used to make jokes about them.'

On the pitch England did marginally better than most of the players had expected, which wasn't particularly well. This was perhaps the first World Cup into which an England team entered without illusions. They didn't know much about the other teams – only that several of them were likely to be superior to their own. And it wasn't that England had poor players: the eleven who lost to Brazil in the quarter-final – Springett, Armfield, Wilson, Moore, Norman, Flowers, Douglas, Greaves, Hitchens, Haynes and Charlton – seem in retrospect at least to be a finely balanced team, full of outstanding individuals. The problem was more that England and the English had apparently lost faith in their style of football. The way they played in the League didn't work at international level; they weren't at all sure why and they didn't know how to play it any other way. They went home as confused by their failure as they were chastened, and in dire need of someone to sort them out. It wouldn't be Walter Winterbottom. Hamstrung by a combination of his own niceness, player conservatism and FA meddling, he finally decided to call it a day after seventeen years of struggling for the helm.

His successor would either need to be adventurous enough to reach out beyond the national culture and incorporate elements of other, foreign footballing cultures into a new British synthesis, or he would need to entrench himself and his new team in the old values and to find some way of translating the strengths of the British game into a formula which could be successful at international level.

To follow the first path would take time and imagination. However, there were still almost four years before the World Cup was staged in England, and this was probably the last time such a choice would be on offer: in future years the combination of almost continual competition and media-led pressure for instant success would make it increasingly difficult for either the FA or their chosen managers to take the long-term view.

In the event the FA was unwilling to take the gamble. Alf Ramsey was their choice, and if few men were less likely than he to offer England and its football an adventurous new beginning, few were better equipped to turn English footballers into world-beaters. As a player he had worked hard and successfully to make the most of limited talents; as a manager at Ipswich Town he had found the tactical ingenuity to make League Champions of a mostly ordinary bunch of players. He had no doubts that he could do the same for England. Even when the nation could call on the likes of Matthews and Finney, he said, 'the team would have been even better with a rigid plan'.

The fact that these great players were now gone did not phase Ramsey. Any plan had to be adapted to the strengths and weaknesses of the available players, and there was always the suspicion that Ramsey empathised more with those some way short of greatness. At Ipswich, he said, he had always had to look at expensive players from the standpoint of how to stop them, and in essence that was his intention at international level. 'His response,' in Eamon Dunphy's words, 'was a formula which stopped good footballers playing.'

Ramsey had found his rigid plan for Ipswich and now needed to find one for England. It would take him several years. Although the decision to appoint Ramsey was taken late in 1962, he stayed on at Ipswich for the rest of the season to break in his successor, and took a firm grasp of the national reins – the rest of the selection committee had finally met its overdue demise – only after England had been unceremoniously dumped out of their first European Nations Cup by the French and beaten into second place in the Home International Championship by Scotland. A reasonable draw with Brazil at Wembley followed, and then Ramsey took the team on one of its most successful European tours.

The Czechoslovaks were beaten 4–2 in Bratislava, then Switzerland 2–1 in Basel. In between these two matches England travelled to Leipzig to play East Germany for the first time. Ninety thousand attended the match which England won 2–1 despite losing Greaves to tonsilitis before the kick-off. A mistake by Gordon Banks, playing in only his fourth international, gave the hosts the lead, but England had several good chances to equalise before Roger Hunt scored with a thunderous shot from Terry Paine's pass. The second half belonged mostly to England, and after Bobby Charlton had put them ahead from a goal-mouth scramble they coped fairly comfortably with a late German rally.

England played 4-2-4 on this tour, and it worked. In the first two games Charlton and Paine played on the wings, with Milne and Eastham in midfield; in the third game Charlton and Douglas were the wingers and Kay and Melia the men in the middle. Bobby Moore first captained England in Bratislava, and three other future World Cup regulars – Gordon Banks, Ray Wilson and Bobby Charlton – were by now established members of Ramsey's team. Jimmy Greaves was also there, the one truly world-class goalscorer the country possessed. It all seemed highly promising, and the organisation off the field reflected the improved performances on it – the FA had even arranged for a doctor to accompany the tour. Everything appeared to be a lot less sloppy and a lot more professional.

England began the next season in the way they'd ended the last, thumping four past Wales, eight past Northern Ireland (Greaves scoring four, Paine three) and in the interim defeating a Rest of the World team 2–1 in an exhilarating match at Wembley staged to celebrate the FA's centenary. There was a blip at Hampden in April when England, much to Ramsey's annoyance, went down to a simple header from a corner; but Uruguay, Portugal, the Republic of Ireland and the USA were all dispatched in May, the Americans by a 10–0 scoreline guaranteed to wipe away the last memories of the 1950 debacle. At the end of the month a confident England arrived in Brazil for a four-nation tournament featuring the hosts, Argentina and Portugal.

The bottom fell out. Brazil hit five past them in the first match, the recently-beaten Portuguese held them to a 1–1 draw in the second, and Argentina – playing 4–3–3 – delivered the *coup de grâce* with a 1–0 win in the third. Ramsey admitted that there was 'a gap in our respective standards of football', but didn't believe that anything useful could be learned from the way the South Americans played. The England party were given the choice between watching the Brazil–Argentina final or spending an afternoon on the beach and somewhat predictably chose the latter. There they were comprehensively dazzled, just as Finney and his team-mates had been fourteen years previously, by the astonishing skills of the local children.

Four-two-four had seemed to work so well, and catered for the wingers English tradition demanded, yet now looked a much less certain bet. If Ramsey understood one thing fully it was defence, and he knew he had the beginnings of a first-class unit. However, no defence was good enough to play behind a midfield in constant danger of being out-manoeuvred by superior touch, mobility and positioning. So what system, what 'rigid plan', could he could put in its place?

One possible answer arrived almost by accident. In February 1965 two of Ramsey's favourite wingers, Bobby Charlton and Liverpool's Peter Thompson, were prevented by their clubs from attending a three-day England training camp. Ramsey took the opportunity to experiment, pitting an under-23 team playing 4-2-4 against a senior eleven playing 4-

3-3. The latter ran riot and gave the manager much cause for thought. Such a system looked more solid, more defensively sound, and would also solve the problem created by Bobby Charlton's preference for the increased involvement of playing inside to being stuck out on the wing waiting for someone to give him the ball.

The system was certainly worth a try at international level, and in the second game of that summer's post-season tour Ramsey gave it one. The opponents, nine years on from Duncan Edwards's panzer impersonation in the Olympic Stadium, were West Germany.

In the seven years that had passed since their third-place finish in the 1958 World Cup, West Germany's record had been less than impressive. Between 1958 and 1962 they won fourteen out of twenty-four matches, but the opposition was generally weak; and the team's showing in the 1962 World Cup was uninspiring. After qualifying without undue difficulty for the knock-out phase they went out at the first opportunity, their physical long-ball style proving no match for the more skilful Yugoslavs. This was the end of the line for Schäfer and Erhardt, the last survivors of the 1954 World Cup winners, and the next great West German team would slowly coalesce around goalkeeper Hans Tilkowski, defenders Karl-Heinz Schnellinger and Willi Schulz, and forwards Helmut Haller and Uwe Seller – all of whom, in 1962, already had several years' international experience.

Despite this sold backbone the national team's efforts continued poorly. West Germany did not enter the 1962–4 European Nations Cup, and only fourteen international fixtures were arranged between July 1962 and February 1965 (compared to twenty-seven played by England), of which a mere six were won, all against relatively weak sides. This was an important time of transition for German football, though, at both club and national level. In the late summer of 1963 the first national league – the Bundesliga – was launched and in the following June, after a staggering twenty-eight years, Sepp Herberger finally passed on the national coach's baton to his assistant, Helmut Schön. Throughout this period both coaches added new young players to the experienced core: Wolfgang Overath and Reinhard Libuda arrived in 1963, Wolfgang Weber in 1964, and Bernd Patzke and Horst-Dieter Höttges early in 1965.

The game with England scheduled for 12 May was to be held in Nuremberg, where the national team had never yet been defeated. This time the omens were far from good: more than half of Schön's best team were absent through either injuries or club calls. Patzke and Weber had recently broken legs; Seeler and Brunnenmeier, reckoned to be the two best forwards, were both missing with less serious injuries; Schnellinger, Haller and the experienced Szymaniak were all wanted by their Italian clubs. The eleven finally chosen by Schön had only sixty-seven caps between them, forty-five of which were owned by goalkeeper Tilkowski and centre-half Schulz.

England were not much better off. Both Manchester United and Liverpool had important European ties, and the eroded status of the friendly international was well illustrated by the higher priority accorded to the club games. Ramsey had been deprived of Peter Thompson, John Connelly and the recently capped Nobby Stiles; in addition, injury had ruled out Bobby Charlton, Gordon Milne, Johnny Byrne and the promising but as yet uncapped Norman Hunter. It may well have been the enforced lack of wingers which persuaded Ramsey to try out the rough 4-3-3 formation, with Alan Ball, George Eastham and Ron Flowers in midfield, and Terry Paine, Mick Jones and Derek Temple up-front.

Almost from the outset it appeared to work. A Jones goal was denied in the second minute because another forward had strayed offside, and soon after that the Leeds centre-forward forced Tilkowski into a fine save. The England defence looked solid; the midfield and forwards looked like they were enjoying the new tactics. In the thirty-fifth minute Temple went past Piontek and pulled the ball back from the by-line for Paine to shoot home from eight yards. Now all England had to do was to keep a clean sheet and the defence, with the help of a little luck, duly obliged. Gordon Banks wrote much later that this was the day he thought he had 'arrived', and he gave much of the credit to the four men in front of him – George Cohen, Jack Charlton, Bobby Moore and Ray Wilson – who had now established themselves as the first-choice defence. Banks, Moore and Charlton all had particularly good games in Nuremberg, and although the Germans went close on more than one occasion (Krämer hit the bar in one half, the post in the other) they stuck to their task with enormous resolution.

After the match Helmut Schön said how impressed he was by England's work-rate and defensive organisation – items of praise which were to become commonplace over the next five years – and paid particular tribute to the young Alan Ball, who had made his England debut in Belgrade three days earlier. The English papers were also pleased for the most part. The *Express* trumpeted 'a great, encouraging day'; the *Mail* thought it 'a display of wonderful promise'; and even the hard-to-please Brian Glanville announced himself at least half satisfied with England's progress under Ramsey.

Only the *Sun* dissented, though not over the matter of England's quality. Their football correspondent opened his coverage of the match with the news that England's visit had caused 'the biggest buzz in this ancient burg since the War Crimes Tribunal' (a piece of tactlessness which would have done the later paper of the same name proud), then took England to task for playing it rough. 'I could not hear myself type when German left-winger Heinz Horning was floored crudely by an unrecognisable Englishman who stretched out a hand from a scrum to pull the man down', wrote Steve Richards. He also claimed to have seen Paine give Höttges 'a taste of unarmed combat' which left the German full-back 'sinking into the turf in agony'.

No other English paper carried similar accusations, and in the absence of a full film-record it's hard to evaluate the truth of this one. The England team certainly contained several players with a reputation for less than angelic behaviour, and it is possible that what Richards described was the first visible sign of something which would become increasingly clear as the years went by: that Ramsey's changes were something of a devil's bargain involving both loss and gain. His captain, Bobby Moore, admitted that there was 'a hardening process going on in the England team'. Neither he nor any of his team-mates, he said, 'cared too much about whether we lived up to a "Good cricket, sir" image'. The marriage of toughness and fair play which had informed English football since its beginnings was about to suffer a particularly rough patch.

11: treadmills and flying-machines

In the weeks before and after England played in Nuremberg, further evidence was offered of the choices facing English football. On 1 May Leeds and Liverpool delivered a Cup final full of hard work, endless running and unremitting physical commitment carried to the edge of the law and beyond. Equally dedicated fans no doubt revelled in the tension, but those who loved football found little flair or inspiration to lift their spirits. 'I am told that this match was the logical development of "method" football,' Frank Wilson wrote in the *Mirror*. 'I am told that if we are to survive the rigours of the World Cup we must forget individualism, the brilliant flashes of inspiration which transform a tread-mill into a flying machine . . .' Brian James was equally scathing but also unsurprised. 'Leeds and Liverpool did not play like this because they were at Wembley,' he wrote in the *Mail*. 'Rather, they were at Wembley precisely because they play like this . . . Any team with application to match its ambition can create a Leeds or a Liverpool – a Denis Law is produced only by a capricious fate.'

Yet a week after England's victory over West Germany, club sides representing the two nations fought out a European Cup-Winners' Cup final at Wembley which enchanted players and spectators alike. Alan Sealey scored both goals in West Ham's 2–0 win over Munich 1860, the first with a thunderous drive from the edge of the penalty area and the second with a quickly taken rebound after Tilkowski had parried a header from the young Martin Peters. The goals came late in a thrilling contest, though, and it was the style of overall play, the commitment to open, flowing football, which most distinguished the game.

This was the night that Ron Greenwood repaid the footballing gods for showing him the Hungarians in 1953. West Ham's movement both on and off the ball evoked memories of the great Magyar team and threw into even greater relief the soul-numbing sterility of the recent Cup final. 'Our principles were justified,' manager Ron Greenwood said. 'We proved that football at its best is a game of beauty and intelligence. Players and ball were in happy harmony, while skill and method flourished together. Ideas and passes flowed. For me it was fulfilment.' And for the players, too. Geoff Hurst remembered 'time and time again grinning at a German opponent in sheer joy at the end of a great movement by either team . . . and getting back a smile of complete understanding. If only it could always be like that!'

The Munich 1860 manager could have said the same, because his team played their full part in creating the spectacle. As he claimed after the game, with home advantage they might well have won themselves.

Though there was no doubt which way Alf Ramsey's vote would go when it came to England's football future, he remained seemingly uncertain of which tactics to employ and which players should implement them. England played six matches before facing the West Germans again in the return friendly at Wembley in February 1966, and in the first four of them he reverted to 4–2–4 formation, without conspicuous success. Ramsey then switched back to 4–3–3 for the visit to Madrid in December, playing without a single recognised winger for the first time. The resulting 2–0 win over Spain was far more impressive than the scoreline suggested and apparently finally decided him against 4–2–4.

The defence was more or less settled by this time, with Banks in goal and Stiles playing in front of a back four comprising Cohen, Jack Charlton, Moore and Wilson. Bobby Charlton, now in midfield, and Jimmy Greaves up front appeared certain of their places when fit, but the remaining three spots were still up for grabs. The choice of Greaves' principal striking partner presented a particular problem; Mick Jones, Barry Bridges, Joe Baker, Roger Hunt and Alan Peacock were all given an opportunity to impress in the games before Christmas. Following a bout of jaundice Greaves himself was unfit for several of these games and was not considered ready for a recall by Ramsey for the return against West Germany. Instead, the manager gave yet another young hopeful, the previously uncapped Geoff Hurst, his chance to stake a claim.

With the World Cup now less than five months away this match was inevitably deemed relatively unimportant in itself – both managers saw it more as a vital step in the process of preparing for the great event. That said, it was still the English versus the Germans and there were places and pride to play for. The former had no desire to lose their unbeaten record against the old enemy just prior to a World Cup, while the latter could hardly have wished for a better morale-booster than an end to their long record of failure against England.

Ramsey's chosen team was his most negative yet, with Leeds' Norman Hunter drafted in to partner Jack Charlton in central defence and Bobby Moore moved up into midfield alongside Nobby Stiles, Bobby Charlton and Alan Ball. Only Roger Hunt and Geoff Hurst clearly played as front-men in an essentially 4-4-2 formation, and to add insult to injury Nobby Stiles was allotted the No. 9 shirt. It was 'a team that makes the final break with football tradition', Ken Jones wrote in the *Mirror*.

Their German opponents had been weakened by club-calls and injuries. There was no Schnellinger, Haller or Seeler; only Tilkowski, Schulz and Syzmaniak, winning the last but one of his forty-three caps, had much international experience. In midfield, youngsters Günter Netzer and Franz Beckenbauer were winning their third and fourth caps respectively, and up front Borussia's Siggy Held was making his debut. None of them shone particularly brightly in a match marked by England's shading, through tenacity and sheer force of numbers, of the midfield battle, and the failure of both sides to turn their few chances into goals. England's were mostly missed by the hyperactive Alan Ball. He headed straight at the Tilkowski when well-placed to pick his spot, and then shot wide from inside the area after Stiles and Hurst had combined to set him up. Between these two misses he put a perfect cross onto Hurst's head, only for the West Ham striker to unerringly pick out the German keeper.

The only goal of the game came just before half-time. A long cross from the overlapping Cohen found Hunt. His header, though weak, was too well-directed for Tilkowski to hold, and Stiles forced it over the line from very close range.

For most of the second half, play was confined to midfield but with twenty minutes to go the West Germans started pushing more men forward and the Wembley crowd had its first sight of how slick Beckenbauer and Netzer could look in combination. Their forwards' finishing, however, proved almost as woeful as England's, and when substitute Heiss did find the net – gleefully volleying home after Held had flicked on a Krämer cross – the referee disallowed the goal and inexplicably awarded a corner instead. The crowd booed this decision but England nevertheless finished with a flurry of their own, Hunt first heading against the bar and then shooting ludicrously wide when put clean-through on goal by Ball.

The final whistle sounded with England's unbeaten record against German national sides still intact, though this wasn't evident in the reaction of the Wembley spectators, many of whom jeered the team all the way back to the tunnel. This was not the sort of football they wanted to watch. It lacked finesse and ingenuity, it lacked the more eye-pleasing skills, it even lacked goal-mouth excitement. Moore's move from defence to midfield had reduced the former to one-dimensionality without greatly enhancing the latter, and the forwards who might have provided the missing qualities – Greaves, Eastham and Byrne, to name but three – had all been deliberately omitted. This was 'for the purpose of priming the newcomers', Brian James thought; but all three were still absent five months later when the two nations met again in the World Cup final.

Other managers came, somewhat reluctantly it seemed, to Ramsey's defence. Bill Nicholson and Tommy Docherty agreed that 'tight systematic football' was 'dulling the game', but if it worked – if it won England the World Cup – then the fans would no doubt come to accept it. Ramsey himself was already quite satisfied. He had stopped the Germans from scoring and almost stopped them from playing. England had won, and that should be entertainment enough for any Englishman. He thought it had been 'very unfair' of the crowd to boo, and had found it 'most extraordinary' that they should do so after the disallowing of a visiting team's goal. Would they have preferred a glorious defeat to the victory they got? he seemed to be asking, as if it were self-evident that these were the only two options.

Two weeks later Manchester United showed that there were others. They had beaten Benfica only 3–2 in the first leg of the European Cup quarter-final at Old Trafford, and many observers feared the one-goal advantage would prove insufficient in Lisbon's Stadium of Light. There, however, Matt Busby's team scorned any thought of playing for safety and produced one of the most exhilarating displays of attacking football in their history. George Best scored twice in the first twelve minutes, the second time after a coruscating run through half the home defence, and United won 5–1. Of course, neither Best nor Law was English, and perhaps England really did lack players of comparable quality, but the suspicion remained – and the fate of Jimmy Greaves in the World Cup would go a long way towards proving it correct – that in any case Ramsey would always prefer the relative certainties of stopping the other side playing to the joyful uncertainties of encouraging a flair-fuelled attack.

Fittingly during a season which would end with an Anglo–German World Cup final, there were seven Anglo–German club-clashes in European competition, more than in any year before or since. Five were won by the English, two against West German opposition and three against East German. In the European Cup Manchester United beat Vorwaerts to reach the quarter-final; in the Fairs Cup, Chelsea, Leeds and Everton beat Munich 1860, Lokomotiv Leipzig and Nuremberg respectively. In the Cup-Winners' Cup, holders West Ham beat the East German Magdeburg in the last eight and found themselves up against the West German Borussia Dortmund in the semi-final.

This Borussia side, which would finish runners-up in that year's Bundesliga, featured Tilkowski in goal, Held up front and a wide player with a ferocious shot who had only just won his first cap, Lothar Emmerich. He was currently the top scorer in the Bundesliga, and at Upton Park he showed why: West Ham, ahead since just after half-time, were still straining for a second with five minutes to go when Emmerich swung his lethal left leg and almost broke the net. Two minutes later he did it again. West Ham travelled to Dortmund hoping against hope, but in the first minute of the second leg Emmerich hit the bar with a header and slammed home the rebound. Borussia went on to win 3–1 on the night, 5–2 on aggregate, and book themselves a place in the final against Liverpool.

This, the Merseyside club's first European final, was played in atrociously wet conditions at Glasgow's Hampden Park before a rain-reduced crowd of only 42,000 mostly Liverpudlian supporters. It proved a fairly even contest, with Liverpool's power and determination matched by Borussia's greater inventiveness with the ball. The West German side went ahead in the sixty-third minute, Held firing high into the top corner from twenty yards after Emmerich had lobbed the ball into his path. Liverpool equalised only five minutes later, Thompson centring for Hunt to net from close range. The goal stood, though the German players – and the *Daily Mail* correspondent – were certain that the ball had crossed the line before Thompson centred. Hunt had a golden opportunity to wrap up the game in the last minute of normal time, but over-elaborated and the chance was lost.

In extra time Liverpool again pushed forward. Borussia's defence held firm, though, and soon into the second period they went ahead with something of a freak goal. Tommy Lawrence had rushed out to punch clear and succeeded only in finding Libuda, who blasted it back from forty yards out, straight over the stranded keeper and into the net. Liverpool kept trying, but to no avail.

While their fans thought Liverpool had been unlucky, wiser heads realised that there was a lesson to be learned from this match. Both German goals had originated in quick interplay between Emmerich and Held, and it was exactly these sorts of skills which Liverpool had lacked. 'If they are to win in Europe they must find those higher graces in attack,' the *Times* correspondent wrote. In later years they would do just that; but in May 1966 many feared that England's experience in the imminent World Cup would echo Liverpool's – that hard work, spirit and all-round competence would ultimately prove insufficient.

For the moment, however, England seemed to be set fair. In early April they came away from Hampden with a 4–3 win; Ramsey had moved Moore and Bobby Charlton back into the centres of defence and midfield respectively, and played John Connelly as a wide attacker. The team chosen to play Scotland included nine of the eleven who would line up in the first World Cup match, but only four of them were in the eleven who beat Yugoslavia 2–0 a month later at Wembley. Ramsey chose three out-and-out strikers – Greaves, Tambling and Hurst – and also gave a first cap to West Ham's Martin Peters. England again looked good, leaving Ramsey with much to chew on in the weeks of waiting which followed.

By early June when the squad set up camp at Lilleshall they were down from forty players to twenty-seven, and on the eve of their pre-tournament tour two weeks later their number was further reduced to twenty-two. The tour itself was a victory parade, albeit one enjoyed at the expense of three weak Scandinavian teams and Poland. Greaves scored four against Norway, each a gem in its different way, which helped allay the doubts that had haunted him since his bout of jaundice earlier in the year. England returned home full of confidence, secure in the knowledge that they had at least one magician in their attack.

The competition itself was already steeped in controversy. Over the last thirty-four years England's triumph in the 1966 World Cup has assumed a legendary, almost mythical status; therefore subjecting it to reasoned examination is not an exercise calculated to win friends. The fact that England has not won anything since has provoked a tendency in the average Englishman towards over-protectiveness of his country's sole great football achievement. But – and it is a big but – few non-Englishmen see the events of 1966 in quite the same way, and any honest chronicler of the competition has to raise a critical eye above the national parapet.

For a start, the refereeing arrangements were anything but fair. Twenty-three referees were chosen to officiate: seven from England, three from the other constituent parts of the United Kingdom, five from other parts of northern Europe, three from southern Europe and five from Latin America. This disproportionate preponderance of referees versed in the north-European style of playing was probably (rumours and subsequent practice seem to bear this out) further accentuated by instructions given to all the referees urging them to go easy on north-European-style heavy tackling. The end result was to put the southern European and particularly the Latin American sides at a definite disadvantage. Brazil started the competition as favourites yet were virtually kicked out of it, and the Latin Americans as a whole harboured a fairly righteous grudge about the whole business for decades. England and West Germany, on the other hand, both derived crucial advantages from the chosen style of refereeing in at least one match.

England's progress to the semi-final was anything but triumphal. They drew 0–0 with an unadventurous Uruguay; looked like failing to score against Mexico until Bobby Charlton pulled one of his specials out of the bag; and then scraped through with the help of a palpably offside goal against nine fit Frenchmen. They played 4-3-3, a different winger partnering Hunt and Greaves in each of the three games, and looked desperately short of inventiveness. The victory over France was further marred by an appalling tackle from Stiles that should have seen him sent off but that instead led to England's second goal and deprived the French of their best player, Jacques Simon.

Despite this less than glorious start, a large part of the country was now caught in the grip of an ugly chauvinism which in the quarter-final match against Argentina overflowed from the terraces and on to the pitch. I was at that game and have rarely experienced an atmosphere so full of self-righteous malevolence. If the Argentinians had managed to rise above themselves and concentrate on their football they would probably have won: few in attendance – including many members of the England team – doubted that they were the better players. As it was, they met England's hard and often unfair tackling with their own battery of vicious and niggling off-the-ball tricks (thirty-three fouls were committed by Englishmen, nineteen by Argentinians). In addition to this Argentina's captain, Rattin, for reasons that were at least understandable, showed so little faith in the referee's impartiality that he got himself sent off for persistent dissent.

With Greaves injured, England were fielding their World Cup final eleven for the first time in a clear 4-4-2 formation – and even against ten men struggled to dominate, never mind score. Prompted by the brilliant Onega, Argentina, meanwhile, looked dangerous on the break, but the ten men were eventually worn down. Thirteen minutes from time a beautifully flighted cross from Peters was elegantly glanced into the right-hand corner by the leaping Hurst. It was the one bright moment in a deeply soured afternoon.

After the match the Argentinian players piled disgrace on disgrace, urinating against the tunnel walls, spitting at FIFA officials and trying to batter their way into the England dressing room. When interviewed soon afterwards, Alf Ramsey claimed that during the match the Argentinians had 'acted as animals', a remark that would do more to undermine England's progress in the 1970 World Cup than any mistakes his players might make on the pitch.

But Ramsey and his team had reached the 1966 semi-final and had yet to concede a goal – the defence was proving as solid as the attack was inadequate. They were to meet Portugal, whose progress had been just as chequered as England's. The Portuguese had overcome a Hungarian team weakened by injury to their goalkeeper, had practically kicked Brazil out of the tournament, and then somehow had pulled back a three-goal deficit against the North Koreans in their quarter-final. At Wembley both sides were on their best behaviour and a thrilling match played in excellent spirit was narrowly won by England.

West Germany had reached the final with almost as much difficulty as the English. Netzer was missing from the German squad (as he would be again in 1970), but Franz Beckenbauer soon made his presence felt with his two goals in the 5–0 demolition of Switzerland. A turbulent 0–0 draw with Argentina in which Jose Albrecht was sent off by the Yugoslav referee was followed by a narrow win over Spain, and in the quarter-final Uruguay were dispatched by the seemingly comfortable margin of 4–0. In fact the Latin Americans should have already been two up when they conceded a goal to a lucky deflection, and were then denied what looked a clear penalty when Schnellinger handled on the line. The Uruguayans were let down by fate and an English referee and lost their heads; soon after half-time they'd had two men sent off. Even against nine men the Germans didn't manage to score a second until the seventieth minute.

In their semi-final against the Soviet Union, West Germany found themselves once more facing nine men: one Russian had crippled himself with an attempted foul and another had been expelled for a wild kick. Yashin almost single-handedly kept the lead to a single goal for a long period, but was finally beaten by a fairly innocuous Beckenbauer free-kick. The crowd at Goodison, which had ten days earlier seen Hungary and Brazil provide the tournament's single feast of gorgeous, flowing football, jeered West Germany off the pitch.

In the final where England had picked up a reputation for boring play and brutal tackling, the Germans had enhanced their existing reputation for over-acting and provoking opponents. Neither had given spectators any reason for thinking that football was a beautiful game.

12: the fatal victory

Given the frenetic outpouring of nationalism and worse that had accompanied England's progress to the final, the country could conceivably have witnessed an eruption of bad feeling towards the enemy of two world wars and a million comic strips. It didn't happen. Perhaps the old illusion that politics and sport belonged to separate universes still had influence; perhaps the last war was now a sufficiently distant memory. Or perhaps the Germans no longer made such good enemies as they once had: both their values and their football were too similar to England's own – in the hot light of unreason it was easier to hate the Latin nations and their sensuous skills and their general untrustworthiness.

Allusions to history were made, of course, but they didn't seem malicious. On the eve of the final Peter Lorenzo reminded *Sun* readers that 'as the Fatherland are embarrassingly aware, England have never lost to Germany – at soccer either', while Hugh McIlvanney in the *Observer* thought former coach Herberger's recipe for defeating England sounded like a script written by Rommel. On the whole, past events were kept in the background. Neither Ramsey nor his players made any reference to history, though one assumes it must have occasionally entered their thoughts. Jack Charlton later admitted that just before kick-off he found himself thinking how strange it was that 'we had waged a war for six years against Germany . . . and now we were preparing to do battle on the football field'. He and his team-mates were possibly inhibited by the knowledge that Gordon Banks had a German wife and therefore would not have appreciated a stream of anti-German vilification.

Though the rampant English nationalism was not directed specifically against them, some Germans were concerned about it. Werner Schneider, a well-known German TV commentator, thought the English behaviour had gone well beyond simple support of a football team. 'Perhaps we have learned our lesson in World War Two,' he said. 'Perhaps we think more than other people how mad this thinking is. You would expect this from countries who have nothing else . . . but in England it is strange and sad.'

What the Germans did not say, maybe because they were unaware of it, was that the weight of the past fell more heavily on them. It was they who had been spurned by their opponents at the beginning of the century and they who had been defeated and disgraced in two world wars. If the West Germans went into the 1966 final with something of an inferiority complex – and their tactics suggested that they did – then it was one borne out of more than football.

The West German team showed only one change from that which had played in the semi-final – a fit-again Höttges returned in place of Lutz at right back – while the English line-up remained the same. Greaves was fit but wasn't recalled, Ramsey ultimately proving true to his creed: genius was unreliable, a willingness to run was not. Arguably the finest English striker of all time was found surplus to requirements.

Helmut Schön made a similar decision with the West German side. Together with Wolfgang Overath, Franz Beckenbauer formed the creative hub of the team, yet was given the negative role of stopping Bobby Charlton.

Shorn of a considerable part of their ability to surprise, the two teams resembled each other more than ever. 'The English and German styles, in fact, are highly similar,' the *Times* correspondent wrote, as if it were a new discovery. 'Both believe in the hard tackle, both go for the ball fairly, and both will play till they drop.' In the *Mail* Brian James believed that the Germans were just as fast and just as fit as England. 'For the first time in the tournament, England can only win if they are more skilful than their opponents.'

Entire books have been written about the 120 minutes of football which comprised the 1966 World Cup Final; thirty-five years later English players are still being awarded honours simply for having taken part. Specific moments in the game seem forever engraved on both English and German retinas, and with good reason: after stumbling their way to the final the two teams provided a classic contest. It was hardly a feast of individual skills, but both sides gave their all in a roller-coaster match full of tension and goals. While England had the added joy of winning, even in Germany the match is remembered better than many later victories – many a German football fan can still recite from memory the names of all twenty-two who played that day.

It began well for the West Germans, who had a reasonable chance as early as the second minute. Siggy Held received a pass from Emmerich inside the area and had space and time to turn and shoot narrowly wide, which didn't augur well for England's much-vaunted defence. Minutes later Wilson only just headed off a Seeler surge in the penalty area, and England players generally were giving away the ball with alarming regularity. When they did attack, Stiles attempted to play a one-two with Hunt, only for the Liverpool man to turn so ponderously that a German defender had no trouble picking the ball off his toes. At the other end Seeler, Held and Emmerich were combining far better, and to the English pessimists observing the game these seemed like archetypal moments; the Germans had the better technique and sooner or later they would make it count. They might look like English players (most of them did) but their defenders looked so much more comfortable on the ball, and in midfield only Bobby Charlton came close to matching the arrogant composure of Beckenbauer and Overath.

Nine minutes had gone before England posed a serious threat, which came, unsurprisingly, from the air. Two crosses in quick succession produced near-panic in the German penalty area, and then a twenty-five-yard drive from Peters brought a flying save from Tilkowski. Another shot from the same player flew wide and then at the other end disaster struck for England. Held, on the left midway inside the English half, swung a long right-foot cross towards the far side of the penalty area. Ray Wilson could have simply left it, but he either misheard or misunderstood Banks's shout to that effect. Though he could have glanced it into touch, he instead headed it weakly forward and down, right to Helmut Haller on the edge of the area. The West German controlled the ball with one touch and hit it with the second, a ground-shot of no great power. It could have been stopped by either Jack Charlton or Gordon Banks, but both left it to each other and Banks's final despairing dive was far too late. Thirty-four years later one is struck by the similarity between this failed save and Bonetti's in 1970; the difference, of course, being that in 1966 England went on to win.

Not that victory for England seemed a very likely outcome at this point in the game. Haller and Beckenbauer were stroking the ball around with added assurance, throwing England's poor passing and ball-control into even greater relief. For a few minutes England were looking dangerously down-in-the-mouth, and it took a wonderful piece of quick thinking from Moore and Hurst to revive them. Moore was advancing in the inside-left channel, desperately looking for someone open to pass to when Overath fouled him. He looked up and took the kick almost instantly, floating the ball in for the equally quick-thinking Hurst to head home from only eight yards out. Tilkowski was flat-footed on his line, the German marking non-existent. Two defensive lapses had cancelled each other out, and England were level.

The game now swung from end to end, with half-chances for both sides. Twice Seeler beat Moore to high crosses, heading the first into Banks's arms, the second wide. Bobby Charlton picked up a deflected Ball shot and made space for himself on the edge of the area, but his shot was uncharacteristically weak and was easily saved. In the twenty-sixth minute a lovely piece of German play saw Seeler take a pass from Beckenbauer near the centre circle, spin away from Moore's challenge and slide a near-perfect thirty-yard pass inside Wilson for the speeding Haller, who was just beaten to the ball by the alert Banks. For a short time the two teams looked less alike, the Germans almost pulling off a couple of dangerous one-twos around the penalty area, England seemingly content to throw high balls forward for Hunt and Hurst to run down. Then Charlton managed to thread a lovely ball into the box where Hunt was headed off only by Weber's quick challenge.

The Germans did seem vulnerable to the high ball. The English players had concluded before the game that Tilkowski was a bit of a 'Dracula' – he didn't like crosses. He certainly showed little inclination to come for them. When Hurst, standing on the six-yard-line, rose to beat two defenders to an innocuous-looking cross from Cohen, Tilkowski didn't venture off his line. On this occasion, though, his reflexes made up for his caution and the ball was scrambled away.

This heralded five minutes of fruitless England pressure but they were then fortunate to only concede a corner when Ball and Cohen made successive mistakes. From Held's kick the ball eventually reached Overath on the eighteen-yard-line; his instant half volley was parried by Banks to Emmerich, who shot powerfully into the England keeper's midriff as he rushed out to narrow the angle. Minutes later the Dortmund winger was almost through on goal when he was stopped by Moore's brilliant covering tackle; and at the other end Hunt contrived to volley a Hurst knock-down straight at Tilkowski from only eight yards. If there was one moment in the match when the heart cried out for Jimmy Greaves, this was it.

Half-time arrived, and with it the chance for players and crowd to get their breath back. Both sides had missed four reasonable chances and taken one, and if the West Germans had looked marginally the better team going forward, they had also had obvious problems in coping with the aerial threat from Hurst. Beckenbauer's close marking of Bobby Charlton had made them both largely peripheral figures, but it was still too early to judge which side had suffered more as a result. In defence Bobby Moore's performance had been outstanding, and had only emphasised how unique an English player he was. Indeed, in many ways he didn't seem like an English player at all.

The second half began with a flurry of England pressure, though a good break by the Germans was halted only by a narrow offside decision. The first real chance of the half fell to Beckenbauer, but his shot from the edge of the area was as weak as Charlton's had been in the first half. Then Hurst chested the ball down for Peters to sky his shot over from twenty yards. The game was now being played in sudden spurts, with long lazy interludes in which the players conserved their strength.

Sixteen minutes into the half Stiles committed the first bad foul of the game, a dreadfully wild challenge on Haller who milked it for all it was worth. The incident apparently lifted England, who during the next fifteen or so minutes gradually began to look the more likely side. In one attack Bobby Charlton looked as if he'd been obstructed close to goal; in another, Hunt's pass was inches away from putting Hurst in on goal.

England stepped up another gear. A Charlton run saw Beckenbauer divert the ball to Hunt; he turned neatly and slipped it out to Ball, whose cross cum shot was touched behind by Tilkowski for a corner. Ball's kick was headed out to Hurst, lurking in the far corner of the area. His attempted shot spun up off the lunging Höttges's boot and dropped as invitingly as any ball could drop for the on-rushing Peters a mere six yards from goal. It was not exactly a classic move, but England were 2–1 up with only twelve minutes remaining.

The West Germans tried to lift themselves, to little apparent effect. A Schnellinger shot was easily saved by Banks, then six precious minutes passed before a real chance was created, Weber heading it weakly wide. The Germans pressed forward leaving gaps at the back, and with four minutes left England should have sealed their victory. Instead, Hunt put his pass just behind Charlton's stride and the chance went begging. Two minutes later Overath shot narrowly wide. It seemed like it was all over, but a Jack Charlton foul on Held some thirty yards from goal – the Englishman later claimed that his opponent had made a back – offered the Germans a final lifeline.

Emmerich's kick eluded the wall but was half-stopped by Cohen; Held got a foot to the loose ball which cannoned off Schnellinger and finally fell for Weber, almost as invitingly as Höttges's deflection had fallen for Peters at the other end. He scooped it in and West Germany were alive once more. The English players complained bitterly that a German had handled the ball – Schnellinger, Held and Haller were each accused by different parties – but the film of the incident suggests that any such contact was unlikely to have been intentional.

The whistle went, the players collapsed in a heap, and Ramsey came out with his famous exhortation: 'you've won the World Cup once, now go out and win it again.' They did just that. Sides that come back at the death of normal time usually find themselves reinvigorated by their escape, but the thirty minutes of extra time clearly belonged to England. They pressed forward from the outset, Ball bringing a tip-over from Tilkowski in the first minute; Bobby Charlton, set up by Peters, striking the post in the third; Hunt cutting in from the left and shooting just past the far post in the fifth.

After eight minutes Held went past Jack Charlton and reached the by-line, but none of his team-mates had the energy to keep up with him so there was no one to cross to. This was the one moment of German threat in the first period, and it was followed almost immediately by another goal for England. Stiles fed Ball on the right wing and his first-time cross found Hurst, his back to goal, on the corner of the goal area. He pulled it down beautifully with his right foot, shuffled his feet as he turned and hit the ball as he fell. It crashed on to the underside of Tilkowski's bar, bounced down onto the line and out, whereby Weber headed it back over the bar to safety. The English – particularly Hunt, who was standing some eight yards out – appealed for a goal; the Azerbaijani linesman was flagging. The Swiss referee consulted him and gave the goal.

There's no escaping the fact that this was a bad decision, and all the English players' effort to claim otherwise were about as convincing as Maradona's excuses twenty years later. The notion that Hunt would only have instinctively appealed for a goal if the ball had crossed the line was particularly ludicrous, as any observer of professional footballers would know: most seem more inclined to appeal for a throw-in when they know the ball has rebounded off themselves. Nor was Hunt the favourite to pick up the rebound – Weber was. It has been claimed that the film evidence is inconclusive, but all the footage I have ever seen shows quite clearly that between a third and a half of the ball did not cross the line. And I have never met a neutral, let alone a German, who believes that the goal should have been given.

But it was given, and if anyone deserved such a huge slice of luck at this stage it was England. Even if they had only hit the woodwork for the second time in ten minutes, that was a damn sight more than the West Germans had achieved. And in the final five minutes of the period, stunned by what fate had dealt them, they didn't trouble England at all.

In the second period West Germany did come into it a little more, though there was still no incisiveness to their attacks and the best they could manage until near the end was a pair of long-range shots from Beckenbauer and Held. Four minutes from time Emmerich's control echoed that of Hunt's earlier in the match, letting him down in a good position, and two minutes later Seeler was inches away from contact when Haller knocked down a Schulz cross. It was their final throw. With the seconds ticking away Moore launched one last accurate long ball from defence to the free-running Hurst, and he simply blasted it past Tilkowski's right shoulder, a Roy of the Rovers special to provide a memorably fitting climax. England had won, and on the day they had narrowly deserved to – undeserved goals notwithstanding.

The West Germans proved themselves good losers at the celebration banquet, congratulating the England players and insisting that they had no complaints. The English media, on the other hand, proved rather less worthy winners. Those, like Danny Blanchflower, who had the temerity to criticise the manner of England's victorious tournament were met with cries of 'traitor'. As several journalists had predicted in February, Ramsey, his team and his tactics went from villains to heroes overnight when they won the World Cup.

True foreigners were allowed their say – not that many of the English were listening. Puskas tactfully suggested that after their victory England would 'still be wise to bring in coaches to improve their individual technique'. Pelé, who had been give next to no protection by officials, thought the tournament had been 'a revelation' in its 'unsportsmanlike conduct and weak refereeing'. England, he added, 'did not have the best in the field'.

Following England's victory, journalists and fans across the world had an anxiety attack. Was this the way football was going, with all those beautiful skills buried under an avalanche of physical strength, stamina and negative tactics? Outside Britain the worries did not last long, because it was clear to most that home advantage and a few great players, rather than Ramsey's tactics, had been the crucial factors in England's success. National coaches and academies around the world didn't scramble to follow England's example: on the contrary, they set their minds to producing an attacking game which would render it an historical irrelevancy in less than ten years. And nowhere was this more true than in West Germany, where the lessons of this World Cup were to produce a radical re-think of footballing priorities, a re-think which would eventually lead to the first clear divergence between the English and German styles of play.

Ramsey's greatest fortune had been in the few outstanding players available to him; and his greatest achievement, perhaps, in placing them at the heart of his team. Banks, Moore and Bobby Charlton would have graced any national team in 1966, and would probably have flourished in any tactical formation. Ball and Peters, by contrast, were what lifted Ramsey's tactics beyond their natural ordinariness: each would work himself into the ground for the team; each would provide levels of skill and vision not normally associated with mere 'runners'. Like Roy Keane in the current Manchester United team, they each offered two players in one, and as such were virtually priceless.

Though Ramsey's team survived and prospered for another five years, English football in general paid a wide cost. The old values of toughness, speed and a never-say-die attitude had been reinforced, but the insistence on fair play which had always accompanied them would weaken as the game became more thoroughly professional. The need for British footballers to emulate the superior technique of so many of their foreign counterparts, which were apparently so palpable prior to the World Cup, now seemed a mere gilding of the lily.

Ultimately the real loser in 1966 was English football. Ramsey's success reinforced English insularity and reduced what willingness there was to learn from abroad, thus condemning the national game to the status of a backwater. Having potentially offered football such a glorious future, the Hungarian example was damned and left, by the English at least, to the dustbin of history. The 'total football' which so enchanted football lovers in the 1970s would neither be born in England nor find a home there: the players to make it work would not be available because the football spawned by Ramsey's success had no need of them.

13: waves to mexico

'Nineteen sixty-eight was something of a watershed year. Steam was being phased out from British railways; and British troops disappeared from that part of the world affectionately known as 'East of Suez'. The Troubles began in Northern Ireland; John met Yoko; and Royal Mail officially recognised that at least half of its deliveries were Second Class. Rather more significantly, the whole world suddenly appeared to be in turmoil, with revolutions of one sort or another threatening both the major socio-economic systems. The Vietcong's Tet offensive made a mockery of American military pretensions, and the assassinations of Martin Luther King and Robert Kennedy raised questions about the whole direction in which American society was heading. Similar questions turned the streets of Paris into a battleground, and another outpouring of dissent in Prague forced the Soviets into a dramatic exposé of the corruption at the heart of their own system. Everything seemed up for grabs, nothing was certain.

And on the first day of June the England football team finally surrendered its long unbeaten record against Germany.

The game was a friendly, and had been scheduled for a mere four days before England were due to meet Yugoslavia in the semi-final of the newly christened European Championship. Though mindful of the national desire not to lose the record, Ramsey was clear where his priorities lay, and the England side showed many changes from that of two years before. Cohen, Wilson and Jack Charlton, all nearing the end of their international careers, gave way on this occasion to Keith Newton, Cyril Knowles and Brian Labone. Tottenham's Alan Mullery, who had often taken on Stiles's role during the previous year, and Bobby Charlton, who had just given his all in the European Cup-final win over Benfica, were both rested, along with Hunt and Peters. Banks, Moore, Ball and Hurst were still there, along with Manchester City's Colin Bell and two wingers, Bell's team-mate Mike Summerbee and Liverpool's Peter Thompson.

England had lost only once since the World Cup, going down 3–2 to an ecstatic Scotland at Wembley in April 1967. That sole defeat, however, would have cost them their place in the European Champion-ship finals had the Scots not carelessly dropped points in their matches with Wales and Northern Ireland. The West Germans had lost twice in the same period – a qualifier in Belgrade and a friendly in Bucharest – and had failed to reach the finals after being held to a scoreless draw by Albania in Tirana. As a result this match was probably more important to them than to England, but they too had a severely weakened team.

Over the last two years several soon-to-be-prominent players had been introduced by Schön – striker Gerd Müller and goalkeeper Sepp Maier from Bayern Munich, full-back Berti Vogts and striker Josef Heynckes from Borussia Mönchengladbach, wingers Jurgen Grabowski from Eintracht Frankfurt and Johannes Lohr from Cologne – but only Vögts and Löhr were available for this game. Netzer, Höttges, Schulz, Seeler and Held were all missing for one reason or another, and only Weber, Beckenbauer and Overath survived from the World Cup Final team. This was a team decidedly short on experience, and when the English players saw their opponents' team-sheet they must have fancied their chances. The 1966 final was still fresh in the memory, and the club meetings between the two nations that season hardly suggested a German resurgence. Nottingham Forest had beaten Eintracht Frankfurt 5–0 on aggregate, Liverpool had put eight past Munich 1860 at Anfield, and Second Division Cardiff City had given the mighty Hamburg a serious scare in the semi-final of the Cup Winners' Cup, only conceding the deciding goal in the very last minute of the second leg at Ninian Park. English football, generously defined to include the Welsh, was still on a roll.

More than 79,000 spectators packed into Hannover's Niedersachsensta-dion for a match which produced few echoes of the World Cup final. The German fans were disappointed by the England omissions, upset by

Jakob clears his goalmouth, 1935. © *Hulton Getty*

London Transport advertising poster for the game at Tottenham.
© *London Regional Transport, UK 1990*

The shameful salute, 1938. © *Illustrated London News*

A teenage Uwe Seeler chased by Staniforth, 1954. © *Hulton Getty*

The incomparable Bert Trautmann.
© *Allsport*

Colin Grainger scores in Berlin, 1956. © *Hulton Getty*

Moments of triumph, 1966. © *Allsport*

Lee accelerates between Vögts and Schnellinger, 1970. © *Allsport*

Maier claims the ball, 1972. © *Empics*

Hudson and Ball celebrate. © *Empics*

Leeds fans, French police, 1975. © *Empics*

Keegan leaves Vögts for dead in the European Cup Final, 1977. © *Empics*

Paul Mariner on the ball, 1982.
© *Empics*

Gary Lineker scores a Gerd Müller goal, 1990. © *Allsport*

Out on penalties, 1996. © *Allsport*

Shearer scores the only goal in Charleroi, 2000. © *Empics*

the (later rescinded) announcement of Uwe Seeler's retirement from international football, and finally enraged by England's less than friendly approach to the game. The first half was most notable for two tackles – a late one by Labone which left Weber dazed for some time, and a gratuitously violent assault on Overath by Norman Hunter. In between times the Germans did the majority of the attacking without posing many problems to a typically solid England defence, and Beckenbauer and Moore, so alike in their casual arrogance, looked a cut above all the other players on the pitch. Just before half-time there was a flurry of half-chances at either end, but Beckenbauer shot over and Bell's header narrowly went past the angle of bar and post.

The second half continued in the spirit of the first. A violent body-check by Labone on Beckenbauer was followed by more brutal English tackling and more German theatrics. Ramsey waxed sarcastic about the latter after the match, but said nothing about the former – he never had ascribed to the old public school notion of 'playing the game'.

The game dragged on, only to be briefly enlivened by the invasion of a lone spectator, who was pushed in the face by the referee, knocked to the ground by a linesman and finally rescued from the match officials by the police. Hurst then went close with a header and promptly disappeared back into the ponderous anonymity from which he had briefly emerged.

This proved the last England throw. The West Germans dominated the last twenty minutes and finally managed, albeit fortunately, to score the goal their greater ambition warranted. Beckenbauer picked the ball up midway inside the English half, drifted past one Englishman in that deceptively unhurried way he had, one-two-ed his way past another, and let fly with his left foot from the edge of the area. Banks had been screaming at Labone to close the German down, and had purposefully left a wider space on his left for Beckenbauer to shoot at, but could only watch, wrong-footed, as the shot deflected off Labone's knee and into the other side of the goal.

There was no comeback in the final eight minutes. After thirty-eight years of attempts to do so a German national team had beaten England, and their fans duly celebrated. While it had not been a performance to remember, an important psychological barrier had been broken: the Germans had long suspected that English invincibility was a myth, and now they had proved that to be the case.

The English saw little significance in the result. They had lost in Europe for the first time in more than five years, which was hardly anything to be ashamed of. The Germans had been more inventive in midfield, but that was scarcely surprising in the absence of Bobby Charlton and Martin Peters. The team flew south to Florence for the match that mattered: their semi-final with the Yugoslavs. Wilson, Peters, Charlton, Hunt and Mullery all returned to the team, but Ramsey decided to play with five men in midfield and only Hunt up front. The tone was set as early as the fourth minute when Norman Hunter committed a disgraceful foul on the opposition playmaker Osim that reduced him to a virtual passenger for the rest of the match. The Yugoslavs retaliated in spades, and the match settled into a midfield kicking contest which they eventually won with a late goal from Dragan Dzajic. In the final minutes Mullery, goaded into retaliation by yet another appalling foul, became the first England player to be sent off in a full international.

England were out, and if they sought any compensation for the fact in West Germany's earlier exit, it would be for the last time. There would be fifteen more World Cups and European Championships in the twentieth century, and England would finish behind the Germans in each and every one of them.

If anyone had predicted such a gloomy future for the English national team in the summer of 1968 he would have been laughed at. England were still the World Champions, still had great players, and their record in the two years leading up to the next World Cup bore comparison with the best. They lost only one out of twenty matches – to Brazil in Rio – and if the tally of thirty-four goals scored suggested continuing problems in attack, a mere eleven conceded seemed proof of continuing defensive soundness.

West Germany's record was slightly inferior: they played eighteen and lost two in the same period, with a goal difference of 33–16. Twelve of the thirty-three, however, were scored in one match against Cyprus, and at club level the West Germans continued to under-achieve. In seasons 1968–9 and 1969–70 the best they could manage was two semi-final defeats in the European Cup-Winners' Cup, whereas English clubs won the Fairs Cup twice, the Cup-Winners' Cup once and reached two

European Cup semi-finals. The two nations only came head-to-head on two occasions: Leeds trounced Hannover 7–2 on aggregate in the Fairs Cup; Manchester City defeated Schalke 04 5–2 on their way to winning the Cup-Winners' Cup.

England's visit to Latin America in the summer of 1969 was reasonably successful. A draw with Mexico, a win over Uruguay and a narrow loss to Brazil were respectable results; and the tour gave most of the players who would take part in the following summer's World Cup a chance to experience conditions in the host country. Nonetheless, in PR terms it was a disaster. England's popularity was already low in Latin America, where both real and imagined slights still rankled from 1966, and a major effort was required to reverse the situation. Alf Ramsey, xenophobe *par excellence* was the last person to knowingly ingratiate himself with foreigners, and the FA should have had the sense to realise as much. Instead, they simply tossed him like a lighted match into a cauldron of combustible feelings.

Ramsey stayed true to type. Asked in 1969 if he had any message for the Mexican people, he replied that a band had been playing outside the team's hotel until five in the morning, that a promised motor-cycle escort had failed to arrive, and that the players had been abused and jeered when they went out to inspect the pitch. 'I would have thought that they'd be delighted to welcome England,' he added, as if any other reaction was virtually inconceivable. A few days later after a 'B' international in Guadalajara, he shooed a bunch of Mexican journalists out of the dressing-room area with the unsympathetic zeal of a pest-control officer.

This was not the way to win friends and influence Mexicans, yet when the team returned for the World Cup a year later, the PR assistant Ramsey so obviously needed had not been appointed; the British tabloid press had a heyday ridiculing the local hotel arrangements; and the Mexicans, already disposed to dislike the English, duly went to town. After Bobby Moore's arrest in Colombia on a trumped-up theft charge and Jeff Astle's arrival at Mexico City airport looking (deceptively, as it later transpired) much the worse for drink, one Mexican journalist happily dubbed England 'the team of drunks and thieves'. In a much-belated gesture England strips were handed out to local kids at a training session, but Ramsey then wasted the good work by refusing to talk to local journalists. 'Arrogant and inaccessible' was the predictable verdict, but the latter was unfortunately less true in one sense than others: apparently forgetting their experience with the all-night band a year earlier, the English had booked themselves into a city-centre hotel. The parties in the street outside would be long and loud.

Meanwhile, up in Leon, Helmut Schön and his party were charming the pants off the locals. When the time came for the great rivalry to be resumed, his team would enjoy as much 'home advantage' as England had enjoyed so decisively at Wembley four years earlier.

This time they met in the quarter-final, after England had come second in Group 3, West Germany top of Group 4. England opened against Romania with six survivors of the 1966 team: Banks, Moore, Ball, Peters, Hurst and Bobby Charlton. Blackburn's Keith Newton and Leeds' Terry Cooper were the regular full-backs now, more skilful on the ball than Cohen and Wilson though perhaps less defensively sound. Brian Labone was an adequate replacement for Jack Charlton at centre-half, Mullery a more constructive 'destroyer' than Stiles, Francis Lee, in English conditions at least, a more mobile but less clinical striker than Roger Hunt. It was a slightly more attack-minded team than its 1966 predecessor, or had the potential to be so.

The Mexican crowd booed England on to the pitch, and the Romanians apparently took this as a cue to kick England players up in the air at regular intervals; they were lucky to still have eleven men on the pitch at half-time. England never looked in trouble, but took longer than they would have liked to wear down the opposition, Hurst scoring the only goal of the game in the second half. Next England met Brazil – the only time in the history of the World Cup that the two countries have met. It was a match worthy of its uniqueness (perhaps the best that England ever played under Ramsey) despite the fact that England lost, by a single goal. Moore was magnificent, Mullery not far behind him in his control of Pelé; and only bad misses from Ball and Astle towards the end prevented England from grabbing a draw.

England needed to beat Czechoslovakia to ensure a place in the quarter-finals – and duly did so, but it was painful to watch. Labone, Hurst and Lee were rested, and it took a highly dubious penalty, converted by Allan Clarke, to settle the match. 'How long can England persist with tactics essentially negative in theory and largely negative in practice?' Brian Glanville asked in the *Sunday Times*. 'How long can they eschew wingers when wingers are doing so much for other sides?'

One of the other sides in question was West Germany, who had three excellent wingers in their squad: Reinhard Libuda, Johannes Löhr and Jurgen Grabowski. Schön claimed to have arrived in Mexico with only 'the idea of a team'; if that was the case, he had soon sorted one out. Beckenbauer had been persuaded to play in midfield rather than as *libero*, leaving that role to either Schulz or Schnellinger. Meanwhile a potential squabble for the centre-forward's shirt between the veteran Seeler and the Bundesliga top-scorer Gerd Müller had been averted firstly by making them room-mates, and secondly by convincing Seeler that he had more to offer the side as an attacking midfield player. With Cologne play-maker Overath also in midfield and two of the three wingers always in the team, West Germany had a lot of attacking options, as demonstrated in the group games.

After surprisingly conceding a goal to Morocco, West Germany came back to win 2–1 with goals from Seeler and Müller. In the second game, against Bulgaria, the attack cut loose, Libuda running riot on the right wing and Müller hitting a hat-trick in a 5–2 win. They met the much-fancied Peru in the group decider and refused to let the Latin Americans set up their close-passing movements just outside the area, destroying them with a lethal combination of wing-play and Müller's predatory instincts. Libuda, Löhr and Seeler all found the Bayern striker with crosses, and all three were dispatched past the lamentable Peruvian keeper. Müller had now scored seven times in three games: five more goals than the two scored in total by the entire England team.

When on the eve of the quarter-final Schön said that games between the two nations were always 'physical affairs' because their football was 'so alike', he was speaking the truth but not the whole truth. Certainly both sides tackled hard and ran their hearts out, but Schön's use of ball-playing wingers to set up attacks was very different from Ramsey's reliance on overlapping full-backs to fill the same role, particularly at high altitude in the heat of a Mexican summer.

The English press were seemingly even less inclined to drag up the non-footballing past in 1970 than it had in 1966, though Hugh McIlvanney, writing in the *Observer*, believed that history was still taking its toll on the Germans. Whenever the two nations met, he said, 'echoes of previous battles sounded in blood'. This might be regrettable, but it was also real, and McIlvanney had no doubt that 'the unique tensions that pulse beneath the surface on these occasions have always done more damage to Germany than to England'.

In every other respect the Germans looked favourites to win. Form and virtual home advantage certainly favoured them, and the choice of an Argentinian referee was not likely to fill English hearts with confidence. Finally, the news only hours before the game that Gordon Banks had been forced to withdraw with a stomach upset was bound to deflate the England players and boost their opponents. Chelsea's Peter Bonetti was a fine goalkeeper, but only a week earlier Banks had enhanced his reputation as the world's best with a save from Pelé which almost defied belief. His mere presence would be sorely missed.

'Like Wembley in 1966', Brian James wrote in the *Mail*, 'León's stadium was packed with people overflowing with emotion, but the feeling was for Germany, not England.' The game itself had a false start: a free kick was no sooner awarded to England than the referee decided the ball needed changing. When the new one arrived, Moore punted it straight into Sepp Maier's arms, the first mistake of many in an untidy and somewhat fractious first twenty minutes.

Peters headed weakly at Maier from Hurst's cross; Beckenbauer misdirected a through-pass for Müller; another English cross failed to reach its target. In the fifth minute a first overlapping run from Newton produced a cross which Maier held at the second attempt. The West Germans were trying to set their own pace, striding around and attempting sharp one-twos, but the England players were not letting them settle on the ball.

The sharp tackling was not improving tempers, and in the ninth minute there was an incident between Maier and Francis Lee. The English TV commentator decided that nothing had happened and that Maier was trying it on, but after examining Maier's face the referee agreed that contact had been made, allowed the trainer on and booked Lee. A bad tackle by Peters on Beckenbauer followed, then Cooper was upended by Vögts. Fifteen minutes had passed without a single chance being created.

Instead, there were more fouls – Ball on Overath, Müller on Ball. A half-hit Charlton drive was easily saved by the sprawling Maier, and at the other end Seeler, found beautifully wide in the area by Overath, had his cross blocked by Moore. The German wingers had hardly been in the game, and neither attack appeared to be capable of a penetrating move. Moore at the one end and Schnellinger at the other seemed imperiously in charge.

As the half reached its mid-point things began to improve. Bonetti had to move swiftly to punch away from Seeler, Charlton reached the by-line only to scuff his cross, and Beckenbauer shot narrowly wide. Müller almost succeeded in acrobatically volleying a Beckenbauer chip which drifted over his shoulder, and Höttges just managed to prevent Charlton shooting from the edge of the area. Opportunities to make chances were finally occurring, if not the chances themselves.

Then England scored a truly wonderful goal. Mullery picked up the ball on the left hand side of the field in his own half and swung a forty-yard-pass to Newton on the right touch-line. Newton advanced slowly, Overath retreating in front of him, and then threaded a perfectly weighted ball into the penalty area, roughly in the direction of the near post. Mullery, who had run some fifty yards since first releasing the ball, met it on the half-volley about ten yards from goal and swept it past the helpless Maier. It was the Tottenham man's first and last international goal.

The Germans pressed forward for the next few minutes, during which Beckenbauer almost put Seeler in, but there remained a lack of sharpness to their forward play. England reverted to the predictable, and sent long balls into the corners for Lee to chase or urged the full-backs forward on the flanks. Neither gambit looked like producing much and the match as a whole settled back into stalemate, with the score-line the only reminder that one moment of brilliance had illuminated it. The first half drew to a close with Beckenbauer and Löhr both shooting wide, Lee failing to climax a penetrating run with a shot, and a Newton cross causing consternation in the German area.

The teams trooped off in search of liquids and wise words from their managers. Schön had more to worry about than Ramsey: Müller had hardly got a kick, Libuda and Löhr had been pulled inside by the need to match England's four-man midfield. Ramsey would have noticed that the thirty-three-year-old Bobby Charlton had faded in the last fifteen minutes, and that Peters had been only slightly more effective than in the group games. That said, the defence in general and Moore's covering in particular had been as accomplished as ever.

Schulz came on for Höttges at the beginning of the second half, but there was little time for him to pick up the pace before England scored another good goal. In the forty-ninth minute the overlapping Newton, fed by Hurst, lifted a precision cross to the far post, and Peters, arriving as unexpectedly as only he could, pushed the ball between Maier and the near post. Two–nil to England.

The West Germans looked momentarily with stunned. On the touch-line Schön took seven minutes to make up his mind, then brought on Grabowski for the largely ineffective Libuda. Straightaway the Eintracht winger forced Cooper to block the hardest shot of the match, and for five minutes or so the West Germans kept England in their own half. Bonetti made a fine catch from Löhr's cross, and a jinking run by Grabowski saw a Löhr shot rebound off a defender to safety.

The pressure faded, and Hurst narrowly missed out on crosses from Charlton and Lee. With more than an hour gone the game in midfield was slowing significantly with England at times apparently intent on reducing it to walking-pace. On the touch-line Colin Bell could be seen getting ready to replace one of England's tired midfield runners. The superstitious Francis Lee noticed him with alarm: the same player had been warming up when Brazil scored a week earlier.

In the sixty-fifth minute, however, it was England who could have scored a third. Ball clumsily stepped on the ball when a Peters cross found him close to the penalty spot, and then Charlton, running at the German penalty area, jinked inside Overath and swerved past Fichtel before letting fly an under-powered shot from twenty yards. The England players were now walking the ball around in the middle of the pitch, effectively an invitation to the Germans to come and get it.

They did. Beckenbauer advanced through the centre-circle, fed Fichtel to his right, and received a return ball about forty yards from goal. He rounded Mullery almost diffidently and let fly from just outside the box, a low shot of medium power which Bonetti would have saved ninety-nine times out a hundred. This time he dived over it, and the West Germans were back in the match.

After the game almost everyone, English and Germans alike, would swear to a man that if Banks had played then England would have won. They might well have done, but it's a foolish argument. If Banks had played as well as he usually did then it seems unlikely that Beckenbauer's shot would have beaten him, but the same was true of Bonetti. And even Banks made the occasional bad mistake – he had made one with Haller's remarkably similar shot in the 1966 World Cup final. According to Alan Mullery, none of the players blamed Bonetti: 'The goal was just as much my fault – I allowed Beckenbauer to accelerate past me and get in a shot.'

A mistake had been made and Ramsey proceeded to compound it by taking off Bobby Charlton and bringing on Colin Bell. Mullery thought that 'Bobby was fitter than any of us', and that more to the point the West Germans were scared of him. 'As soon as Bobby went off the Germans couldn't believe their luck, and Beckenbauer was released into a more positive role . . .' Beckenbauer agreed. 'How glad I was to see the back of Bobby Charlton!' he said later.

The largely Mexican crowd began picking up their support for the West Germans, and Bonetti took another good catch from a Grabowski cross. A Löhr centre from the other wing was headed over by Seeler and Grabowski, who was now giving the rapidly tiring Cooper a torrid time, 'almost broke free again on the right. However, England were far from finished as an attacking force: Bell had a good shot saved by Maier before delivering a cross which could have finished the match, Hurst's glancing header passing a few agonising inches outside the far post.

A minute later the Germans almost equalised. After receiving a pass from Löhr, Müller turned Newton and shot powerfully from ten yards, only to be denied by a fine diving save from Bonetti.

With eleven minutes to go Ramsey made another even more baffling substitution, removing Peters and sending on Hunter. This swap was ill-advised in itself – with Charlton already off the pitch Peters was England's only source of the unexpected. If the Germans equalised it would effectively condemn the two exhausted full-backs to another forty minutes of play.

Within a minute they had done just that. A long cross by Grabowski

was headed out by Labone and volleyed back into the area by Beckenbauer. Müller's efforts to twist and turn himself into a shooting position
ended with the ball breaking loose to Löhr on the left-hand corner of the
area, and his intended flick rebounded out to Schnellinger, some forty-
five yards out in the inside-left channel. He floated a long cross towards
the far post and Seeler, running away from the ball towards the goal line
while trying to keep sight of the approaching ball over his shoulder,
somehow managed to back-head it up and over Bonetti and into the far
corner. The watching Lee thought the ball simply hit the back of Seeler's
head, but even he had to admit that it needed superb timing to make any
sort of contact. In reality it was a brilliant goal; sixteen years of international experience had enabled Seeler to make his own luck.

England looked increasingly rocky, and two minutes later Beckenbauer and Müller skilfully combined to produce the best move of the
match, ending with the former shooting inches wide of the near post.
Löhr was cut down by Newton and headed Overath's free kick narrowly
over before both teams settled for playing out the few remaining minutes.

The initiative now lay with the West Germans. Ramsey tried to revive
his troops as he had done four years earlier, but to his eternal regret
Mullery couldn't prevent himself from pointing out that it hadn't been a
hundred degrees in the shade at Wembley.

Yet it was England who made more chances in extra time. In the first
period they had two golden opportunities, but Hurst headed a Bell cross
over the bar, and Labone skied his shot from only ten yards out. In return
the West Germans managed only a twenty-yarder from Beckenbauer
which Bonetti tipped over, and some good runs by both wingers which
failed to produce any end-result. Many of the players were now looking
drained, and the fresher substitutes seemed the likeliest source of a goal.

So it proved. In the third minute of the second period the relatively
fresh Grabowski beat the exhausted Cooper once more on the right and
crossed to the far post. Löhr beat Newton to the ball and headed it back
over the stranded Labone for Müller to hit home an acrobatic volley from
no more than five yards. It was the perfect poacher's goal, and again
Bonetti had no chance.

Far from lying down and dying, England roared back. Lee burst past
Schnellinger on the goal-line and centred for Hurst to net the ball, but an
offside flag had already been raised – probably correctly. With the

Germans now repeating England's mistake of sitting back, the latter forced two corners, following the second of which Bell took a low cross from Hunter, turned Vögts, and was about to pull the trigger when he was blatantly pulled down by Beckenbauer. It was as clear a penalty as penalties get, yet the referee simply waved play on.

Still England were not finished. Mullery put a twenty-yarder just over; a Hurst knock-down was swept high and wide by Ball. The minutes ticked away, the exhausted West Germans going to ground at the slightest provocation. In the very last minute a viciously swerving drive by Newton was flicked over by Maier, and from the resulting corner a Mullery drive just missed the angle of bar and post. There was to be no drawing of lots – the Germans were through.

The England players could hardly believe it. 'We were the better side by far,' Jack Charlton said, although he had stopped watching after the first German goal. 'It wouldn't be so bad if we had lost to a great team,' Alan Ball lamented, 'but they were nothing.' The manager agreed. 'The whole thing was unreal, like a freak of nature,' Ramsey thought. Stupid defensive lapses had cost England the match, and there was no legislating for those. If he could do it all over again he wouldn't change a thing.

The English press was in general understanding. Though Ramsey was taken to task for his alienation of the Mexican public, his selection of teams which lacked an adventurous edge and his inept handling of the substitutions, since the press also felt that England had deserved to win this particular game it was hard to offer more fundamental criticisms. England's all-running style might have been ill-suited to Mexican conditions, but the West Germans had played an equally physical game and were widely praised for winning an English-style victory. England had been 'beaten by the very quality that made them champions', wrote Brian James in the *Mail*; 'on the day the Germans had as big a heart, as great a determination as England', Albert Barham echoed in the *Guardian*. A few commentators gently pointed out that West Germany had more players willing to take on opponents than England, but the overwhelming feeling was that it was luck not a gulf in skill that had been the crucial factor, and on this particular occasion the assumption was probably correct.

The parallels with 1966 were quite striking. Both had been essentially even matches for the first ninety minutes; both had been virtually decided by terrible refereeing decisions in extra time – Hurst's second goal in 1966, Bell's denied penalty in 1970. On both occasions the two teams had fought each other to the point of exhaustion and beyond, and in 1970 this proved fatal to both losers and victors. The drained West Germans were in no state to play another two-hour game three days later, and duly went out to the Italians.

On his return to London a few days later, Ramsey announced that England's chances of winning the World Cup in West Germany four years hence were 'very good indeed.'

14: a german bobby charlton?

In retrospect, the trilogy of Anglo–German meetings in July 1966, June 1970 and April 1972 could be seen as benchmarks in English football's slow fall from grace, but at the time few recognised the earlier matches as such, and the gulf in quality revealed by the third came to most as a terrible shock.

On the eve of the game there was certainly no clear evidence that England had suffered a precipitate decline. On the contrary, they were unbeaten between the two German games and had qualified for this two-leg European Championship quarter-final with some ease. Most of the players from 1970 were still in the team – eight of those who had played in León turned out in April 1972 – and if few of England's recent newcomers were bursting with flair, there was no denying Roy McFarland's excellence at the heart of the defence or Martin Chivers' explosive power. The departed Bobby Charlton was clearly irreplaceable, but generally speaking the team looked as strong as it had in Mexico.

This was fortunate, because England's preparations for this match were anything but ideal. It was five months since the national team had last played, and the pressures of League football had ensured that Ramsey's access to his players was utterly inadequate. There would not have been time to re-shape the team or bed-in new players, even had he wished to do so. Ramsey, probably to his secret delight, had no choice but to rely on both the understanding which already existed between his veterans and the style of play which had served them so well in the past.

In the event he was deprived of McFarland's services at the last moment – possibly through injury; probably through Derby's determination to have him available for a League Championship decider two days later – and he was forced to hurriedly shuffle his pack. Rather than replace McFarland with another true centre-half he moved Hunter back into that position, thus weakening both the defence and the midfield, which now had no obvious ball-winner. He could have brought Mullery in to provide the latter but decided instead to persist with three ball-players – Bell, Ball and Peters. This was only the first leg, after all, and England would probably need to take an advantage to Berlin.

West Germany had also qualified for this quarter-final quite easily, and had themselves only lost once since Mexico: 2–0 to the always difficult Yugoslavs in Belgrade. But they too had their problems. Reinhard Libuda and Klaus Fichtel, the two Schalke players who had been such important members of the squad in Mexico, were implicated in a bribery scandal in 1971 and were never again asked to represent their country. The squad that arrived in England towards the end of April 1972 was riven with disputes. Sepp Maier was apparently not talking to Bayern team-mates Beckenbauer and Müller after being blamed for club defeats at the hands of Glasgow Rangers and MSV Duisburg, and the five players from Borussia Mönchengladbach were all part-time sales reps for *Puma* and so were refusing to wear the *Adidas* boots traditionally worn by the German squad. This was not ideal preparation for a crucial game against England.

Of course, the student of German football would have taken all this gossip with a pinch of salt and concentrated instead on the players available to Helmut Schön. Günter Netzer, who had been recalled to the national team in November 1970 (he had been injured for the World Cup but had also often been omitted by Schön on the grounds that he was too individualistic) was said to be still worried by a knee injury. Netzer was Schön's only major concern – Höttges and Held were still around, and Maier, Beckenbauer, Grabowski and Müller were entering their prime, unlike most members of the England team.

Four other important players had been introduced or re-introduced during the past year: Borussia Mönchengladbach's Herbert Wimmer and the Bayern Munich trio of Georg Schwarzenbeck, Paul Breitner and Ulrich (Uli) Hoeness. The inclusion of the latter three raised the number of Bayern players in the team to five, and this, together with the almost telepathic relationship which existed between Mönchengladbach's Net-zer and Wimmer in midfield, made for a wonderful level of understanding within the team. It also offered a creative blending of two contrasting styles: Mönchengladbach's more swashbuckling approach and Bayern's reliance on venomous counterattack.

Many of them were also great players in their own right. Bobby Robson had described Beckenbauer as the best player in Mexico two years earlier, and he had improved since then. In April 1972 the English press was full of commentators who thought that Beckenbauer was wasted as a mere sweeper, but they would be taught otherwise over the next few years as Bayern and West Germany carried all before them. Ron Greenwood got it right: 'A *libero* should lead from the back and that is why it is a specialist's job – a job that wouldn't be wasted on the best player in the side. Franz Beckenbauer was the first and the finest. He saved many games for West Germany but he won them even more.'

He was also fortunate in the players alongside him. Three in particular were every bit as important to this German side as Banks, Moore and Charlton had been to Ramsey's England in their finest days. Gerd Müller was one of the greatest strikers of all time, an awkward, clumsy-looking mover with a positional sense and a rarely matched ability to hit the target with either head or foot. Paul Breitner was a player who could defend, create or strike with equal facility, the best full-back to emerge from the 'Total Football' revolution which had spread from Holland to Germany in the wake of the success enjoyed by Cruyff's Ajax. Günter Netzer was West Germany's Bobby Charlton in more ways than one, a man who loved to run at the heart of defences, who could hit wonderfully accurate long passes and play the sharpest of one-twos. He was, as all such players tend to be, often accused of insufficient commitment, but his awareness and vision were remarkable.

While these were the four stars of Schön's revitalised West Germany, there was hardly a weak link in the team. Grabowski and the veteran Held were still there to torment England's full-backs; Wimmer and the brilliant young Hoeness to link with the advancing Beckenbauer and Netzer in midfield. The Bayern stopper Schwarzenbeck was solid as a rock; Sepp Maier the safest goalkeeper in the national team's history. This was a team with everything, the team many Germans today still consider the finest they ever had, and it was about to fall on an unsuspecting England.

With hindsight the English press comment which preceded the game is almost comic. Writing before the teams were announced, Brian Glanville thought that the Germans would defend and that McFarland would look after Müller. His advice to Ramsey – that he should drop Hurst and Peters and play Mullery in midfield as a ball-winner – was predictably ignored.

Though Glanville's colleagues, writing on the eve of the game and knowing the West German line-up, had no excuse for not realising that the Germans would attack, only Jeff Powell in the *Mail* thought it worth mentioning that a foreign team at Wembley was planning on taking the game to England. He didn't think it would make any difference, of course: Chivers and Lee would soon lose their man-markers, Beckenbauer would wilt under the sudden pressure, and England would win 3–0. There would be no repeat of 1970's 'outrageous fluke'; over a two-leg tie 'class' would indubitably tell. Others were not quite so sanguine: in the *Sun* Peter Batt was only expecting England to win by a single goal; in the *Daily Mirror* Ken Jones merely predicted victory; and in *The Times* Geoffrey Green was just reasonably optimistic, provided that Chivers played 'on top of Beckenbauer' and that England as a whole put pressure on the 'suspect Maier'. In the same paper Bobby Moore was quoted as saying that England would win both games.

The game was played at Wembley on a Saturday evening. Several showers had fallen during the day and there would be further brief and somewhat half-hearted spells of rain during play. According to Hugh McIlvanney, the pitch looked 'lush as an Irish meadow'.

Virtually from the kick-off the West Germans, wearing green for the first time against England, began spraying accurate ground-passes across the glistening turf, and almost immediately a bad back-pass from Ball won them a corner. It came to nothing and for a few deceptive minutes England propelled themselves forward, mostly by means of the long ball. Chivers was much in evidence, particularly with his long throws, from one of which Hurst headed on for Maier to make a simple save.

Then in the eighth minute the Germans made the first in the series of surging attacks which made their first-half display so memorable. In this instance it was Wimmer robbing Bell and racing forward, drawing in two defenders before slipping the ball wide to Hoeness on the left. Though his cross from the by-line was too long, Grabowski pulled it back from the other flank for Held whose weak shot just eluded Müller's flailing boot on its way to Banks.

The ball swung back to the other end, where England's build-up was noticeably much slower than that of West Germany. Both this attack and the one which followed it ended in easy catches for Maier. As it became apparent that Schwarzenbeck, Höttges and Breitner were not having any great difficulties in coping with Chivers, Hurst and Lee, Beckenbauer felt increasingly free to move forward and join Netzer, Hoeness and Wimmer in their sweeping attacking moves. From one of these, a Grabowski-Held one-two was narrowly foiled in the area; from another, Hoeness skipped past Hughes only to be dispossessed by last man Hunter. A minute later Netzer and Wimmer almost brought off a double one-two, and just after that Netzer galloped forward from the halfway-line and exchanged twenty-yard passes with Hoeness before being blocked just outside the area. Bobby Charlton was obviously alive and well – and playing in a German shirt.

It was exhilarating stuff and the Wembley crowd, like the one which had watched the Hungarian match nineteen years previously, was beginning to feel torn between admiration for the opposition and anxiety for the immediate fate of their own team. Netzer and Wimmer created a shooting chance for Grabowski, and his twenty-yard effort was deflected over. From the corner the ball ran out to Hoeness, and his centre was mispunched by Banks almost on to the boot of the lurking Müller.

For a couple of minutes there was some respite for the England defence. Chivers, suddenly free on the right wing, still failed to get a cross in and had to settle for the first of three corners in quick succession. None offered any real threat and the Germans moved swiftly into their most breathtaking attack yet. Netzer picked up the ball from Beckenbauer ten yards outside his own penalty area, accelerated away from Lee and headed for the England goal. He swept past a stationary Ball, half stumbled his way between Moore and Bell about twenty yards outside the England penalty area and slipped the ball to Grabowski, whose first-time pass to Müller was only just intercepted by Hunter.

Two minutes later a low Beckenbauer shot troubled Banks more than it should have and brought back echoes of 1970. England managed a deflected long-shot from Emlyn Hughes which dropped on to the roof of the net; then it was Breitner's turn to carry the ball from his own half into the England penalty area, where he shot weakly from no more than twelve yards.

A goal seemed inevitable, and another run by Netzer almost brought one. Once more he carried the ball all of fifty yards, straight at the heart of the England defence, before sliding it through to Müller. Running between Hughes and Hunter, the Bayern man looked to have no chance of making contact yet somehow got his foot between Hughes' legs and on to the ball, and Banks was forced to push it round for a corner. It was an astonishing run by Netzer and an astonishing piece of poaching by Müller, and the goal which arrived, somewhat fortunately, a minute or so later was fully deserved. Moore made the crucial error, prodding the ball back towards his own goal-mouth and an alert Müller. He slid it to Held, who set up the shot from Hoeness which was deflected past the wrong-footed Banks by Hunter.

This spurred England to greater efforts. Lee was offered three half-chances at the other end: he had a header tipped over; clumsily chested the ball down too far in front of himself with only the keeper to beat; and had a volleyed shot saved. Despite such evidence of England pressure, the overall impetus still clearly lay with the West Germans. Müller was now dropping deeper and sowing even greater confusion in the England defence, while Breitner and Wimmer seemed to be everywhere. Netzer and Beckenbauer were strolling around as if they owned the centre of the field, offering a vivid contrast to their English counterparts, Ball, Bell and Peters, who apparently lacked the higher skills needed to compete.

Maier continued to catch all the crosses England threw at him, in spite of close attention from Chivers or Hurst. The Germans continued to mount their flowing moves through the middle. In the thirty-seventh minute England's Route 1 tactics almost came off with a Hurst flick from Moore's long ball almost putting Bell in on goal, but seconds later the West Germans went even closer, Beckenbauer and Müller working a one-two on the edge of the area to create space for Grabowski, who was robbed at the last moment by a highly dubious challenge from Hughes.

Peters shot wide from distance then weakly from close in; a beautiful dummy from Hoeness was wasted by Wimmer's bad cross; and one more flowing move ended with Grabowski shooting just wide. The teams went off at half-time with only one goal separating them, but it could have been four or five without flattering the visitors. The West Germans had played like a team of all talents, a team moreover which revelled in its own skills. There had been a languid contempt in the way they had hopped and skipped over flailing English tackles and had lazily propelled the ball across the grass with the outside of the foot. The English had slung in their crosses and fought for them, banged their balls hopefully forward and fought for those too, and had been rewarded for such effort by an inevitable crop of quarter- and half-chances. They hadn't produced a single coherent ground-move, hadn't purposefully opened the way for a single clear shot. They were banging on the door in the hope it would give way; the Germans tried key after key in the lock.

The second half began with another Netzer run and the sort of cheeky chip which no English player on the pitch would have tried. One English player on the bench, though, *was* prone to such flights of fancy. This was Manchester City striker Rodney Marsh, for whose introduction the crowd had been intermittently calling throughout the first half. They began renewing their demand after Hurst had shot wildly over from a Hughes cross. At the other end Müller, sent in by Held on the left-hand side of the penalty area, appeared to have been brought down by Hunter but the French referee waved play on.

Perhaps this discouraged the West Germans, or perhaps their adventurous attacking was beginning to take its toll on the sapping turf. Either way, this was their last big move for fifteen minutes. England pressed forward and obliged with their first incisive move of the game: Hughes and Hurst exchanged passes before the latter almost brought off a tight one-two with Alan Ball. Four minutes later Rodney Marsh was brought on in place of Hurst, his mere introduction raising the English tempo. Another good run and pass by Hughes – emerging as England's best player on the night – set up Bell for a twenty-five-yarder which went wide, and when Moore hit a long and hopeful cross from the right into the far reaches of the German penalty area the Liverpool defender clipped the bar with a first-time cross-cum-shot. Both he and Madeley were now fully engaged attackers, but for all the added England pressure there were still no real openings being created and the Germans looked as dangerous as ever on the break. Two swift raids were stopped by fouls on Müller and Held and a third ended with Müller screwing his shot just wide of the near post.

Marsh was making his presence felt. In the sixty-sixth minute he tried to go past someone and was immediately fouled. A few minutes later a lovely piece of play saw him juggle with the ball, send Höttges the wrong way with a dip of the shoulder and almost put Bell through on goal. An England equaliser, barely conceivable in the first half, now looked almost likely, and when Maier made a mess of a corner, for the first time showing signs of fallibility, Höttges had to clear off the line from Marsh's header.

Three minutes later England did equalise. The move, as most of the English papers readily admitted, began with an unpunished foul by Ball on Wimmer. Bell picked up the loose ball, swung a good pass across the field to Peters and, like Mullery in 1970, kept running. Peters returned the compliment, finding Bell with a lovely diagonal ball into the penalty area, and Maier could only palm the Manchester City man's first-time shot into the path of club-mate Francis Lee a yard or so from goal. England were, almost unbelievably, on level terms.

With a second leg in Berlin to come and thirteen minutes remaining the Germans could have been forgiven for at least trying to shut up shop. Instead, they took the game back to England. Beckenbauer surged forward again, feeding Netzer who was inches away from slipping Müller in between Hughes and Hunter. At the other end Marsh took the ball past Höttges in the German penalty area and found Beckenbauer waiting for him; upon trying the same manoeuvre four minutes later he lost the ball again. This time it was poked out to Müller, and from deep inside his own half the striker put a perfect ball inside Madeley for the accelerating Held. The covering Moore, unable to match the West German for pace, brought him down. Though it was probably just outside the area, the referee awarded a penalty. Banks guessed right and got two hands to Netzer's kick, but the ball still dribbled in off the post.

The best England could manage in the last six minutes were two long shots, both of which failed to trouble Maier. Then just as the crowd was beginning to accustom itself to a one-goal defeat the West Germans scored again, this time a goal of great quality. Banks threw out to Hughes, who slipped and lost the ball to Held. He found Hoeness, who dribbled across the face of the penalty area, evading challenges by Hunter and Peters, before finding Müller with a great reverse pass. In a fraction of a second the Bayern striker stopped the ball, spun on it, and found the far corner. The Germans had won 3–1, a score line which flattered their second-half performance but which hardly did justice to the gulf in quality which had marked the first half.

The West German triumph at Wembley in April 1972 was a real watershed for both the English national team itself and the expectations which surrounded it. It knocked the incipient cockiness out of English football. In future the predictions of three-goal victories would be confined to visits from Luxembourg or San Marino, and England managers would become accustomed to solemnly declaring, in the face of much evidence to the contrary, that there were no easy games in international football.

'Cautious, joyless football was scarcely bearable even while it was bringing victories,' Hugh McIlvanney wrote in the *Observer*. 'When it brings defeat there can be only one reaction.' The English football world was stunned not so much by the fact of the German victory as by the style with which it had been achieved. England had lost in 1968 and 1970, but in both those matches there had been a rough equivalence of quality on display. This was something different, something altogether more wor-rying. England had been utterly outclassed by a nation who traditionally played English-style football. How had this happened? How had the Germans suddenly become so good?

One answer was that England had made it easy for them, made them look better than they were. Ramsey's failure to play a ball-winner in midfield had given Netzer and co. an easier ride than they deserved, or so some experts claimed. If a tackler like Mullery or Arsenal's Peter Storey had been chosen the result would probably have been very different. This was possibly true, but the same experts – Jeff Powell, for example, in the *Mail* – then went on to criticise Ramsey for not keeping up with the times, for not weaning England away from the 'ugly, hit-and-hurry of the long ball' and introducing 'the measured, controlled, classic football played by the Germans'. Did Powell and his fellow critics really think that Peter Storey could play like Wimmer or Netzer?

They wanted it both ways, but that was because they had missed the point. The difference between the two teams hadn't been the presence or lack of a ball-winner. The *Times* correspondent put it cogently: while England 'fenced and parried sideways' the West Germans 'thrust swiftly forwards through sudden gaps, mounting their sharp breaks from defence on the subtle mobility of three fine midfield ball-players.' The Germans weren't playing a ball-winner either, but their ball-players were so much better than England's. Their technique, positioning, awareness and understanding were all superior. They didn't sling long crosses to the far post in the vague hope that something might transpire, whereas England did little else.

This was not an accident, as Brian Glanville and Brian James pointed out three weeks later in a *Sunday Times* full-page post-mortem. 'Our ball-players have for years been discouraged, both by harsh treatment on the field and by being snubbed and ignored by managers and selectors,' Glanville wrote, and he named Greaves, Shackleton, Marsh and Tommy Harmer as cases in point. 'Even amidst victory in 1966 the shortcomings of our players in the matter of personal skill were evident,' James added.

The Germans had noticed the same thing about their own players, but they had acted to put matters right and raise the technical level of their players. The game in West Germany had been overhauled from top to bottom, with everything geared to the discovery and nurturing of talent from the earliest age. 'It was the mood of the country – the coaches, the players, the spectators, all wanted this,' Helmut Schön said later. England, however, bathing in the glow of their 1966 triumph and the supposed near-miss of 1970, had not addressed the problem. 'They seem to have stood still in time,' Schön said after the April 1972 game. 'Of course, they gave us a fight,' he added, as if that was the least you could expect from an England team, 'but we were far superior technically.'

Brian Glanville summed up the German play in his match report. It was, he said, 'a wonderfully flexible formation and made one think of just how remarkably Latin the nature of German football has become.' This style used a high level of technique to lift the traditional north-European game to a higher level, one in which flair and imagination could not only survive but could also make all the difference. It should have been the blueprint for the transformation of English football, and in the long-term – particularly at club level – there has been slow, steady progress made in this direction. But the English national team has never taken that leap forward which West German football as a whole took between 1966–72; the obstacles have always proved too great.

In 1972 these obstacles included Alf Ramsey's negative tactical approach and the selfishness of club managers, but both were symptomatic of a deeper malaise and the periodic appointment of new England managers and enforcement of greater player-availability has not fundamentally changed matters. English managers are still forced to select from defenders with inadequate technique, and a long procession of 'flair' players have been first lauded as saviours and then condemned for their inconsistency and lack of commitment.

If the 1972 game marked a critical moment in English football history, it also, as Ian Wooldridge pointed out in a wonderfully perceptive article in the *Daily Mail*, proved something of a turning point in Anglo–German relations. Wooldridge began by emphasising how much residual anti-German feeling existed in Britain, and had great fun describing the front page of a current boys' comic to illustrate the point. 'Crikey, a Jerry!' an Englishman exclaims; 'Himmel,' a German in field-grey expostulates in reply and is promptly shot.

The German football team's performance, Wooldridge thought, had completely subverted such simplistic stereotypes, and had done 'as much to drain the poison and bury the hatchet in ninety minutes as the respective Diplomatic Corps of the two countries had accomplished in twenty-seven years'. Again, it was not the victory that mattered, it was the way in which it had been achieved and celebrated. The Germans had played nothing like the brutal and humourless automatons of English legend, and they had accepted the victor's laurels as graciously in 1972 as they had accepted defeat in 1966. 'From the nervous preliminaries to the joyous scenes at the end,' Wooldridge wrote, 'from the Charlie George hairstyles to the occasional small courtesies in the blazing heat of the match, from the cool heads in defence to the glittering flair of the forward line, this was a German team to make nonsense of the pulp magazine conception of the German character and to make a few million adults realise that their prejudices are as obsolete as Bismarck's spiked helmet.'

'NIGHT THAT CHANGED THE GERMAN IMAGE' was the title of Wooldridge's article; and that would have been an apt headline for any of the match reports which followed the second leg, two weeks later in Berlin. Poor England performances away from home have been far from rare over the last fifty years, but few of them have left such a bad taste in the mouth as this one.

Perhaps it was merely the shock of humiliation at Wembley, or perhaps football itself had reached a critical juncture and was unconsciously preparing, in the name of complete professionalism, to jettison those ethical constraints which had always been woven into its spirit. The Arsenal, Leeds and Liverpool players in Ramsey's squad – all of whom had just lost out on either the League or Cup – were said to be depressed, and maybe they all bore giant chips on their shoulders. Ball and Lee had both been even more petulant than usual in the first German game, and the Leeds–Arsenal Cup final which fell between the two legs was a bruisingly squalid encounter even by the standards of the two teams concerned.

Ramsey's negative attitude to the second leg can hardly have helped matters. He had clearly discounted any possibility of the two-goal win needed to take England through; to attack would simply risk another humiliation, and that was unthinkable. The tie could not be saved, but his own face – and those of his players – could be.

The team was chosen accordingly. McFarland was back, having helped Derby to the title just two days after crying off from the first leg, and the abrasive Hunter was shifted forward into midfield where he joined fellow hatchet-man Peter Storey and the ever combative Ball and Bell. Peters' guile and Lee's skill on the flanks were omitted, leaving Chivers and Marsh to soldier on alone up front. This was a team built to destroy. 'LEAVE NETZER TO ME' was Peter Storey's headline promise in Friday's *Daily Mail*.

He kept that promise. By the end of ninety minutes Netzer's legs were a mass of bruises. As a football contest the match was largely uneventful. Chivers had a header scrambled off the line early on, and the Germans twice hit the bar – Held with a thunderous shot and Netzer with a swerving free kick from almost forty yards out – but neither team seemed prepared to take risks in pursuit of a goal. Ramsey had drastically curtailed England's attacking options by his team-selection and the West Germans, deprived of Grabowski due to injury, showed no great desire to build on their already comfortable lead. With Beckenbauer reducing his forward forays and Netzer suffering the constant attentions of Storey they inevitably looked less impressive than they had at Wembley.

England naturally looked much more solid at the back, and if the players had shown a modicum of respect for the spirit of the game, or at worst accepted some responsibility for not doing so, they might have come away from Berlin with some credit.

As it was, they played like thugs and then in true thug fashion blamed their victims. In the last half-hour alone there were violent fouls by McFarland on Breitner and Netzer, by Hughes on Hoeness, and by both substitutes, Peters and Summerbee, on the unfortunate Netzer.

After the match the England players refused all blame. 'If they lost a tackle they just lay there moaning and groaning,' Colin Bell said. 'You knew they weren't hurt.' 'I never thought the Germans would act like cry-babies – they tried to make villains of us,' Alan Ball told journalists.

Few were fooled. Although many of the English papers thought that the Germans had overdone the theatrics, none believed that there was any excuse for the English players' behaviour. 'I felt embarrassed and ashamed by the Englishmen's violent ugly methods,' wrote Alan Hoby in the *Sunday Express*, while David Lacey, writing in *The Guardian*, thought that 'many of the rash, reckless and some downright wicked tackles would have meant an early bath for the miscreants had there been any English official controlling the match.' Peter Batt of *The Sun*, who had been sitting only twenty yards from the touchline, could not accept 'that the Germans were only acting when they went down'; England, he thought, had approached the game 'cynically and, at times, viciously.' In the *Telegraph*, Donald Saunders dealt contemptuously with Alan Ball's 'cry-babies' allegation, saying how much he had admired the self-discipline that enabled the Germans 'to accept so much illegal punishment without retaliation.'

For their part, the Germans seemed more saddened than angered by the England players' behaviour. Schön, who had leapt angrily from his seat on several occasions during the game, coldly accused them of 'brutal tackling aimed at the bones', but Beckenbauer, ever the diplomat, merely pronounced himself 'disappointed' with the 'over-vigorous tackles'. The *Welt Am Sonntag* correspondent spoke for many when he lamented the English players' betrayal of their own country's reputation for fair play, a reputation for which the Germans had once had so much respect.

Something had died in the Berlin rain, and it wasn't just England's hopes in the European Championship.

15: an english günter netzer?

Over the next few years the West Germans, at both club and national level, were the dominant force in European and world football. The national team went on to win the European Championship in June 1972, and two years later, though missing the coruscating skills of Netzer, narrowly defeated Johan Cruyff's wonderful Dutch team to win the World Cup on home soil. In the same period Bayern Munich, with a team which featured Maier, Breitner, Schwarzenbeck, Beckenbauer, Hoeness and Müller, went from strength to strength, winning the first of three consecutive Bundesliga championships in 1972 and the first of three consecutive European Cups in 1974. 'Kaiser' Franz Beckenbauer was indeed emperor of all he surveyed.

Borussia Mönchengladbach, the other great West German side of the 1970s, proved less adept at winning European trophies than Bayern. In 1971–2 they had been knocked out of the European Cup by eventual finalists Inter Milan after a 7–1 home victory was annulled on account of crowd trouble, and the following year they came up against Liverpool in the UEFA (Union of European Football Associations) Cup Final.

Again there was a whiff of controversy: heavy rain forced the abandonment of the first leg at Anfield after half an hour, with the Germans easily holding their own, and when the game kicked off anew on the following evening Liverpool manager Bill Shankly had changed his team, putting in John Toshack to partner Kevin Keegan up front. The Welsh striker's prowess in the air set up two goals for Keegan in the first thirty-two minutes, and if Keegan had also converted a first half penalty the tie would have been virtually settled by half-time. Mönchengladbach, who included national team members Heynckes, Netzer, Vögts, Wimmer and Bonhof, had their chances, Danner hitting a post in the first half and Wimmer shooting high when clean through in the second, but they never fully came to terms with Liverpool's aerial threat, and centre half Larry Lloyd headed a third from a corner in the sixty-second minute. Three minutes later Mönchengladbach were awarded a penalty. Ray Clemence's save from Heynckes' kick was compared by many who saw it with Banks' save from Pelé in Mexico.

In the second leg Mönchengladbach, and particularly Netzer, who had been criticised for playing too negatively at Anfield, attacked Liverpool with imagination and gusto. They were rewarded with two first-half goals from Heynckes but despite the almost constant pressure in the second half, they proved incapable of finding the aggregate equaliser. Liverpool's nine-year pursuit of a European trophy had at last been rewarded.

The Merseyside club were also crowned as League Champions that season, and duly entered the European Cup in 1973–4. In the first round they surprisingly struggled against Jeunesse Esch of Luxemburg, and in the second they went out to a brilliant Red Star Belgrade team, beaten both home and away by demonstrations of dazzling virtuosity. The strength of purpose and commitment which had so narrowly seen Liverpool through against the more skilful Mönchengladbach was on this occasion insufficient, and Shankly was perceptive enough to realise that at the highest level it always would be. A few weeks later at a now famous meeting of the 'Boot Room' team which guided Liverpool, it was decided that their style had to change – that a more Continental approach, with less reliance on the long ball and more on close control, must be adopted. Liverpool would attempt the leap forward which the Germans had taken and England had flunked, and they would reap the greatest rewards for their courage in doing so.

England, meanwhile, had stumbled along for another eighteen months under Ramsey's increasingly atavistic leadership. He finally departed after his team had failed to qualify for the 1974 World Cup (they drew the crucial last game against Poland when only a win would do). It was a performance that summed up his reign, full of sound, fury and non-stop effort, frustratingly devoid of subtlety or finesse.

His ultimate full-time successor was Don Revie, once the originator of Manchester City's daringly progressive 'Revie Plan' but now better known as the driving force behind Leeds United's recent success, which had been built, consciously or not, very much in the image of Ramsey's England. Allan Clarke was a fine poacher, Lorimer a ferocious striker of the ball, but many Leeds players were somewhat robotic and those who weren't were often recognised more for their work-rates and suspect temperaments than for any extraordinary skill with the ball. Admirers claimed that Leeds were a highly professional outfit; detractors that this team had the collective moral sense of a hyena and would do whatever was necessary to win. One Hungarian referee, shaking with rage at the end of a European tie involving the team, thought Leeds the roughest team he had ever seen.

In this light, it looked as though the FA had exchanged a Ramsey with scruples for one without.

The West German visit to Wembley in March 1975 bore striking parallels to the visit just over twenty years before. Once again they were arriving as World Champions and once again they were bringing a team much weaker than that which had actually won the crown. As in 1954, the hosts had much more to prove than the guests.

Interest in the game was certainly high. Wembley sold out and fourteen cinemas had contracted to show the match live, adding a further 40,000 to the audience. Ramsey and the once glorious past had been swept aside during the twelve months prior to the match, and the footballing public was hoping to see a brighter future emerge against the old enemy.

Revie had inherited a side which had already undergone transformations during Ramsey's last few months in charge and Joe Mercer's caretaker period, and made no dramatic changes of his own in his first few months in charge. Only Bell and Ball remained of Ramsey's old guard, the latter surprisingly recalled for this match and, more than a little controversially, given the captaincy to boot. Sunderland's Dave Watson and Derby's Colin Todd were a year into establishing themselves at the heart of the team's defence, and the partnership of Southampton's Mick Channon and Liverpool's Kevin Keegan was becoming a solid fixture in attack.

A Leeds–Ipswich Cup replay had deprived Revie of probable first-choice full-backs Paul Madeley and Kevin Beattie, and new caps were awarded to Leicester's Steve Whitworth and QPR's Ian Gillard. Up front, Malcolm Macdonald was offered another chance to prove he could perform at this level, and, most exciting of all, Stoke City's extravagantly gifted Alan Hudson was given a debut alongside Ball and Bell in midfield.

Hudson's inclusion was some compensation for the absence of other flair players, such as Trevor Brooking, Frank Worthington and Duncan Mackenzie. The former pair had played in England's last half-dozen or so games, but Mackenzie, though one of the most talented players of his generation, was never selected to play for England and often had trouble even making the first team at his various League clubs.

If England were relatively short on flair, so – rather less intentionally – were their West German opponents. Now in his eleventh year as coach, Helmut Schön had lost Grabowski and four Bayern players – Müller, Breitner, Schwarzenbeck and Hoeness – since the World Cup, and their replacements, as soon became apparent, were lacking the same level of inspiration. Players like Bernhard Cullmann, Heinz Flohe and Bernd Hölzenbein, all of whom eventually won a respectable forty or so caps, were efficient, technically excellent 'runners' who would rarely let anyone down, but they were light years away from Netzer, Hoeness and Grabowski. And Müller was of course simply irreplaceable. The most golden of golden periods for the West German national team was coming to an end.

There was still Beckenbauer, though, and as he shook hands with Alan Ball in the centre-circle it was hard to believe that the two of them had first faced each other at Wembley in February 1966. Then, they had been winning their fourth and sixth caps respectively; now, they were winning their eighty-ninth and sixty-seventh.

The match proved a happier one for Ball than for Beckenbauer. England looked more positive, more incisive, right from the beginning, and the German sweeper found few opportunities for going forward in support of his lacklustre attack. On this occasion it was the England midfield players and forwards who caught the eye, and none more so than Alan Hudson. As early as the fifth minute he brilliantly made space for himself in the penalty area only to find his forwards badly placed, and in the twenty-sixth minute it was his beautifully flighted free-kick which was volleyed in by Bell. Later in the half, Hudson's pass sent Macdonald clean through to shoot over the bar, and throughout the first forty-five minutes his overall orchestration of the game, his comfort on the ball, his changes of pace and wide range of accurate passes were reminiscent of a Netzer or a Charlton.

It was a measure of his success that Schön felt obliged to take off the attack-minded Wimmer at half-time and replace him with the more prosaic Kremers. With Cullmann and Flohe also working themselves into the ground, Hudson and his colleagues in midfield certainly had a harder second half. Nonetheless the West Germans themselves looked no more likely to score. They didn't win their first corner until an hour had been played, and at the other end Bell almost punished them for their temerity, only just failing to find the net after Macdonald's shot had been blocked. Five minutes later the Newcastle man did score, heading in after Channon's quickly taken free-kick had sent Ball to the by-line for a far-post cross.

While the Germans did finally manage to exert a little pressure, they never looked like scoring. The two most memorable incidents of the final quarter featured Beckenbauer inelegantly diving to cut out a through-ball with his hand and Keegan finding the underside of the bar with a glorious chip. The crowd went home wondering whether England had been as good as they had looked. Had they just witnessed the first stages of a resurrection?

The papers thought so. 'ENGLAND COME GOOD AGAIN' headlined *The Times*, speaking for them all.

The hero of the hour was Alan Hudson, whom the same paper hoped and believed was 'the man England have been looking for since 1970'. In the *Daily Mirror* Frank McGhee thought that Hudson had strolled through his debut 'with the assurance, the elegance and the efficiency of someone who was born to play at this level'. He was 'here to stay – all the way to the 1978 World Cup'. Even the Germans were impressed. Schön thought the Stoke player had 'good vision', and that with Ball and Todd he could form 'the basis for a very fine England team'. The watching Günter Netzer wondered out loud where the English had been hiding him: Hudson had been 'magnificent' and had all it took to be 'a world-class player'.

There were caveats. David Lacey qualified his praise with the thought that 'not so long ago skills of this sort were accepted as the norm in an England team', and Brian Glanville cautioned against reading too much into one performance against weak opposition.

All that aside, the West Germans had been beaten for the first time since 1966, England had looked good for the first time in many moons, and for a few weeks it was hard to resist a rare and heady sense of optimism.

Two months later Leeds United and Bayern Munich were preparing themselves to contest the first Anglo–German European Cup final in Paris. Bayern were the title-holders, having comprehensively beaten Athletico Madrid at the second attempt in the previous season's final. Their form in the current season, though, had been poor and they were lying only tenth in the Bundesliga. Breitner had left for Real Madrid, Hansen was injured and while Beckenbauer was officially fit, he had been worried for some time by an abdominal strain. Dettmar Cramer, Bayern's manager of only a few months, was pessimistic. 'We are not strong enough for Leeds', he told the press. 'We have no midfield. Our defence has been open like barn doors. Leeds are stronger than us in so many positions.' The Yorkshire side, he added, were identical to England 'in their style and their system'.

Brian Clough had succeeded Revie in the Leeds managerial seat at the beginning of the season, but had lasted just forty-four turbulent days before giving way to the former England full-back Jimmy Armfield. The team recovered well enough from this traumatic start to take the ninth place in the First Division, but it was the first time they had finished out of the top four since their promotion in 1963–4. Hunter, Giles and the combative Bremner had by this point been playing together for ten years, and many of their supporting cast – Madeley, Clarke, Lorimer, Jordan and Eddie Gray – had been around almost as long. If they were ever to win the biggest prize then this was probably their last chance to do so.

Armfield's team selection was cautious, perhaps too much so. Already deprived of centre-half Gordon McQueen because of a moment of retaliatory madness in Barcelona, he decided to sacrifice Eddie Gray's wing-skills for Terry Yorath's beefy presence in midfield. Up front the ever-reliable Allan Clarke was preferred to the mercurial Duncan Mackenzie. Given that Leeds fully expected Bayern to defend and play on the break, the omission of two such gifted attackers is baffling.

Few doubted Leeds' determination, but many doubted their ability to keep the game within legal bounds. Speaking in the *Sun* a couple of days before the game, Billy Bremner poured scorn on the team's critics. He and his team-mates had just watched a video of Bayern's semi-final, and 'the way the Germans steamed in, they've just got to be bloody joking to say we're too rough'. This didn't bode well. In the same paper the next day Arsenal keeper Bob Wilson predicted a match with 'many bad-tempered moments'. This gloomy forecast, he said, was 'based on my first-hand knowledge of the players involved'. Since Arsenal had not been drawn against Bayern in any of their four European campaigns, one could only assume Wilson thought these moments would come from Leeds.

In the event, it took the Yorkshire team four minutes to set the tone. Yorath went straight over the ball and into the shin of Bayern's Swedish international midfielder Bjorn Andersson – at best it was a criminally reckless challenge; at worst the calculated crippling of an opponent. In either case Yorath should have been sent off. As it was, he didn't even receive a yellow card from the incompetent French referee.

Andersson was stretchered off and replaced by Weiss, then four minutes later Reaney was booked for another bad foul. Hoeness was the victim this time, and he too would eventually be forced to retire after a tussle with Yorath added injury to injury. The game was only eight minutes old and already Leeds had sacrificed any moral claim to victory or right to expect justice from the referee. When Beckenbauer clearly tripped Clarke in the penalty area seven minutes from half-time most neutrals delighted in the officials' apparent blindness.

Leeds certainly had most of the possession and made most of the play, but the Clarke incident aside they showed little sign of breaking down the Bayern defence. Without Gray there was no one to get behind the Germans, and a long procession of high balls lobbed into the penalty area were gobbled up by Schwarzenbeck and Beckenbauer. It was the sixty-fifth minute before they created a second real chance, and then Bremner, turning on a Lorimer free kick, put it close enough to Maier for the German to make a magnificent reflex save.

A minute later Lorimer fired home after the Germans had failed to clear a free kick from Giles. Leeds thought they had scored, but an offside Bremner had been close to the line of the shot and the referee rightly disallowed the goal. This didn't sit well with the Leeds fans in the stadium, many of whom took the disappointment as a cue to go berserk. Bayern supporters had been attacked and a supermarket looted before the game; now uprooted metal seating and other assorted missiles rained down on the French police. A policeman and a ball-boy were knocked unconscious, a photographer blinded in one eye.

To make matters worse for the apoplectic fans, Bayern scored. Müller and Torstensson broke out of defence at speed and suddenly Franz Roth was free on the left to shoot past David Stewart and into the far corner. It was an electrifying goal – even the French police clapped, enraging the Leeds fans still further. Eddie Gray replaced Yorath, but the winger had only been on the pitch a few seconds when Kapellmann wriggled his way to the by-line and pulled it back for Müller to strike in typical fashion, spinning and shooting with no apparent back-lift before anyone else could react. The final whistle sounded a few minutes later, and as the Bayern players danced for joy in the centre of the pitch the beaten Leeds team ran over to applaud their rioting supporters.

Leeds were quite unrepentant, even after their fans' subsequent behaviour cost them a four-year ban from European competition. Nor was anyone in their camp anything other than indignant at the fact that they had lost. The referee's decisions had cost them victory, Armfield thought. He was referring to the ungiven penalty and the offside goal, not the lenience accorded to Yorath.

The English papers were inclined to agree: 'No other defeat has ever seemed so cruel or seemed so unfair', Frank McGhee lamented in the *Mirror*. He mentioned Yorath's crippling of Andersson and yet, like his fellow correspondents, failed to make the simple connection: if the Leeds man had been dismissed as he should have been, then who knew whether Beckenbauer would ever have needed to trip up Allan Clarke?

Don Revie was in Paris to watch his old side, and claimed that he hadn't seen Yorath's foul. While TV pundits Jimmy Hill and Bobby Charlton had no such excuse, they too, in Danny Blanchflower's words, 'seemed strangely silent about it'. When England had disgraced themselves in Berlin three years earlier the English press had rightly taken them to task, but loyalty to one's country was apparently becoming more important than loyalty to the old English belief in fair play.

This Nelsonian blind eye also extended to the football itself. Leeds had enjoyed eighty per cent of the possession; nonetheless to assume from that, as many did, that they had out-played Bayern only to be denied by the referee was a judgement worthy of Ramsey. Football was about scoring goals, not keeping possession, and when it mattered a foul-weakened Bayern had shown the skill to score them. Though the referee had been dreadful, his dreadfulness had not significantly favoured either side. Leeds had played unimaginative English football in the worst possible spirit and had deservedly lost. If this was, as the *Sun* claimed, 'the end of a decade of glory and greatness', then football could only breathe a heartfelt sigh of relief.

These two games in 1975 – England v. West Germany in March and Bayern v. Leeds in May – offered highly contrasting views of England's football future: on the one hand a newly confident national side moving in the right tactical direction, on the other a club-side apparently stuck in the tactical past. If the future for England looked bright, the outlook for English clubs in the premier European competition looked decidedly gloomy.

Neither prognosis could have been further from the truth. After the game at Wembley David Lacey, glancing up at the recently installed screen above the seats, saw 'the huge disembodied face of Alf Ramsey . . . like some operatic phantom, gazing down from the gods on a darkened stage . . .' Ramsey was actually taking part in a TV postmortem, but would indeed be haunting England for a while yet. Revie was unable to break away from the fear-fuelled negativity which had marked his predecessor's reign, and failed to qualify for the finals of either the 1976 European Championship or the 1978 World Cup. Alan Hudson, 'the man England had been looking for since 1970', would win just one more cap.

So much for the national team. English clubs, meanwhile, were about to assert a dominance over European club football that only their own fans could disrupt.

16: clubs first, country second

In 1976 Bayern Munich won the European Cup for the third consecutive year, holding on by the skin of their teeth to beat France's St Etienne 1–0 at Hampden Park. Six weeks later most of the usual suspects were in the West German team which lost the European Championship final on penalties to Czechoslovakia. For Beckenbauer, Hoeness, Schwarzenbeck and Wimmer it was virtually the end of the line; for both Bayern and West Germany it was the end of an era. The former's run of Bundesliga Championships had been broken by Borussia Mönchengladbach in 1974–5, the first of three successive titles for the North Rhine-Westphalian team. It was Mönchengladbach whom Liverpool met in the second Anglo–German European Cup final, in May 1977.

The match was a first appearance for both teams at this level, and as such most observers predicted a close match. Some also expected a game of dramatically contrasting styles, but to some extent this was an outdated perspective. Though Liverpool were hardly exponents of 'Total Football', under Shankly and his successor Bob Paisley they had developed into an unusually sophisticated British side. Clemence, Hughes, Keegan, Heighway and Callaghan remained from the team which had beaten Mönchengladbach in 1973, and the newcomers told their own story: Phil Thompson, Phil Neal, Ray Kennedy, Jimmy Case and Terry McDermott were better ball-players than the likes of Chris Lawler, Tommy Smith, Larry Lloyd and John Toshack. Smith would play in place of the injured Thompson in Rome, but the team as a whole would not be lumping high balls forward for a British-style centre-forward to chase – the team didn't have one. It relied instead on the traditional English virtues of determination and commitment allied to constant, intelligent movement, all imbued with a high level of technical competence. They did the basic things, like tackling, passing and finishing, extremely well. There was nothing complex about Liverpool's style; it was simplicity raised almost to the level of an artform.

Borussia Mönchengladbach played to a more flexible formation, the man-markers following their men wherever they went, the *libero* both sweeping and joining in attacks, the midfielders and forwards popping up all over the field. While they seemed the more 'modern' team, they were also an older team, their experienced striker Heynckes was not fully fit and, perhaps most crucially of all, they were afraid of Liverpool in general and Keegan in particular. Their manager Udo Lattek decided, over Vögts' protests, to give the veteran full-back the job of taming Liverpool's live-wire, and compounded this mistake by preferring Wittkamp to the more mobile, more intelligent Stielike in the sweeper position. Keegan would lead Vögts a merry dance, while Stielike's creative skills would be all but wasted in a hectic midfield.

Even so it was far from an easy win for Liverpool. A wonderful pass from Steve Heighway in the twenty-seventh minute picked out an equally wonderful run and precise finish from Terry McDermott, but Mönchengladbach responded to the challenge and eventually secured an equaliser just after half-time, the Dane Allan Simonsen rifling home a glorious shot after Case had mis-hit a back pass. For ten minutes or so the Germans looked a class above Liverpool, and Stielike, clean through with only Clemence to beat, could have given them a mountain to climb. But Clemence made a fine save and soon Liverpool's advantage had been restored, Smith heading home a Heighway corner as the rest of the German defence watched Keegan. Eight minutes from the end Vögts tripped him in the area and Phil Neal put the penalty away with his usual quiet aplomb. Three and a half years after deciding to adopt a more Continental style Liverpool, with a team containing nine Englishmen, had become England's second winners of the European Cup. Don Revie remarked that if Liverpool's triumph had come three years earlier he would have built his England team around their players.

There was no chance of this happening now. Keegan left to play for Hamburg in the Bundesliga, and over the next eight months Paisley signed the three Scots who would form the backbone of his team for the

rest of their golden era: Alan Hansen, Kenny Dalglish and Graeme
Souness.

Nineteen seventy-seven was not a good year for the England team. In
February they were given a footballing lesson by the Dutch which ranked
alongside those previously inflicted by the Hungarians in 1953 and West
Germans in 1972, and later in the year their inability to score enough
goals against Luxembourg saw them fail to qualify for a second consecutive World Cup. The only good news was Don Revie's abrupt
desertion of the sinking ship in the middle of that summer's Latin
American tour.

His successor, Ron Greenwood, had no magic wand to wave, but he
soon created a new atmosphere in the England camp by the simple, and
previously overlooked, expedient of treating the players like grown men.
Their opinions, and those of a whole new brains-trust of club managers –
Bobby Robson, Dave Sexton and Don Howe – were invited and listened
to rather than treated as incipient mutiny, as had often been the case in
Revie's time. Though irrelevant to the final standings, a stylish 2–0 World
Cup-qualifier victory over Italy raised hopes for the future, and when
Greenwood took his team to a snowbound Munich for a friendly international in February 1978 even Helmut Schön was heard to say that he
thought England were improving. Admittedly he spoiled the effect somewhat by adding that the forthcoming match would give his side useful
practice for a potential meeting with Scotland in Argentina, but praise was
praise, and England had had little enough of it in recent years.

When England took the field only Clemence, Watson and Keegan
survived of the team which had bred such optimism in 1975. Manchester
United's nimble Stuart Pearson was now Keegan's partner in attack, and
the midfield in an attack-minded 4-4-2 formation (it often looked like
4-2-4) featured Steve Coppell and Peter Barnes on the flanks, Ray
Wilkins and Trevor Brooking in the centre. There was no obvious ball-
winner in midfield, no hulking target-man to aim for up front. This
looked a team better-suited to attack than defence, and so it proved.
Seventy-seven thousand spectators braved the weather and millions more
watched the game on live TV; all saw England take the game to the West
Germans on their own soil and demonstrate more class and confidence
than any English visitors since the time of Duncan Edwards.

Right from the beginning Wilkins and Brooking controlled the midfield, and the speedy Barnes was soon giving the German defence all sorts of problems. In the sixteenth minute he shot narrowly wide after a scintillating run, and a few minutes later Pearson should have done better with his accurate cross. The West German side included no real replacements for Beckenbauer and Müller, and relied heavily on the rather pedestrian Flohe in midfield. Their two wingers – Rudiger Abramczik and the young Karl-Heinz Rummenigge – were having trouble getting into the game, though the latter's deliberate deflection of a Bonhof free kick in the twenty-sixth minute almost gave West Germany an undeserved lead when it struck a post.

England finally scored in the forty-first minute, Pearson heading a Coppell centre in off the post after fine passes from Wilkins and Neal, and the West Germans came out for the second half in more determined mood. England's defence appeared well capable of keeping them out until a triple substitution by Schön saw the introduction of the Duisburg pairing, Ronald Worm and Bernhard Dietz. Worm had scored against England 'B' the previous night and within minutes had repeated the feat after club-mate Dietz unselfishly squared the ball.

With ten minutes remaining England still seemed set to secure at least a draw, but when Watson conceded a dubious free kick on the edge of their area they allowed their concentration to falter, and Bonhof's quickly taken kick thundered through the still-forming wall and past Clemence. Having looked likely victors for most of the match, England had to settle for the compensation of a fine performance in a narrow defeat. Greenwood announced himself 'not too disappointed', and Schön's assistant Jupp Derwall (who was scheduled to succeed him after that summer's World Cup) thought that the England manager was 'on the way to building not just a good England side, but a very very good one'.

This was good to hear, particularly after recent comments suggesting that England was falling behind the rest of Europe, but after all the disappointments of recent years the English press had learned not to be too optimistic. England had played reasonably well without ever looking particularly incisive and it was, the *Mail* thought, 'a measure of the depths to which England's football had sunk that Ron Greenwood's travelling circus flew home from Munich yesterday celebrating a defeat'.

Greenwood himself was as measured and clear-sighted as usual. He had never wavered from his belief that success lay in marrying the better qualities of European football with English football's own strong points. 'Some of the close combination work the Germans produced against us on Wednesday was breathtaking,' he said, 'and we would be foolish not to try and match it.' England needed to produce players with comparable technical abilities, and he knew only too well that they could not be achieved overnight.

Over the past few decades several British stars had sought success in Italy, some more successfully than others. None had moved to West Germany, however, and for two obvious reasons. The Bundesliga lacked the sun-drenched glamour, the football quality and the financial clout of Italy's Serie A. It was also German, and although the popular equation of 'German' with 'enemy' was slowly fading it was still far from forgotten. It was one thing to accept that the Germans were people just like us, and quite another – particularly for young men of usually narrow experience – to actually go and live among them.

Kevin Keegan's move to Hamburg in the summer of 1977 changed all that, and his lead was followed in subsequent years by fellow England players Dave Watson (albeit briefly) and Tony Woodcock. Both Keegan and Woodcock, the former after a rocky start, proved great successes in the Bundesliga: Keegan helped Hamburg to that first Championship since the national league's foundation in 1963 and a European Cup final; Woodcock established himself as a firm favourite at FC Cologne in 1979–82. Both eventually returned to England with a lot to say about the differences between the two nations' football cultures.

Training, for one thing, was much harder in West Germany. Keegan had a hard taskmaster at Hamburg in the Yugoslav Branko Zebec, and in later years he described sessions which left him unable to walk for days, 'never mind kick a ball'. Zebec was perhaps more extreme than most, but Woodcock also found the training harder than that he had been used to at Nottingham Forest. Another difference was that players who hadn't trained would never be considered for a match, whereas in England the practice of patching people up and sending them out on a Saturday was quite normal.

The West German approach was generally more scientific, the players much more weight- and diet-conscious. Woodcock's team-mates thought

English players inclined to fat, and found much amusement in the fact. He recalled how a German group visiting the England base in Italy during the 1980 European Championship had been amazed by how much food they were given. When they heard the English had stayed there for over a week they laughed and said, 'You've no chance!' The Germans were strict with themselves in terms of what they ate and drank, whereas the diets of most English footballers were still infected by the old machismo right into the eighties. 'Real' men didn't eat quiche, they ate steak, preferably with a large plate of chips and a few pints of beer to wash it down.

At this time the Germans also had the advantage of only thirty-four league games a year, only one cup competition to enter, and a midwinter break. Woodcock remembered that his team-mates used to complain about how 'English weeks' – weeks with two games – took it out of them, and that he himself, unlike most of his England team-mates, was still feeling fresh when they all arrived in Spain for the 1982 World Cup. The West Germans not only got themselves fitter, they also gave themselves a chance to stay that way.

On the pitch the differences were just as instructive. Keegan quickly realised how much more comfortable German players – and particularly German defenders – were on the ball when compared to their English counterparts. And because they were all comfortable on the ball they were more versatile in the roles they could play. 'German defenders didn't just tonk the ball away unless they were under severe pressure', Woodcock noticed; and when the team was trying to breach another team's defensive wall they didn't just toss the ball in. 'All the players were confident to have the ball.' Where English teams would try to force an issue, the Germans would just play it around among themselves, waiting for an opening to appear.

The English relied on speed and hard tackling, the Germans on change of pace. Woodcock's coach told him that constant movement simply signalled his intentions, that he should be more selective in making runs, and that on no account should he waste his energy chasing lost causes just for the sake of looking busy. Woodcock continued this policy when he returned to England only for the coaching staff to scream, 'Get running, you lazy bastard!' Once again English machismo was winning out over common sense.

There were debits too. German man-markers could be too rigid – as

Vögts had been in the 1977 European Cup final – and German goal-keepers, who encounter few high crosses in a normal Bundesliga season, tended to be primarily shot-stoppers. Arguments between players which in England were usually left on the pitch could lead to days of awkward silences. Generally speaking, though, both Keegan and Woodcock seemed highly impressed and were eager to bring the lessons they'd learned home with them.

How to implement them, of course, was something else again. Woodcock doubted if skill-levels could be increased with the ball 'flying around you all the time', and suggested slowing the English game down at little. 'I'm not advocating losing the good qualities we've got,' he said, 'but we do need a bit more subtlety and control in our game.' It could be done. Liverpool, he pointed out, did not play the sort of 'kick-and-rush' English football which his Cologne team-mates had teased him about. Perhaps ultimately what was required were English defenders and midfield players who were as comfortable on the ball as their forwards were. The English game was still far too full of 'good, honest players' who merely worked hard.

Liverpool's 3–1 over Borussia Mönchengladbach in the 1977 European Cup final had been full of exciting, flowing football. That was more than could be said for the next five finals, all of which were won 1–0 by English teams. Liverpool beat Bruges with a typically neat Kenny Dalglish goal in 1978; Nottingham Forest defeated Malmö in Munich with a Trevor Francis header in 1979. Both had beaten German teams in their semi-finals, Liverpool powering past Mönchengladbach yet again and Forest coming back from a 3–3 home-draw with Cologne to snatch victory by a single goal in the Rhineland.

In 1980 their final opponents were Kevin Keegan's Hamburg. Perhaps stung by criticism of Forest's dull performance in the previous year's final, assistant manager Peter Taylor expressed an aspiration to win this one in style. The loss of Trevor Francis, Forest's most skilful forward, with a torn achilles tendon made this a forlorn hope. They defended in depth from the outset, secure in the knowledge that in Peter Shilton they had the best goalkeeper in the world. Indeed, on this particular Spanish night Kenny Burns and Larry Lloyd gave a good impression of being the best central defenders in the world.

Forest attacked exclusively on the break, and in one such first-half foray winger John Robertson drifted inside international full-back Manny Kaltz, advanced unchallenged to the edge of the penalty area and rather surprisingly beat keeper Kargus with a low shot of no great power. Rarely had the shortcomings of German man-to-man marking been more vividly exposed.

For the rest of the game Hamburg strove mightily to get back on level terms, in the second half laying virtual siege to the Forest goal. But Burns and Lloyd dealt with everything the increasingly desperate West German side threw in the air, and Shilton made at least four great saves, including one Milewski which almost defied belief. By the end of the game it seemed as if the old stereotypes had been reversed, with Forest playing like the Bayern Munich of old, content to absorb pressure and launch swift breaks, and Hamburg reduced to the tired English habit of throwing high balls in the general direction of the penalty spot.

After the match, manager Brian Clough insisted that defending well was just as important as attacking well. 'We beat them for application, determination and pride – all the things that portray our football', he added. All of which was true, but on this night Forest had made few friends for English football. As Hugh McIlvanney pointed out somewhat sadly in the *Observer*: 'If Forest had played as the Germans did, and lost, our newspapers would have brimmed with laments over misfortune and condemnations of Teutonic sterility.'

Two years later there was a near-repeat performance, this time with Aston Villa and Bayern Munich in the starring roles, though the Birmingham side's defensive stance was perhaps less voluntary than Forest's. Their regular goalkeeper, Jimmy Rimmer, though competent enough was certainly no Peter Shilton, and a neck injury forced his withdrawal after ten minutes. His replacement, the twenty-three-year-old Nigel Spink, had only appeared in the first team on one previous occasion, and that two and half years ago.

Bayern dominated the game, with sweeper Klaus Augenthaler and the returned Paul Breitner instrumental in many fine moves. However, they were thwarted by a combination of bad German finishing, excellent saves from Spinks and towering performances from McNaught and Evans at the heart of the Villa defence, and once again a single break decided the issue. Gary Shaw fed Trevor Morley on the left; he went past Augenthaler for the one and only time in the game and pulled the ball back for Peter Withe to shoot awkwardly home off a post. A further twenty minutes of German pressure came to nothing, and when the final whistle blew the Bayern players sunk to their knees in disbelief.

It was England's sixth consecutive European Cup win, and if the style of the last five victories had left a lot to be desired, it was hard, in the short term at least, to argue with such an incredible run of success, particularly when the national team appeared to be so incapable of matching it.

17: a loss of nerve, a touch of skill

The West Germans had not had a particularly successful World Cup in 1978 (they went out in the second stage after failing to win any of their three games) but by the time of the 1980 European Championships the crop of players introduced in the mid to late seventies were settling into another formidable-looking team, and they duly won the competition. England had qualified for this one – their first such achievement since 1968 – but a draw with Belgium and a one-goal defeat by their Italian hosts cost them any chance of further progress. By this time Ron Greenwood was showing signs of succumbing to the 'safety first' policy which had condemned his predecessors, and refused a decent run in the team to the nation's most obviously gifted newcomer, Glenn Hoddle. The Tottenham player's priceless ability to unlock defences was not considered adequate compensation for a less than stellar work-rate.

Both nations arrived in Spain for the 1982 World Cup with good recent records: West Germany had only lost four games since the last World Cup – three to Brazil, one to Argentina – and England had won six and drawn one of their last seven. Both were also missing key players, though. The young and highly talented Bernd Schuster, who until recently had provided much of the flair in West Germany's midfield, had been ruled out of the tournament by injury, while both Trevor Brooking and Kevin Keegan were deemed unlikely to play any role in the early stages.

England began well, beating what would eventually prove to be a very good French team 3–1 in the first of three group matches in Bilbao. Rather less convincingly they then beat Czechoslovakia 2–0 and Kuwait 1–0 to qualify for the second round. Whatever the circumstances, three wins were three wins, and that was more than the West Germans could manage. They took Algeria for granted and paid the price with a 2–1 defeat, recovered to beat Chile 4–1 and then played out a disgraceful travesty of a game against Austria, their 1–0 victory sending both nations through.

Neither England nor West Germany were very pleased to find themselves in the same second-round group. It was their Spanish hosts, however, who were probably the most disgruntled of the three teams, having somehow contrived to finish behind Northern Ireland in their own group. The old enemies were drawn to play each other first, with Spain facing West Germany in the second match and England in the third. Since defeat in the opening match would more or less guarantee an imminent exit from the tournament both managers were set to adopt cautious approaches.

The West German camp was as usual allegedly riven with discord. That said, the team at Jupp Derwall's disposal still looked formidable, at least in theory. Most of the players had established themselves over the previous three or four years (only Breitner, Stielike and Rummenigge went back to Euro '76 and beyond) and the defence in particular looked as solid as anyone's, with Uli Stielike sweeping up behind the hard-tackling Förster brothers, Hans Briegel and the attack-minded Manny Kaltz. The midfield players, Stuttgart's Hansi Müller excepted, verged on the pedestrian, but Rummenigge, Hamburg's giant centre-forward Horst Hrubesch and Cologne's darting Pierre Littbarski posed a variety of threats up front, should Derwall take the risk of playing them all. Much would depend on how he assessed the dubious fitness of both Müller and Rummenigge.

Greenwood had similar problems with Brian Robson, Kevin Keegan and Trevor Brooking, all of whom believed themselves fit enough to play at least some part in the game. He gambled on Robson, bringing him back in place of Hoddle, but decided against recalling the two veterans. The team which took the field against West Germany was identical to that which had played the first match against France; it lined up in a typically English 4–4–2 formation, with Steve Coppell and Graham Rix the wide men in midfield, Ray Wilkins and Bryan Robson holding the centre and, whenever possible, moving forward to support the striking duo of Trevor Francis and Paul Mariner.

On the eve of the match the smart money was apparently on England, who Italian manager Bearzot, Johan Cruyff and Franz Beckenbauer all tipped to win. The *Sun*, fresh from its triumphant coverage of the Falklands War, noted that England had 'beaten the Germans at most things. But not in the 1982 World Cup. Not yet.' On the morning of the game the same paper's banner headline – 'ACHTUNG STATIONS' – offered a depressing foretaste of the coming decade; in the text below it John Sadler claimed that 'the best team England has assembled in years just can't wait to get at the Germans'.

When the two teams lined up in Madrid's Bernabeu Stadium the most noticeable omission from the German team was Pierre Littbarski, the man who the England managerial team had feared the most. Nor was there any place for strikers Hrubesch or Fischer; Rummenigge would be a lonely figure up front, receiving what support he could from a five man midfield. Derwall, it was clear, was playing for a draw from the outset, which had to be some sort of tribute to England's slow resurrection under Greenwood.

Whether the English team deserved that much respect was a moot point. For the first ten minutes the two sides sniffed at each like suspicious cats, interspersing easy lateral passes with occasional hopeful balls forward, all of which proved easy for defenders or floated harmlessly out for goal-kicks. While the Germans had more possession it was England who managed the first shots from distance, one easily saved by Schumacher, the other deflected for a corner. Both came to nothing, play switched ends and it was Hansi Müller's turn to find the crowd.

It had quickly become apparent that the heat would preclude ninety minutes of 'kick-and-rush', and yet there were few signs of a more skilful approach in the opening quarter of an hour. The West Germans lacked in ambition, the English – and Paul Mariner in particular – basic ball-control skills. One swift German passing move briefly troubled the England defence, but Stielike was showing no inclination to abandon his place at the back, and what English moves were made were much too slow to worry a full-strength defence. Their first chance, in a match lamentably devoid of them, was not so much created as gifted by fate: Mariner accidentally headed a Sansom cross almost straight up in the air, but it fell almost perfectly for Bryan Robson whose powerful header was acrobatically tipped over by Schumacher. Two minutes later the West Germans created their first opening, Breitner wriggling round Sansom on the right and dropping a fast cross inches away from the lunging Rummenigge's foot on the six-yard-line.

These were rare moments of excitement. While their isolated strikers ran circles in the heat both sides carried on playing neat, unincisive football in midfield; if anyone looked like breaking free he was uncer-emoniously chopped down. There was no malice about it: this was Godfather-style football — nothing personal, just business.

In the thirty-fifth minute a German passing movement down the left found Breitner on the edge of the area. He turned beautifully on the ball and his rasping shot was pushed round the near post by an alert Shilton. From the corner Rummenigge suddenly found himself with ball and space in the penalty area, but failed to react quickly enough. Four minutes later Robson chest-trapped a pass from Rix and half-volleyed wide from twenty yards — a rare sight of goal for England.

No one in the English team was attempting to take the ball past an opponent; no one was trying to get behind the German defence as Breitner had got behind the English defence earlier in the game, and it was hard to see how anyone could score from open play. Just before half-time a mistake from Kaltz did set Francis clear some fifty yards from goal, but Stielike snuffed out the threat with a cynical pull-back, balancing out a similar foul by Butcher on Reinders in mid-half. The two teams went in at half-time to a scattering of boos from the unimpressed Spanish crowd; though both managers were probably happy not to be losing.

The second half began as unadventurously as the first. While the Germans continued playing their neat passes neither Dremmler nor Reinders looked anything more than proficient. Both sides committed several more cynical fouls; both produced periods of pressure without ever looking like they might score. Francis and Mariner were getting no change out of Briegel and Karlheinz Förster and it was becoming increasingly obvious that Rummenigge was far from fit.

It was Reinders, not Rummenigge, who gave way when Littbarski was introduced in the sixty-second minute, and for a few moments it looked like Derwall might be going for the win. The formation remained unchanged, however, and so did the general outline of the battle. If Greenwood wanted to push for victory this was the moment to introduce

Hoddle, but when an England change was eventually made it was Woodcock for Francis, one striker for another.

The dearth of chances continued. Hansi Müller, free on the left, put his cross behind the goal, and at the other end Coppell actually went round his full-back for the first time but then failed to get his cross in. The game was drifting towards its apparently inevitable conclusion when one moment of brilliance almost changed everything. Rummenigge received a pass from Stielike about ten yards outside the England area, was carelessly allowed to turn with the ball, and a viciously swerving shot with the outside of his right foot crashed off the bar and back into play. When the final whistle blew five minutes later the players sunk to their haunches with exhaustion, oblivious to the jeers of the locals.

It had not been a game to set alongside those stirring encounters which the two nations had produced in the past. It had been 'a battle without combat' according to *Le Figaro*, 'a funeral' in the opinion of the Danish paper *Extrabladet*. The format of the tournament had invited both managers to be cautious, and they had duly obliged.

Danny Blanchflower thought that England had blown their best-ever chance of beating the Germans, but at a press conference after the match Ron Greenwood seemed to be more preoccupied with England's success in preventing Manny Kaltz from throwing in a single dangerous cross. Much later he claimed that England in 1982 had lacked 'someone who could provide a flash of brilliance, a player who could suddenly do better than his best and find within himself a moment of rare inspiration or invention', yet few players in postwar English football history fitted this definition better than Glen Hoddle, who Greenwood had failed to use against West Germany and who he would fail to use against Spain.

Two and a half years had passed since Hoddle had enjoyed his auspicious debut against Bulgaria, during which time he had started in only eleven of England's thirty-two games. Such things didn't happen in Germany, according to Tony Woodcock. There the national manager would say, 'This is who I want . . . and it doesn't matter if he has a bad game, he is going to play in the next game – it doesn't matter what the press say.'

In Madrid the West Germans had been deprived of at least some of their flair players by injury, not by unadventurous team-selection, but that didn't stop the English press from finding them mostly responsible for the lack of spectacle. 'It was not the fault of Greenwood's men that the occasion failed to ignite,' Jeff Powell wrote in the *Mail*. 'England had come expecting a contest of high technical quality and lacerating commitment. Instead, they were asked to hack their way through a tactical jungle.' In the *Sunday Times* Brian Glanville took up the same theme, accusing the West Germans of 'horrible sterility' and 'mean-souled fearfulness'.

Meanwhile, preparations were made for the two nations' games against Spain. *The Times* decided that the advantage now lay with England: they were playing second and would therefore know what was required of them. West German coach Jupp Derwall had other ideas: he was sure that his attackers would find it easier to score against Spain than their English counterparts. With Littbarski and Fischer on from the start they managed a 2–1 win, and Paul Breitner for one was convinced that would be enough. The Spanish team, he surmised, could hardly afford to lose three consecutive games in front of their own crowds, while England now needed to win by two clear goals.

In the event, just one goal proved beyond them. Brooking was given only twenty minutes to make an impression and Hoddle no time at all; while the team's failure to score in three hours of play against far from forbidding opposition offered, in Hugh McIlvanney's words, 'a fundamental statement about the game in our country'. There was a shortage of 'creative refinement, in thought and technical execution' which most obviously manifested itself as a lack of inventiveness in and around the penalty area. 'Such sophistication is not encouraged in the Football League,' McIlvanney added, 'where the values of what one Brazilian coach has called "track and field football" predominate.' Ultimately, England simply didn't produce the players that mattered most at this level. As during all World Cups the huge conclave of football journalists produced favourite World XIs by the score, few of which in this instance included an English outfield player.

The West Germans had fewer great players than they'd had in the past. They had more than England, though, and won through to the final by beating France on penalties. This match, which might have been remembered for some wonderful football and a stirring recovery, was utterly soured by Schumacher's criminal – and criminally unpunished –

assault on Battiston. 'THESE GERMAN CHEATS MUST NOT WIN' ran a *Sun* headline before the final, and few neutrals shed any tears when the Germans lost a mean-spirited game to the Italians.

In 1982 at least they were still called Germans; Thatcher, Murdoch and co., fresh from their successful war in the Falklands, were only just setting out on their xenophobic high horses in search of a nastier, dumbed-down Britain. The Second World War was now almost forty years distant, and though its representation in the media often gave new life to those negative images of Germany most associated with it, time was blurring the sharpness of the real antipathies left in its wake. In most British minds the Germans had become one bunch of foreigners among many to be envied, pitied, disliked, admired or complained about, according to personal taste. When the ordinary people of the two nations did meet, which wasn't that often in their own countries, they usually found something to confirm whatever prejudices they might have.

Like the Americans, French, Italians and others, the Germans had a stereotypical identity which was often mocked as a matter of bigoted course but rarely invoked with any deep malice. And as the years went by, the bigotry itself increasingly became a target for mockery. When British viewers watched the famous 'Don't mention the War!' episode of the mid seventies sitcom *Fawlty Towers* they were left in no doubt as to who the real idiots were – and they weren't Basil Fawlty's German guests.

In the early eighties a couple of important TV programmes did further damage to long-held stereotypes. The six hour-long episodes of the German-made U-Boat drama *Das Boot* were watched by some seven million British viewers in 1984, few of whom could have come away from the experience without noticing that in most situations Germans behaved remarkably like anybody else. *Auf Wiedersehen Pet*, the highly successful comedy-drama series about Geordie brickies working in Germany, painted a highly positive view of their hosts; indeed, one sometimes wondered if any people could be as tolerant and under-standing of their fractious guests as these Germans were.

In this series greater German prosperity was more or less assumed, and if that provoked envy it also led to a little soul-searching. In his novel *Nice Work* David Lodge portrayed modern West Germany as 'clean, neat, freshly-painted and highly polished. There were no discarded chip cones, squashed fried-chicken cartons, dented lager cans . . . The commercial architecture was sleek and stylish.' Why the difference? his character asks. The Germans had had the chance to rebuild after the war, but then so had cities like Birmingham, so how come that hadn't ended up sleek and stylish? The answer, according to Lodge's character: 'We were too greedy and too lazy. In the fifties and sixties, when we could sell anything, we went on using obsolete machines and paid the unions whatever they asked for, while the Krauts were investing in new technology and hammering out sensible labour agreements.'

The West Germans simply appeared to be better at making things which both their own and other peoples wanted. And just to hammer home the point, every hour or so Geoffrey Palmer would pop up on TV to remind us, with that telling smirk, that ' "*Vorsprung durch technik*", as the Germans say.'

Less than four months after their match in Madrid, England and West Germany met once more in a friendly at Wembley. Shilton, Sansom, Thompson, Butcher, Wilkins and Mariner retained their places from the England side which had played in Spain; the five newcomers playing alongside them were all relatively inexperienced. With Hoddle, Brooking and Robson all unavailable, new manager Bobby Robson picked Tottenham's Gary Mabbutt to replace Robson in midfield and then shifted him to right-back when Viv Anderson picked up a last-minute injury. West Ham's Alan Devonshire, a wide player with a taste for taking on opponents, was preferred to Graham Rix on the left, but Robson compensated for this piece of daring by selecting the unimaginative David Armstrong to partner Wilkins in central midfield. An unprecedented six black players had been chosen for the squad – 'OUR BLACK MAGIC' as the *Daily Mail* quaintly put it – though only two were in the starting line-up: West Brom's Cyrille Regis, chosen to partner Mariner up front, and Luton's right-sided midfield player Ricky Hill.

Schumacher, Kaltz, Dremmler, Briegel, Rummenigge and the Förster brothers had kept their places in the West German team. Breitner had retired again, Schuster was still working his way back to form with Barcelona, and Stielike was out of favour. Their newcomers were the relatively experienced Klaus Allofs, the twenty-one-year-old prodigy Lothar Matthäus, and two debutants, the Cologne sweeper Gerhard Strack and the Werder Bremen striker Norbert Meier.

The game was played on a damp October evening and proved more entertaining than June's World Cup stalemate. Like most friendly internationals of the modern era, however, it never quite transcended its lack of competitive consequence. England, prompted mostly by Wilkins, attacked for most of the first hour – Hill and Devonshire ran, sometimes successfully, at their markers while Regis and Mariner struggled, usually unsuccessfully, to lose theirs. Mabbutt hit the post with a beautifully struck shot from the edge of the area; Schumacher just managed to tip round an acrobatic header from Hill. One German break, led in thrilling style by the young Matthäus, resulted in Shilton being forced to tip over a header from Meier, but that was all that the Germans produced until the last half-hour.

Playing in the hole behind Allofs, Rummenigge was already beginning to make his presence felt with several thrusting runs at the England back four when Littbarski was finally brought on in the seventieth minute. The tempo of the entire German side went up a notch and within minutes a mesmerising move involving Rummenigge, Allofs and Littbarski had carved England apart. Rummenigge, left with only Shilton to beat, did so with a contemptuous flick of the foot.

Ten minutes later he did it again, this time touching home a fast low centre from the rampant Littbarski. Substitute Woodcock scored a consolation with five minutes to go but, as they had done so often in the past, England had dominated a match in terms of possession only to be beaten by a moment or two of high skill. Brian Glanville's doleful admission that there was no English Rummenigge – and, even more to the point, his implicit assertion that English football was uninterested in creating the conditions which made such players possible – was really all that needed to be said after this match. The new manager was still in his honeymoon period, though, and past experience notwithstanding sterling efforts were made to accentuate the positive. 'It will be surprising if the West German game does not mark the real beginning of international careers for Hill, Devonshire, Mabbutt and Regis,' David Lacey wrote optimistically in the *Guardian*.

Hill, Devonshire and Regis won five more caps between them, and none of the four were included in the next side to face West Germany, in 1985.

18: robson's choice

The period between these two games marked something of a low point in the fortunes of both nations. England failed to qualify for another European Championship, this time losing out to the Danes, and West Germany only reached the finals in France by the scruff of their necks, qualifying above Northern Ireland – who had beaten them twice – on goal difference. In the finals they rarely looked impressive; that said, they were a little unlucky to be eliminated by an injury-time goal in their last group match. Most of the faces were familiar from 1982 and before, although there were two significant newcomers on the international stage: Kaiserslautern's left-sided wing-back Andreas Brehme and Werder Bremen striker Rudi Völler. While Lothar Mätthaus was now a regular in midfield, there was no one with great creative gifts – no Walter, Netzer or Schuster – to play alongside him, and this team, though technically gifted and often ominously efficient, was decidedly unimaginative by West German standards.

In club competition the English sides continued to out-perform their West German rivals. Hamburg finally won the European Cup in 1983, but it was the only German final appearance in all three competitions during these three seasons. English clubs reached four finals: Liverpool retained the European Cup in 1984; Tottenham and Everton took the UEFA Cup in 1984 and 1985 respectively; and Liverpool reached the ill-fated European Cup final of 1985. Thirty-nine spectators died in Brussels' Heysel Stadium when drunkenly rampaging Liverpool fans caused the collapse of a wall, and as a result of the incident English clubs were exiled from European club competition for the following six years. UEFA (Union of European Football Associations) had been lax, the ticketing criminally inept, and the

Belgian police incompetent, but so far as English football was concerned this was a tragedy which had been waiting to happen since the early 1970s. One of its lesser consequences was that it brought to an end remarkable runs of success for English clubs in all three tournaments.

In the nineteen seasons since England's World Cup victory English clubs had won twenty European trophies (eight European Cups, three Cup-Winners' Cups, and nine Fairs/UEFA Cups). In that same period West German clubs had won only nine, Italian and Dutch clubs six apiece and Spanish clubs four. On eleven occasions English and West German clubs had met each other at the semi-final or final stage of a tournament, and Leeds in 1975 had been the only English side to lose.

Yet the English national team had reached the semi-final stage of a major competition only once since 1966, and had failed to even qualify for the finals of four of the last nine tournaments it had entered. The discrepancy between success at club level and failure at international level could hardly have been more striking.

In the week following the Heysel disaster England flew to Mexico for two mini-tournament games with Italy and the host nation and then a further game with West Germany. England already looked virtually certain to qualify for the following summer's World Cup, and this trip was intended to provide both players and management with a better idea of the conditions they would face.

The mini-tournament didn't prove particularly auspicious: England lost 2–1 to Italy and 1–0 to Mexico. Once it was over the three Italy-based players – Francis, Wilkins and Hateley – flew back to join their clubs. Their replacements for the West German match were Leicester's Gary Lineker, Chelsea's Kerry Dixon and Everton's Peter Reid. Lineker was winning his sixth cap while the other two made their first starts at international level.

The West German party only arrived forty-eight hours before the match, barely enough time to shake off jet-lag, let alone acclimatise to Mexico City's thinner air. New manager Franz Beckenbauer, who had taken over as national coach in September 1984, had been against coming to Mexico but the arrangements had been finalised before his appointment. The squad was lacking Bernd Schuster, who no longer had any interest in playing international football.

The game was played in the Azteca Stadium on 12 June. The West Germans had their first good look at Terry Butcher's new defensive partner, Mark Wright, and at the recently-capped forwards, Chris Waddle and Gary Lineker; the English came up against Thomas Berthold, Klaus Augenthaler, Olaf Thon and Andreas Brehme for the first time. All appeared five years later in Turin.

For the first half-hour the match was even. The West Germans' long-range shooting gave Shilton plenty to think about in the thin air, and at the other end both Lineker and Bryan Robson narrowly failed with half-chances. Then a chip from Hoddle was accurately chested into Robson's path by Kerry Dixon and the captain volleyed home. Seven minutes later Wright bundled Uwe Rahn over in the area, but Shilton stretched to turn Brehme's penalty round the post. German heads went down, and when England scored their second some eight minutes into the second half it was obvious that they lacked the basic energy for one of their famous fight-backs.

It was Terry Butcher of all people who made that goal, running into a gap left by Augenthaler's hesitation and putting in a shot which Schumacher could only parry. Dixon was on hand to net the rebound and thirteen minutes later he added a third, sending a fine looping header over the goalkeeper's outstretched hand. Rahn hit a post with another long shot, though by this time travel and altitude had clearly caught up with the Germans and thus England coasted to only their second victory over the old enemy in almost twenty years.

It seems unlikely that either manager learned very much from the game, but the team at least had learned something about playing with Hoddle. 'They said that he should have been working back on the right-hand-side,' David Lacey reported, 'but because he had been so good on the ball they had covered for him.' On the other hand, Bobby Robson 'continued to put emphasis on the Tottenham player's work-rate'. In the 1986 World Cup both England and West Germany did better than most observers had expected. England were nearly out after losing to Portugal and holding Morocco to a fortunate draw, then recovered well to beat Poland and Paraguay and so set up the quarter-final tie with Argentina in which Maradona's hand played such a crucial role. They lost, but in the last twenty minutes, with Barnes belatedly brought on to attack the Argentine defence, they looked better than they had for several years.

West Germany went two stages better, though eventually made the same mistake as England in offering Argentina more respect than they deserved. Mätthaus was wasted shadowing the unshadowable Maradona, and although the West Germans pulled back a two-goal deficit they too went down by a single goal.

Losing to the ultimate winners was no disgrace, and England had other more specific reasons for optimism. Lineker, Beardsley, Barnes and Waddle had developed into four attackers of real quality, players who would have a fair chance of getting into most international elevens. Both Barnes and Waddle were willing to take men on, and Beardsley was a throwback to the golden age of English inside forwards, full of cheek, trickery and skill on the ball. Most crucially of all, Gary Lineker was rapidly turning into the best English striker since Jimmy Greaves, although the comparison which most readily came to mind was with West Germany's Gerd Müller. They both had a low centre of gravity, thick thighs and shortish legs, the same deceptive awkwardness of movement, the same instinctive positioning and lethal finishing. Lineker was not as good in the air and his goals-to-chances ratio was not quite so high, but at long last England had a poacher who could poach at the highest level.

At least three of these four featured in most of the matches England played in 1986–7. In midfield Bobby Robson usually permed two or three from Bryan Robson, Glen Hoddle, Peter Reid and Forest's Steve Hodge, but in defence Terry Butcher was the only certainty. Viv Anderson and Kenny Sansom were gradually giving way to Gary Stevens and Stuart Pearce, yet Robson remained uncertain who best to play alongside Butcher in the centre. He was sure of his preferred formation, which remained 4–4–2 despite occasional attempts by the players to interest him in the sweeper system.

Most of these players were in the squad which travelled to Düsseldorf in September 1987 for the third friendly between England and West Germany in five years, but both Bryan Robson and Terry Butcher were ruled out by injury. Robson chose the young Tony Adams to partner Gary Mabbutt in the centre of defence, and gambled on playing both Waddle and Barnes in a very attack-minded 4–4–2 line-up.

The West German team which faced them had undergone a major transformation since the World Cup fifteen months before. Schumacher,

Jakobs, Briegel, Magath, Rummenigge and the Förster brothers had all played their last international in 1986, leaving only Brehme, Littbarski, Allofs and Völler of the old familiar faces. Three relative newcomers who went on to enjoy long international careers were Stuttgart central defender Jurgen Kohler, Cologne central midfielder Guido Buchwald and Schalke playmaker Olaf Thon. It was hoped that the latter would supply the creative imagination which had lately been lacking in West Germany's play, but on this occasion he would have to do without the help of the injured Lothar Matthäus.

If Beckenbauer's team looked experimental on paper, it looked devastating on grass. Right from the kick-off the West Germans poured forward, displaying far too much speed of movement and thought for the slow-moving England back-line. Adams in particular was soon being given a torrid time by the mobile Völler, who hit a post and wasted two other chances in the first twenty minutes. Thon also missed badly and Brehme shot narrowly wide before Littbarski ended the suspense with a dipping, swerving shot from twenty yards which left Shilton grasping at air. England, overrun in midfield and giving a fine impression of a colander in defence, conceded another in the thirty-fifth minute when Littbarski somehow contrived to curl a corner straight into the net.

It could have been four or five by this time, but a few minutes before half-time Beardsley and Lineker – 'the world's best strikers,' as Beck-enbauer had called them before the match – combined for the latter to prod the ball home. The second half began with more English pressure, and for a while it seemed possible that England might share the spoils. However, the West Germans held out, and in one of their own frequent attacks substitute Wolfram Wuttke cut inside Anderson and made it 3–1 with a crashing drive into the far corner.

The balloon of English optimism deflated. It was 'a rude awakening' according to the *Mirror*, which further suggested that Robson think again about introducing a sweeper system. The *Guardian*, like most English papers, paid tribute to the Germans as it lamented its own: 'England were well behind the West Germans in terms of sure first touch on the ball combined with imaginative running and breathtaking changes of pace.' The *Sun*, having headlined one pre-match article 'THE BATTLE OF THE KRAUTS' (the earliest evidence of the word's resurrection I could find) now turned its boyish charm on 'dithering boss' Bobby Robson. He should dispense with Shilton, Sansom, Hoddle, Reid and Barnes, the paper demanded, and bring in Chris Woods, Tony Dorigo, Neil Webb, David Rocastle and Franz Carr.

This was mostly nonsense: the game in Düsseldorf had merely shown that the gap was still there and that England still fell below the highest international standards in basic technique, *not* that Robson had picked the wrong players. And at the European Championship finals in West Germany nine months later the same truth was broadcast to the world as Robson's team went down to three consecutive defeats. England could claim ill-fortune at the hands of the Irish and point out that no one else would find a way to cope with Gullit and Van Basten, but no one was really listening.

In the summer of 1988, with the national team humiliated and the tabloids screaming for the manager's head, and with the clubs which had carried all before them still doing penance for Heysel, the future looked bleak for English football.

In May 1990, with the World Cup only three weeks away, England lost 2–1 to Uruguay in a friendly. Just under 40,000 fans were at Wembley to see the game, but most of their over-forty compatriots reading the scoreline could have recreated a broad outline of the match in their minds: the pattern was becoming that familiar.

As was so often the case, there seemed to be two Englands on display. One thundered forward, threw accurate passes all over the field, tackled hard and covered intelligently, soared to meet balls in the air, hustled and ran until the final whistle. The other lunged at the ball only to find that a foreigner had somehow magicked it away, looked lost at sea whenever opposing forwards ran at the penalty area, and clearly had no clue when it came to penetrating a defence arranged differently from the ones they encountered each week in the domestic league. England fans had been watching this schizophrenic beast have its ups and downs ever since the Hungarians first confirmed the diagnosis in 1953, and thirty-seven years later few could have had any great expectations of the next few weeks in Italy. A decent showing, perhaps; some sort of humiliation just as likely.

For once this was the pessimistic view. Much to the probable chagrin of the *Sun* there had been progress made under Bobby Robson's supervision. For one thing he had qualified England for three major tournaments in a row, which was more than anyone else had ever done. For another, he had a clear idea – as Greenwood had – of the direction in which English football should be heading. The problem, as ever for an England team manager, lay in the short-term; players with wonderful technique might be ten a penny in twenty years' time, but what was he supposed to do with the bunch available to him now?

Ramsey, Revie and ultimately Greenwood had reluctantly accepted that the players they had were not good enough for the sort of football which crowds and purists loved, and had settled with varying degrees of reluctance for embellishing the basic British style with whatever touches of class they could find. At international level this strategy had with one unrepeatable exception failed. Robson was luckier than either Revie or Greenwood in the quality of players at his disposal, but were they good enough to take the great risk, to play the great sides at their own game, to fight skill with skill?

He wasn't sure, and his ambivalence was plain to see. The part of him that loved football, that loved sheer class, showed in his continual selection of flair players like Barnes and Waddle. The part of him that was more afraid of failure showed in his reluctance to try the sweeper system which many of the players now favoured, and in his slow acceptance of Paul Gascoigne as the hub of a possible team. Robson was worried that his defenders lacked the flexibility and technique to make the sweeper system work, and he was worried that the undeniably 'special' Gascoigne wasn't reliable enough.

By May 1990 Robson had been convinced by Gascoigne – or perhaps simply persuaded that a certain level of unreliability was the price you paid for genius – but as he led England to Italy for the 1990 World Cup the other questions remained unanswered. Would England revert to Ramseyesque type or would they surprise the world and themselves? Robson himself seemed as much in the dark as everyone else.

English tactics were not the only thing up in the air in the early summer of 1990. Over the previous year the communist system in Eastern Europe had finally seized up like an old car engine and the Iron Curtain had been reduced to little more than fallen flakes of rust. The boundary between East and West Germany, the front-line of the Cold War for more than forty years, was suddenly redundant and though unthinkable only a few months earlier, German reunification seemed just a matter of time.

The instinctive reaction in some quarters was to throw up their hands in horror. In a *Times* leading article towards the end of 1989 Conor Cruise O'Brien wrote that 'the Fourth Reich, if it comes, will have a natural tendency to resemble its predecessor.' Why it should echo Hitler's murderous Third Reich – rather the Weimar Republic, the Kaiser's Second Reich or for that matter the Holy Roman Empire – was not clear, but *Times* readers were left with the definite impression that military aggression and concentration camps were likely to be on the agenda of any newly reunified Germany. Not surprisingly, the German press was outraged. Nonetheless O'Brien, who should himself have known better, was certainly articulating what a lot of English people vaguely feared.

While the wars were long since over their consequences lingered on, and at moments like this they came back to haunt Anglo–German relations, no matter how normal those now appeared to be. Britain had started the century in its own estimation at least as the world's fattest of fat cats, and was ending it as a slightly mangy member of the dominant group. This fall from grace could be traced, somewhat deceptively but nevertheless very obviously, to the strain imposed by two German-instigated World Wars. Britain's decline was the Germans' fault, and to many it was becoming increasingly clear that they hadn't paid a high enough price for their guilty behaviour. For such people each new display of German prosperity was a slap in the face, and reunification seemed a positive punch in the mouth. It was like seeing a murderer emerge from jail: all thoughts of the sentence already served were overtaken by reawakened memories of the crime. Of course he would kill again. Of course the Germans would be at it again. European integration, which was supposed to make everyone more tolerant of each other, would simply be the means by which they finally got everyone under their arrogant thumbs.

It would be nice to report that this mindset was restricted to those who had actually lived through the war or its immediate consequences. Sadly it was not. For one thing, some tabloids were happy to encourage such xenophobic scaremongering; for another, the images derived from a century of conflict, though fading, were still reaching the youngest members of both societies. The majority of historical works for children were still based on violent conflicts, and the two wars against the Germans loomed larger than any other.

The Germans, of course, had their own distorted views of the English. Emer O'Sullivan summed up those images of England and the English to be found in German children's fiction since 1960. It was always foggy, always raining, in a countryside dotted with castles. The ham-and-egg breakfasts and afternoon teas were excellent, the rest of the food disappointing. Englishmen were thin, 'often red-headed and sporting freckles', sipped sherry and whiskey and talked endlessly about the weather and never about feelings. They were frequently arrogant, always nationalistic, and prized their freedom even above good manners and discipline. The two qualities they respected most were a love of animals and fair play.

Most stereotypes contain a few grains of truth, this one being no exception. Still, it represented a ludicrous distortion of reality. The English stereotype of the Germans was no less ludicrous but was different in one crucial way. The Germans might not be associated with cruelty as such (as they often had been in earlier decades) but they were still very much identified with war. And reunification brought the war back, if only for a short time. It was 'sexy again', I was told by a literary agent around this time, and indeed one of the best-selling novels of the next couple of years was Robert Harris's *Fatherland*, set in a world that followed a fictional Nazi victory, a world in which reunification would never have been an issue.

Eventually the released murderer would be forgotten again, but in June 1990, for the first time in many years, the conditions were there for a major Anglo–German spat. It needed only a spark to set the pile of past grievances alight. Or perhaps a football match.

19: no shroud in turin

An English appearance in the semi-finals looked a distant dream – a distant nightmare, perhaps – after the opening match in Sardinia, a typically lumpen draw with Jack Charlton's more-English-than-the-English Republic of Ireland side. 'NO FOOTBALL, PLEASE, WE'RE BRITISH' ran one Italian headline, but in the second game against Holland Robson and his team surprised everyone – including, one suspects, themselves. Perhaps persuaded by the players' inclinations, perhaps by worries about what Gullit and co. might do to a flat back-four, Robson opted for the sweeper system, playing three at the back, two wing-backs, four in midfield and only Lineker permanently up front. It worked a treat, particularly for the first half hour, and Holland, who had been expected to win the game, were slightly fortunate to escape with a draw.

Robson went back to a 4-4-2 formation for the dire 1–0 win against Egypt which put England through to the last sixteen, and then reverted once more to the sweeper system for the match against Belgium. 'All the players want to play it,' Gary Lineker said at the time; 'I don't think there's one player in the squad thinks we should play 4–4–2.' Robson may have been swayed by such unanimity, or he may have needed no convincing at all. He may have just thrown his hands up in the air and reckoned that it was better to lose with style than without it. Either way, England embarked on the most exhilarating of rocky rides, and for the first time in many years became a team worth supporting for the way they played football.

They were fortunate to beat Belgium and Cameroon – the first with a sublime volley from David Platt, the second with two pieces of Lineker playing at his most Müller-ish – but in both instances they would have been equally unlucky to lose. These were thrilling, open affairs in which each team sought to win by serving up their best, not dour, sclerotic contests in which one or both teams sought only to stop the other from playing.

With Brazil and Holland stuttering, Italy bowed under the weight of home expectations, and Argentina too reliant on a fitful Maradona, only West Germany seemed capable of playing with equal abandon. They demolished Yugoslavia and the United Arab Emirates in their first two group matches, took it easy against Colombia in the meaningless third, and then overcame Holland in an acrimonious match in Milan.

Since England's visit to Düsseldorf in 1987 Beckenbauer had added two more crucial pieces to his jigsaw: the diminutive Cologne play-maker Thomas Hässler and the rangy, Italian-based striker Jurgen Klinsmann. The latter, a fast, intelligent runner and excellent finisher with either his head or his feet, had struck up a fine understanding with Rudi Völler. Brian Glanville thought they lacked the giants of the past – Brehme and Augenthaler were pale imitations of Breitner and Beck-enbauer – but the defence was full of experience and in midfield Matthäus was approaching his prime. When his penalty took them past Czechoslovakia and into a semi-final with England few were prepared to bet against them.

'The Germans have all the qualities the English hold dear: strength, speed, spirit, character and an undying will to win,' David Lacey wrote in the *Guardian*. 'They also,' he added, 'have better players and a more consistent strategy.' There was no arguing with this last comment – the Germans had been playing their system for twenty-five years, England had played the system for only three games. Indeed, the Germans hardly appeared to be aware that any change had been made. 'The English play the same way they played twenty years ago,' Rudi Völler said on the eve of the match. 'We must play fast up front. We won't get so many chances in the air so we will have to keep the game on the ground.'

The truth of Lacey's other assertion – that the West Germans had the better players – was more open to doubt than at any time in the last twenty years. There was no denying that the West German defenders and wing-backs were more comfortable on the ball than their English counterparts, but if Lineker, Beardsley, Waddle and Gascoigne had been born in bierkellers they would have given their West German counterparts a good run for their places. These were, as the game would amply demonstrate, evenly matched teams.

In England the team's progress to the semi-final had been watched with rising incredulity and mounting excitement, and for some the chance to blow off xenophobic steam proved too good to waste. In the past the English press had always refrained from using the opportunity of an Anglo–German contest to indulge in sales-boosting rants, but this time around the *Sun* and the *Star*, weakened by ten years of self-vulgarisation, were unable or unwilling to resist the temptation.

'HELP OUR BOYS CLOUT THE KRAUTS' the *Sun* suggested to its readers on 3 July. Bernard Manning claimed that 'if their football was as bad as their sense of humour they wouldn't be in the World Cup'. Clive Dunn was wheeled out to recite his *Dad's Army* catchphrase, 'They don't like it up 'em'. There was a plethora of plays on the words 'Hun' and 'Kraut' and a whole page was given over to changes in Germany since 1966. These generally boiled down to the Germans getting richer, though space was saved for the illuminating information that the average German bust-size was thirty-eight inches. In case anyone forgot that there was a football match in prospect, Bobby Robson and Franz Beckenbauer were given marks out of ten for looks, brains, sex appeal, and 'love records'. On the following day – the day of 'the big hun' – a cartoon showed Hitler screaming 'Victory or the firing squad!' at the emerging German team, while elsewhere in the paper it was all put into context for the history-conscious reader: 'We beat them in '45, we beat them in '66, now the battle of '90.'

The coverage in the *Star* was even more tasteless. Their headline on 3 July was 'NOW FOR THE KRAUTS!', and their most perceptive feature a spoof-piece by Herr Flick, the Gestapo officer in TV's Resistance sitcom *Allo Allo*. His 'Twenty-one vays vy ve Germans vill beat ze English' included stamping on Lineker's toes with jackboots, the Germans' previous experience stealing sunbeds on Spanish beaches, and simple justice: 'You beat us at our national sport TWICE so it's time ve beat you at yours.' On the eve of the match the paper triumphantly revealed that the English group New Order were racing up the German charts – 'ENGLAND CUP SONG BLITZES THE KRAUTS!'

It was, as they say, all in fun. It was also as sad as it was puerile.

The stampede home from work caused near-gridlock on London's North Circular in the early evening, but by the approach of kick-off a good proportion of the English were in front of their TVs and the nation's streets were eerily deserted. Prince Charles and Diana were letting eight-year-old William stay up for it, and even his great-grandmother was said to be watching at Clarence House. Many prisoners were allowed to stay later than usual outside their cells; and the aircraft-carrier *Ark Royal* was sailing as close to the mainland as possible in order to boost its TV reception. In the Rumbelows boardroom a few men were sweating about the possible result for reasons of their own – before the competition began they had offered full refunds on all purchases of TVs, videos and satellite dishes in the event of an England victory. It had looked a safe bet then; now, with a suspension-crippled Argentina already waiting in the final, it looked anything but.

The first minute was hardly encouraging for Rumbelows. Butcher nearly got on the end of an England corner inside the six-yard-box, and when the ball ran out to Gascoigne he forced the German keeper Bodo Illgner to put it behind. More corners, a break by Beardsley on the left, and a flowing link-up between Lineker and Gascoigne all followed in quick succession. England were moving and passing the ball with the fluency which had so often escaped them, and Waddle in particular was catching the eye.

The first threats from the Germans arrived soon after the ten-minute-mark. A jinking run from Hässler ended with his shot deflected narrowly wide, and then Klinsmann's incisive passes for Völler and Matthäus were efficiently intercepted. The English defence, with Butcher acting as sweeper, Mark Wright on Klinsmann and Des Walker on Völler, was looking comfortable.

England pressed forward again, and first Waddle, then Pearce, got to the by-line. Waddle's centre was headed away, then Pearce's nipped off Lineker's toe by the alert Jurgen Kohler. A few minutes later a Waddle free-kick was headed out; Gascoigne met the clearance on the volley and Illgner went down on his knees to save. There was no doubt that the English had enjoyed more of the ball in the first twenty-five minutes and that they had indeed sprayed it about with some style. However, they hadn't turned their advantage into decent chances and the Germans continued to look intermittently dangerous, as when a neat Matthäus back-heel almost put Thon through in the centre.

England wasted a three-against-two situation when Platt was dispossessed and then two Völler crosses forced the English defence to demonstrate its solidity once more. Another Waddle cross just evaded Platt and the advancing Pearce shot well wide with his weaker right foot. The game passed the half-hour mark still evenly balanced, although it had been apparent for several minutes that the West Germans were beginning to get more of the ball.

Their progress was interrupted in the thirty-second minute when Rudi Völler was injured in a fair challenge from Des Walker. In the next couple of minutes Kohler was forced to take another cross off Lineker's toe and Waddle, not realising the whistle had already gone, almost succeeded in chipping Illgner from nearly fifty yards. These attacks marked only a temporary setback for the West Germans, who clearly held the initiative for the rest of the first half. A twenty-five-yard drive from Thon brought Shilton to his knees even before Karlheinz Riedle came on to replace the long-departed Völler, and soon Matthäus was burrowing through the centre only to be pulled down by Parker. From the free-kick the ball travelled to Augenthaler, whose powerful shot was tipped over without undue difficulty by Shilton. When the whistle brought an end to an ultimately even first half it was probably the English who were the more relieved to hear it.

The West Germans opened the second half in the way they had ended the first, pinning the English back into their own half yet still not looking particularly penetrative. Occasionally England would break forward but they too lacked incision, and when Waddle did slip Parker in on the right-hand side of the area his control let him down. Once again the gulf in ball-technique between English and Continental defenders was sadly apparent.

Gascoigne meanwhile was showing signs of blowing a fuse and one of the linesmen very obviously tried to calm him down. He had committed a couple of bad fouls in the first half, but had been sinned against even more – he ended the game winning more than twice as many free kicks as anyone else.

The West Germans began to raise the tempo, and in the fifty-fourth minute fashioned the first good chance of the match – Thon shooting too straight and too weakly from a good position inside the area. A dangerous cross from Hassler was headed over his own bar by Wright, and another sweeping move ended with Thon hitting a twenty-five-yarder wide. He, Hässler and Matthäus were now running almost unopposed at the England defence, and for the first time in the game a goal seemed imminent.

One came, though not through any great football on the Germans' part. Hässler was running across the pitch, about five yards outside the penalty area, when Pearce's rather foolish lunge took his trailing leg. Brehme's hard-hit free-kick spun off Parker's block, looping up and over the desperately retreating Shilton and just under the bar. It was a freak goal, but it also marked the culmination of almost half an hour of West German pressure.

England surged back − the goal was still being re-examined on TV from every conceivable angle when Beardsley just failed to make contact with a lovely pass from Waddle. Two minutes later Pearce almost glanced in one free-kick from Gascoigne, then the man himself hit the wall with a centrally-placed second. Reuter was brought on for the limping Hässler, presumably to give the Germans more bite in midfield, but England continued to assert more pressure; only a slight misjudgement from Waddle prevented him running on to a great through-ball from Gascoigne. Two minutes later the Marseille winger's trailing leg was clipped by Augenthaler in the area, but the referee waved play on and the English players made no great protest.

With twenty minutes remaining Robson pulled off Butcher, put on Everton's Trevor Steven, and reverted to a flat back-four. Though England continued to have the lion's share of possession − Waddle was spraying passes around like a re-born Bobby Charlton − few half-chances were made, let alone prime opportunities. Beardsley hit the wall with another free-kick from just outside the area; a Wright header from a corner was easily gathered. The minutes ticked by and the West Germans looked increasingly willing to go down and stay down whenever physical contact was made.

Finally England scored, a goal borne of both luck and genius. Wright fed Parker on the right and he hit a long, hopeful ball into the penalty area − exactly the sort of ball that England, to their credit, had been mostly eschewing. With Kohler, Augenthaler and Berthold surrounding the lonely Lineker, Parker had no right to expect that anything good would come from this one. Nevertheless, Kohler somehow managed to fluff his clearance and the ball fell for Lineker rather than Augenthaler or Berthold. He juggled it to the left with his thigh and in almost the same movement shot low under the lunging Kohler's leg and past the helpless Illgner. It was a goal Gerd Müller would have been proud of.

The last ten minutes saw the West Germans pressing forward again, but no more chances were made by either side. As in 1966 and 1970, extra time was required to divide the teams – this time with the added possibility of penalties.

The West Germans played the first half of the extra thirty minutes as if they wanted to settle the match with a real goal or two. Within the first couple of minutes an English corner caused some concern in the German area and a typical Gascoigne run almost created an opening, but from that moment on it was all West Germany. After Reuter and Thon had combined to send Brehme clear, Klinsmann's header from his cross brought a great reaction-save out of Shilton, the first difficult save made by either goalkeeper in the entire game. A second fine chance presented itself two minutes later, Klinsmann spinning on a wonderful chip into the area by Augenthaler and hitting it narrowly wide of Shilton's left-hand post. Only seconds after that another dangerously swerving Brehme corner was put behind by Walker. England were under the cosh and it seemed only a matter of time before the twisting-turning Klinsmann either scored, made an opening for someone else or won himself a penalty.

England suffered another handicap in the tenth minute. Reuter made the most of an undoubted foul by Gascoigne and the latter received his second booking of the tournament. Now even if England made the final he wouldn't be there, and the famous tears started to flow. Lineker made his equally famous 'I think he may be about to blow' signal to the touchline, and indeed Gascoigne appeared to be in a daze for several minutes, during which time the West Germans continued to pour forward. Both Thon and Buchwald shot wide from a distance, and then out of the blue England went closer than Klinsmann had gone. Trevor Steven's header found Chris Waddle in space in the left-hand corner of the penalty area, and his first-time shot cannoned off the bottom of Illgner's far post and back across the six-yard area just too quickly for Platt's lunging foot.

The near-miss seemed to give England a lift, and during the opening half of the second period they looked the better bet. David Platt headed home a Waddle free-kick only to be judged offside; he was then unfortunate to be hit on the heel by a Beardsley through ball and headed a good chance from Parker's cross over the top. The pendulum swung back for the last time: Waddle in particular suddenly looked shattered, while the West Germans surged forward once more. A curling shot from Thon was well saved by Shilton; Brehme blasted just over after a one-two with Riedle; a rampant Klinsmann was brilliantly dispossessed by Walker. A blocked Matthäus shot ricocheted out to Buchwald on the edge of the D, and his carefully placed shot came back off Shilton's left-hand post. One goal each, one strike against the woodwork each. The two teams had to be separated by penalties.

Robson thought Gary Lineker and Stuart Pearce were his best penalty-takers, and duly allotted them the two kicks he thought most crucial: the first and the fourth. Lineker scored, as did Beardsley and Platt, the West Germans responding each time with kicks that gave Shilton no chance. Pearce's attempt, hit down the middle at knee-height, rebounded back into play off the diving Illgner's legs; Thon put the Germans one up with another perfect kick. Chris Waddle had to score just to keep England alive.

Waddle had never liked taking penalties, and had an appropriately low success-rate. He was also exhausted: the semi-final 'felt as if it had been going on for hours'. When he subsequently watched the moment on TV he was struck by how much noise there was; at the time it had felt as if he was 'stepping off the edge of the world into silence'. He had made the decision to simply blast his kick, but his body-shape was all wrong and the ball took off like a plane, still rising as it left the camera's field of vision. England would not be playing in their second World Cup Final.

They did win the tournament's Fair Play Award, which was more than could be said for their supporters. Turin was expecting trouble from the fans on the spot, but few anticipated the mayhem which spread through the home country in the hours after the game. Three people died and 600 were arrested as police fought rioters in sixty towns. Many German-manufactured cars were damaged; and in Brighton a few German students were chased through the town by two hundred youths. England's defeat precipitated these events only in the sense that it offered an excuse. In West Germany victory brought forth the same sad, moronic responses on both the fourth and eighth of July. Deprived of English-manufactured cars to attack, they carried Nazi flags around and took their alcohol-fuelled anger out on Vietnamese and Turkish immigrants.

In England, mainstream reaction to the team's exit was almost as extreme. Seventy thousand supporters greeted the team when it arrived back at Luton Airport; another 150,000 lined the twenty-mile route around the Bedfordshire town. Gallant defeats, it seemed, were as good as victories, particularly after years of defeats that were anything but.

The football press were less ecstatic. England's skilful performance was lauded, but not to the skies. It was generally agreed that though neither side had deserved to lose, the West Germans had probably shaved a tight contest; it was also widely felt that the overall quality of football in this particular World Cup was lower than usual. West Germany's victory over Argentina in a drab and dirty final did nothing to dispel these feelings – if anything it put previous performances in an even more depressing light. For all the excitement of England's run there was perhaps less than met the eye in the nation's top-four placing. There were yet again no Englishmen in the World XI chosen by the International Journalists' Panel in Rome.

There was, however, one undeniable source of hope for the future. As far as England was concerned the 1990 World Cup had seen in Paul Gascoigne the emergence of a saviour, and for the next few months he was almost permanently parked in the national spotlight. His tears became legendary, his potential apparently unlimited. Bobby Robson, now retired as England manager, called him 'one of the finest English players ever to emerge'; the *Daily Mail*, rather more conditionally, thought that Gazza 'gave every sign that, with the onset of maturity, he can become one of the game's truly great figures'.

Nine days after the match in Turin, England's newspapers were again reporting on an Anglo–German conflict. Cabinet minister Nicholas Ridley, always something of a Thatcherite loose cannon, had given an interview to *The Spectator* which did very little to further the causes of peace, love and understanding between the two nations.

The occasion of his wrath was a British visit by the president of the Bundesbank to discuss European monetary union, which was, Ridley warned, 'a German racket designed to take over the whole of Europe' and as such had to be thwarted. The European institutions were utterly undemocratic and giving up British sovereignty in their favour was completely unacceptable. He was 'not against giving up sovereignty in principle, but not to this lot. You might just as well give it up to Adolf Hitler, frankly.'

It was put to Ridley that Chancellor Kohl was preferable to Hitler. The cabinet minister mulled over his answer, then said that he wasn't sure he 'wouldn't rather . . . er . . . have the shelters and the chance to fight back than simply being taken over by *economics*'.

Perhaps his views were coloured by the Second World War, *The Spectator* editor Dominic Lawson suggested. 'Jolly good thing too,' Ridley told him, adding for good measure that he had recently visited Auschwitz. England's role had always been to keep the balance of power in Europe, he went on, and now that the Germans were so 'uppity' it was more necessary than ever that she went on doing so. And as for the president of the Bundesbank running the British economy, well, the thought of British people 'being bossed by a German – it would cause absolute mayhem in this country, and quite rightly, I think'.

This hotchpotch of policies and prejudices was given different receptions in different quarters. The *Frankfurter Runschau* generously proposed that everyone needed time to get used to the current changes in Germany; the leader of the German Liberals suggested that either Ridley was still angry about the result in Turin or he had been drunk. In England it was accepted by many that Ridley's outburst was only the tip of a rather ugly iceberg as far as Conservative Party opinion went, and the *Guardian* gave reasons for believing that the prime minister shared Ridley's sentiments. In recent months Mrs Thatchar had apparently made a number of sharp remarks about staff who bought Volkswagens and had also made occasional references to 'the Fourth Reich'. The *Guardian* was not sympathetic. People like Ridley and Thatcher had not even fought in the war: 'Their fear and distaste is secondhand, a mixture of economic alarm, get nationalism, and Colditz re-runs on TV.'

Much the same line was followed in the *Mail*, the *Mirror* and the other broadsheets – *The Times* pointed out with barely concealed glee that a goodwill delegation from the minister's constituency was leaving for Bavaria that day – but the *Sun* and the *Star* were not so willing to denounce Ridley. 'IT'S WAR: GERMANS DEMAND RIDLEY'S SACKING OVER

HITLER STORM' ran the former's headline, and the paper also carried a reproduction of the *Spectator* cover showing a wall-poster with a face half-Hitler, half-Kohl. It didn't go as far the *Star*, which had Kohl goosestepping in a coal-scuttle helmet under the headline 'UP YOURS, HELMUT!' and an editorial claiming that Ridley had 'talked a lot of sense'. The 'Krauts' were apparently 'the Rottweillers of European politics'. And when East and West Germany united they would be 'running in a pack, savaging Eurocrats into doing their bidding'. Neither 'French poodles' nor 'British bulldogs' would stand a chance.

The following day both the *Sun* and the *Star* published polls supposedly proving that vast majorities of their readers supported the resigning Ridley, but the *Guardian* refused to accept that there was substantial antipathy towards the Germans. On the contrary, the paper's writer believed that the public had become bored with 'the stereotypical evil Kraut', and that any perusal of current comics, books and films would bear this out. The Germans did have 'an image problem', however, as they had recently discovered themselves. A NOP survey of British attitudes to Germany commissioned by the Goethe Institute had revealed that the first thing fifty per cent of Britons thought of when the subject of Germany came up was the Third Reich.

With Ridley gone the story may have died a natural death had *The Independent on Sunday* not had another angle to offer. Margaret Thatcher, it seemed, had done more than mutter about a 'Fourth Reich': in March she had invited a group of experts to Chequers to discuss the possibility, and the paper had a leaked memo of their mental peregrinations.

There were many qualms about the forthcoming reunification. Some of the experts thought Germany had undergone a sea-change after 1945; others believed that 'the way in which the Germans threw their weight about in the European Community suggested that a lot had still not changed'. A list of the Germans' 'less happy' characteristics was included. Though it did not include an irrational tendency to believe that Hurst's second goal should have been disallowed, that was the rough intellectual level. According to this brains-trust the Germans were insensitive to the feelings of others, obsessed with themselves, had a strong inclination to self-pity and a longing to be liked. Angst, aggressiveness, assertiveness, bullying, egotism, sentimentality and an inferiority complex were said to be abiding parts of the national character.

'Three Reichs and you're out!' as one joker put it in the *Sunday Times*. A poll in that paper showed that although fifty-five per cent of respondents were worried that a unified Germany would become Europe's dominant power, only twenty-three per cent actually opposed reunification. It was generally agreed that Germans were more arrogant, aggressive and hard-working than the British, and that the latter were more tolerant, reserved and peace-loving than the Germans.

In the broadsheets the debate spluttered on into a new week, but the tabloids had already found other prejudices to appeal to. On Wednesday 18 July the final obstacles to German unification were resolved at a six-nation meeting in Paris, and football fans could start wondering just how powerful the unified German team was going to be.

20: the penalties of failure

The optimism engendered by England's performance in Italia '90 lasted about fifteen months. In that time the national team went twelve games without defeat, and although much of the opposition was far from stellar – four of the matches were against Australia, New Zealand and Malaysia – qualification for the European Championship in 1992 seemed already assured. And the new manager, Graham Taylor, was apparently building on Bobby Robson's success.

This was an illusion. The FA could hardly have made a worse choice than Taylor, a manager so at home in the domestic game yet so at sea anywhere else. In Dublin for his third match in charge, he dropped Paul Gascoigne on tactical grounds, and it soon became apparent that 4–4–2 was the only formation in which he had any real faith. Early in his reign Taylor told Chris Waddle that he expected to see white paint on the soles of his boots at the end of a match: the man whose roaming had so worried the Germans in Turin was supposed to wear himself out running up and down the touch-lines for ninety minutes. Not surprisingly, Waddle soon found himself joining Shilton and Butcher among the ranks of former internationals.

Taylor was unfortunate to lose Gascoigne, for whom the onset of maturity proved an elusive dream. After almost single-handedly steering Tottenham to the FA Cup final in 1991 he chose the Wembley occasion to comprehensively blow a fuse. He committed two spectacularly dreadful fouls in the first fifteen minutes, the second of which put him out of football for over a year.

In the event, only four of those who had won the nation's admiration in Italy – Paul Parker (now playing in central defence), David Platt,

Trevor Steven and Gary Lineker – were on duty at Wembley for the
September friendly against Germany which burst Taylor's bubble.
Beardsley, like Waddle, was out of favour; Wright, Walker, Pearce
and Taylor-favourite John Barnes were injured. Their replacements –
Lee Dixon, Tony Dorigo and Gary Pallister at the back, David Batty and
John Salako in midfield and Alan Smith up front – were competent,
uninspiring English League footballers to a man. To the casual observer it
looked as though Taylor had cunningly conspired to remove each and
every trace of flair from the team he had inherited from Robson.

The Germans had retained most of theirs. Rudi Völler was missing,
along with exciting newcomers Thomas Helmer and Matthias Sammer,
but manager Berti Vögts, who had taken over from Beckenbauer the
previous summer, was able to reinforce eight of the team which had
played in Turin with the former East German Thomas Doll and new stars
Stefan Effenberg and Andreas Möller. It looked a formidable line-up, and
so it proved. Matthäus, Effenberg, Hässler and Möller were soon knocking the ball around with their usual crisp precision, the England midfield
chasing shadows. A Buchwald header and a Doll shot had both flown
narrowly wide before England managed an attack.

The Germans missed a hatful of chances in the first half, but England
had a few of their own. One Lineker shot on the turn gave Illgner
trouble, and a while later the Tottenham forward looked clean through
on goal until Brehme hauled him back. The Germans occasionally looked
vulnerable to crosses, and Platt even hit the bar with a header, nonetheless
there was no denying the overall superiority of the German play. Just
before half-time they made this point with the decisive goal, Doll jinking
his way past Salako and Parker before dropping a perfect cross onto the
grateful Riedle's head.

The second half was more of the same, the Germans stroking the ball
around, the English huffing and puffing and wondering why the house
didn't blow down. Taylor thought they should have blown harder.
'What we lacked was someone with the hardness to say, "Right, let's give
them a fight,"' he said after the match, a piece of arrant nonsense that
should have earned him the sack on the spot.

The watching Bobby Moore knew better. 'The Germans gave us a
soccer lesson,' he said, and pointedly wondered out loud whether anyone
would learn from it. Their defenders 'moved comfortably into midfield,

the midfielders slotted easily into front positions and they all passed and controlled the ball with great technique'. Though Moore knew there was no point in expecting English players to suddenly play like that when they pulled on an England shirt; the improvement had to run right through the nation's football. 'Some people regard our game as a fast-flowing spectacle,' he argued. 'That's fine, but it bears no comparison with German expertise.' The English game had to find the time to develop players' basic skills.

When the two teams competed in the following summer's European Championships in Sweden the difference in expectations was apparent in the treatment accorded the two managers: Berti Vögts took as much criticism for Germany's defeat in the final as Graham Taylor received for England's one goal in three dismal games. Things didn't get any better for England in 1992–3, and by the time the two met again, in a four-nation tournament in the US, qualifications for the 1994 World Cup finals was looking extremely unlikely.

The core of the West German team which won the World Cup in 1990 survived to defend the trophy in 1994, and the team facing England in Detroit's Pontiac Silverdome on 19 June 1993 contained only three unfamiliar faces: Dortmund defender Michael Schulz and Bayern midfielders Thomas Strunz and Christian Ziege. England's team, by contrast, contained only three reminders of Italia '90: David Platt, John Barnes and an out-of-form Des Walker. Of the rest only Nigel Martyn, Paul Ince and Paul Merson looked likely to prosper at this level, always assuming they managed to stay on an even keel off the field. Gascoigne had been left behind in Europe, supposedly at his club Lazio's insistence, but there were rumours that England's saviour was drinking his talent away and that Taylor, in consequence, had not tried very hard to get him released.

In their first match of the tournament his team had lost 2–0 to the hosts in Boston, and four days later ran Brazil to a satisfying 1–1 standstill in Washington. The Germans, who had beaten the USA 4–3 and shared six goals with the Brazilians, went into this final match needing a win to take the tournament; England wanted at least a point to avoid the wooden spoon.

Much of the pre-match publicity concerned the roofed stadium and its pitch, which was put together like a jigsaw with thousands of hexagonal pods. The grasses – a blend comprising eighty-five per cent Kentucky bluegrass and fifteen per cent rye – had been grown in South California, transported east in four giant trucks and then planted in the interlocking pods. After each game all these were laboriously carted out to the parking lot where growing conditions were better. The stands had room for 62,000 and were full for the occasion. There was no shortage of support for England, as the booing of the German national anthem made depressingly clear.

The game itself was England's seventh without a win, the worst such run since 1958. Taylor's selection of four defenders and six midfield players – albeit six with real talent – was strange in prospect, and if there was intended method in the apparent madness it failed to shine through. 'The Germans' basic technique; as Joe Lovejoy wrote in *The Independent*, 'was, as ever, infinitely superior, their passing and movement on another plane . . . they might have had the game won inside twenty minutes.' Riedle, Möller and Effenberg all missed good chances before the latter, beautifully found by Matthäus, left Pallister for dead and coolly beat Martyn.

The Germans then went into cruise control and England fought their way back into the match. A ferocious Merson volley was tipped over by Illgner; then Ince, set free on the left by Barnes, pulled the ball across goal for a Platt tap-in. Surprised, the Germans moved back up a gear and re-asserted their superiority but couldn't find the net until seven minutes after half-time, when Klinsmann bundled home the rebound from Ziege's half-saved shot. There was more huffing and puffing from England and more Matthäus-inspired breakaways from the Germans, but no more goals for the mostly American crowd. On the following morning the *Sun* lamented that three years into Taylor's stewardship England had 'NO TEAM, NO SHAPE, NO HOPE.'

Though the outlook was on the surface much rosier for the Germans, in fact the team Vögts had inherited was rapidly approaching its sell-by date. It performed badly in the following year's World Cup finals, going out to unfancied Bulgaria in the quarter-finals, and by the time Euro '96 came around the faces were mostly new ones. England did not need to qualify for a tournament on home soil, but if radical changes were not made over the next three years the most likely outcome for them was acute embarrassment. A new manager was needed, along with a new approach and new players.

While the national team was in the doldrums, English club football was enjoying a renaissance in more ways than one. Manchester United and Aston Villa had been allowed back into both the Cup-Winners' and UEFA Cups in 1990–1; and a year later Arsenal had renewed the English challenge for the European Cup. Manchester United's immediate success in the Cup-Winners' Cup heralded something of a false dawn: English clubs won only one trophy in the next six seasons. However, it was generally agreed that in the long-run the renewal of involvement in the European game could only help English football.

Much the same could be said of the involvement of European and other foreign players which the birth of the money-generating Premiership would eventually do so much to promote. The first foreign superstar to grace English League grounds (Scotsmen, Irishmen and Welshmen excepted) pre-dated the Premiership: the French maverick Eric Cantona joined Leeds during the 1991–2 season and spent a frustrating year wondering why Howard Wilkinson wouldn't let him show what he could do. Eventually Alex Ferguson and Manchester United took the risk which English football as a whole needed to take and lived to reap the benefits.

The second great foreign star to join an English club; and one more relevant where this book is concerned, was a much less risky proposition. Jurgen Klinsmann had all the attributes an English striker needed: he was fast, strong, brave, good with his feet and his head and possessed of apparently limitless energy. He also had better technique than most English players of his type dream about. As a footballer he offered living refutation of the oft-heard proposition that strikers had to be either one thing or the other – strong or nimble, providers or poachers, threats in the air or threats on the ground. Klinsmann had it all.

His influence as a German was probably greater than his influence as a footballer. With his handsome chiselled face and Aryan blond mane he actually *looked* like the English idea of a German, and his televised propensity for diving in major tournaments had not sat well with many English fans. When he came to Tottenham in the summer of 1994 you could almost hear the sound of knives being sharpened up and down the country and sense the fervent hope that this arrogant Nazi cheat was about to be taken down a peg or two.

Klinsmann, however, much to many people's disappointment, turned out to be a delightful man: a footballer who played in different countries because he enjoyed learning about other cultures; a Greenpeace supporter who drove a Volkswagen and charged nothing for interviews; a man who seemed unfailingly courteous and unusually adult for a footballer. He even had an almost British sense of humour, as evidenced by the 'diving celebration' he mockingly introduced to celebrate his English goals.

In fact, the more the English knew about Klinsmann the less like a typical German he appeared to be. Which, of course, is how stereotypes are broken down.

Klinsmann returned to the Bundesliga after only one season in the Premiership, but was back in England a year later as captain of Berti Vögts' 1996 European Championship squad. He was almost thirty-two years old himself and many of his team-mates were growing similarly long in the tooth. Jurgen Kohler, Matthias Sammer, Thomas Helmer, Thomas Hässler and Andreas Möller were all around the thirty-mark; even young hopeful Oliver Bierhoff was twenty-eight. The younger new men – players like Borussia Dortmund's Steffen Freund, Bayern's Mehmet Scholl and Werder Bremen's Marco Bode – were all competent enough in the athletic German tradition yet lacked the class of their predecessors. While this German squad looked like it might prove effective it was decidedly short on individual brilliance.

The pressure on Berti Vögts to succeed was tremendous – every other German coach since the war had won a World Cup or European Championship – and his life wasn't made any easier by the traditional pre-tournament turmoil in his squad. This time it was the absent Lothar Matthäus who lit the blue touch-paper, with a diatribe against Bayern team-mate Klinsmann who he accused of planning to desert the club and who he blamed for his own exclusion from the German squad. Now, with the first match looming, Klinsmann and other Bayern players were busy faxing club president Beckenbauer with the demand that he distance himself from Matthäus.

Rather more amusingly, the German squad were the subject of

complaints from British fellow guests at their luxury hotel near Maccles-
field: it seemed that some players had neglected to cover themselves in the
sauna. 'In Finland all you need is a glass of schnapps,' Berti Vögts
explained, 'and in Russia you just need a hat.' In England, he now
realised, 'you must have trunks'.

For all their problems and for all their advancing years, the Germans
looked good in their first match against Czechoslovakia. Without
Klinsmann, they won more comfortably than the 2–0 score-line suggested, and occasionally even managed to look stylish. Reuter, Möller
and Ziege were all impressive, but the one man who stole the eye was
sweeper Matthias Sammer, the first German in that position not to be
utterly overshadowed by the memory of Beckenbauer. He scored in the
next game, a 3–0 demolition of Russia which also featured two goals
from the returning Klinsmann, one a spectacularly taken shot on the
move with the outside of the right foot.

After two matches the Germans were basically the team to beat, but
during their next two games – a goalless draw against Italy in the final
group match and a narrow 2–1 win over Croatia in the quarter-final –
they became increasingly pedestrian. Injuries were taking a large toll, and
by the eve of the semi-final Vögts' squad was looking more than a little
depleted. Kohler, Bobic, Basler and Klinsmann were all ruled out, while
both Hässler and Reuter were carrying injuries.

England had meanwhile been enjoying another roller-coaster of a
tournament. They looked dreadful against the Swiss in the opening
draw and were lucky against the Scots in the second, the ball rolling off
the spot just as McAllister stepped up to strike the penalty which would
have put his side level. Instead, England went 2–0 up only seconds later,
Gascoigne brilliantly flipping the ball over Hendry's head and sweeping it
exultantly into the net.

This moment of impish genius was the springboard for a performance
against Holland which ranked with any England had achieved since 1970.
In front of a delirious Wembley crowd the Dutch were simply outclassed,
Shearer and Sheringham scoring twice each in a 4–1 victory. For a few
days it really was possible to believe that Terry Venables – manager now
for over two years – had, as Trevor Francis said, 'dragged England out of
the Stone Age'. The defence was as solid as ever, and in Gareth Southgate

the team had a central defender who looked unusually comfortable on the ball. The four in midfield – Darren Anderton, Paul Ince, Paul Gascoigne and Steve McManaman – were all capable of much more than mere application, and up front Sheringham's brain and touch acted as a perfect foil for Shearer's physical aggression and explosive finishing. This was a team which more closely matched English and Continental strengths than any of its predecessors.

Then came Spain, and a match which England were lucky to take to penalties. A Spanish goal was disallowed for no apparent reason, and England's stars against Holland looked like one-dimensional caricatures of themselves. Gascoigne and McManaman kept running into trouble; Sheringham appeared to have no idea where anyone else was; Platt, deputising for Ince, looked like a hundred other midfield journeymen. This was the old England, devoid of imagination or any compensating pace, huffing and puffing and hoping that the foreigers didn't suddenly throw a patch of real football at them. While the penalties went England's way, it was clear that a similar performance against Germany would see them out.

Not that anyone in England could easily admit to such doubts. These were the first major championships which the nation had staged since 1966, and the jingoistic mood which accompanied them was a shriller, less self-conscious version of that in evidence during England's only World Cup triumph. The flag of St George was everywhere, and the infantile xenophobia which had marred the tabloids' coverage of the 1990 World Cup was back in force.

This time the *Daily Mirror* was the chief culprit. Reducing the noble art of journalism to a few rancid puns and clichés had paid off for the *Sun*, and for once the *Mirror* was determined not to be left behind. The Spanish were the first victims. Two days before England's quarter-final match *Mirror* readers were treated to 'ten nasties' that Spain had given Europe: these included syphilis, which had been brought back from America by Columbus; the carpet-bombing of Guernica; flamenco dancing; and paella. Of course, Columbus was Italian and Guernica had been bombed by Germans, but *Mirror* writers weren't about to let facts spoil their piece of prejudice. 'What do you call a good-looking girl in Spain?' the paper asked. 'A tourist,' came the answer. The writer was obviously blind as well as stupid.

All this served as a starter for several days of concentrated German-bashing. On Monday 24 June the front page featured Pearce and Gascoigne in soldier's helmets, the headline 'ACHTUNG! SURRENDER', and a wordy declaration of 'football' war on Germany which parodied Chamberlain's declaration of the real one in September 1939. There were pages more of the stuff inside; it was as if the *Mirror* had scraped together every boys' comic cliché of the last fifty years and laid them end to end.

On the following day two whole pages were devoted to a long moan about England's grey strip (the Germans had won the toss to decide who played in white) and endless comparisons between 1966 and the present. Another double page was given to a piece of visualised wishful thinking – Alan Shearer's head superimposed on Hurst's goalscoring body. Kevin Keegan, who had dared tip Germany to win in his German newspaper column, was firmly taken to task under the headline 'KEEGAN KRAUT OF ORDER'.

The coverage in the *Daily Star* was on similar lines, but somewhat surprisingly the *Sun* had sought out higher ground and was now busy congratulating itself on maintaining 'a jingoistic approach rather than a xenophobic one'. 'I think we can get away with blitzing Fritz,' editor Stuart Higgins observed ingenuously, 'but talk of war is in a different league.' The *Mail* took the opportunity to denounce jingoism; the *Express* and *Independent* both carried pro-German pieces. On Monday *The Times* tut-tutted at the tabloids' excesses; on Tuesday it gleefully revealed that *Mirror* editor Piers Morgan had been forced into an apology by angry readers and advertisers. Vauxhall, it transpired, had been sufficiently offended by their Monday editions to withdraw future advertising from both the *Mirror* and the *Daily Star.*

Across the Channel the German tabloid *Bildzeitung* responded in kind to the *Mirror* challenge, posing a list of questions for the English to answer. 'Why do you look like freshly cooked lobsters after one day on the beach?' the paper asked. 'Why have you never won the European Championship?'

It was all pretty ludicrous, all extremely childish. Hopefully Paul Ince spoke for most of the players when he said that they didn't 'regard the Germans as the enemy and don't like some people treating it as World War Three'. Venables agreed. He pleaded – mostly in vain, as it turned out – for the Wembley crowd to respect both national anthems, and stressed that this was a football match and as such had nothing to do with what had happened fifty years before. 'Some things, for this game and the Spain one,' he said, 'have gone too far. Insulting people's mother country is not funny.'

In the final scene of the epic film *El Cid* the dead Charlton Heston is propped up in the saddle so that he can lead his troops into battle; in June 1996 there were rumours that a comparable role might be found for the injured Jurgen Klinsmann. There was never any real chance of him playing, but the rumours were illustrative of a genuine German concern – how were they to win with such a depleted side and without their talismanic captain?

Right from the kick-off it was clear that they had no intention of attacking England on a broad front. Both sides lined up in an approximate 3–5–1–1 formation, but the German midfield five boasted much more defensively minded players. The idea was for both Freund and Eilts to sit just in front of the two withdrawn wingbacks, the two man-markers and the sweeper, creating an almost impenetrable barrier. For attack they would rely on swift two- and three-man breaks.

The plan suffered a severe blow after less than two minutes. A cross was headed out to Ince, and his answering volley was acrobatically punched over by Köpke for a corner. Gascoigne sent in an in-swinger from the left, Adams flicked on at the near post, and Shearer bullet-headed it past the hapless Germans. The crowd erupted, as much with surprise as with joy. This was beyond the wildest English hopes.

It took both sides several minutes to recover their composure, and then it was the Germans who slowly started to push forward. Their formation was obviously more fluid than England's, yet there was no sense of threat in their neat passing and movement. They seemed to be what many commentators had said they were: an efficient but essentially uninspired bunch of athletes.

And then, just as surprisingly, Germany also scored. Helmer and Möller worked a one-two on the left-hand edge of the penalty area, Helmer slipped it in low, and there was Kuntz, reaching the ball ahead of Pearce and stabbing it past Seaman from seven yards. The trick was hidden in the names: Helmer was one of the defensive man-markers. Neither English nor German central defenders had joined in attacks like this prior to 1966, but in the intervening years the Germans had acquired the technique and the willingness to do so. While it had been a simple goal for Kuntz, thirty years of football education had gone into its making.

England continued to reply on raw inspiration, and a few minutes later a glorious dummy by Gascoigne almost created an opportunity. Anderton and McManaman were having a hard time getting into the game, but the former finally got in a cross which was headed over by Shearer. A short period of England pressure produced a couple of corners, and one pulled back along the ground for Sheringham's shot was eventually cleared off the line by Reuter.

The game now entered a long period of scrappy play with both sides unable to string more than a couple of passes together, let alone create chances. Scholl shot weakly after breaking through in the inside left channel, but the third good opportunity of the half was created by England in the forty-second minute. Anderton, set free on the right by Platt, measured his cross well, and Shearer put his header only a foot or so wide. The half ended with England slightly on top, though overall there had been little between the sides.

The second half brought more of the same. England were more inclined to press forward, but German tackling and covering continued to frustrate all their efforts. There was as yet no sign of any German threat and their lack of attacking ambition was well illustrated when Möller broke at speed only to find he had far out-stripped any potential support. That said, the Germans did create the first good chance of the half, Helmer shooting wide from less than fifteen yards when Eilts pulled the ball back from the by-line.

Reprieved, England returned to the attack, and a Gascoigne cross was just too high for Platt. Real chances continued to elude England, and it was the seventieth minute before they got another sniff of goal, Helmer robbing them with a last-ditch tackle after a Gascoigne-Anderton one-two had slipped the former into a great shooting position. Helmer, injured in the process, was off the field for five minutes, a fact which apparently made little difference. German lack of ambition and English inability to break down a well-organised defence combined to deadening effect, and over the last twenty minutes of normal time the game drifted towards a seemingly inevitable stalemate. A Platt shot at the death briefly raised English hopes; however, like so many of the night's efforts, it ended up wide of the mark. As in Turin, there would be extra time, though not necessarily thirty minutes' worth. The 'golden goal' rule now applied: the first team to score would win.

Those who had sat through the preceding ninety minutes weren't too optimistic about the prospects. Surely with so much riding on a single mistake England would now become as cautious as the Germans and the game would simply congeal. To their eternal credit, both sides went into extra time with a renewed commitment to attack, and the first period produced more goal-mouth excitement than the rest of the match put together.

England were the first to go close. Ince found Platt on the right, and he sent McManaman to the by-line with a great pass. The cross was fast, low and a few agonising inches behind Anderton at the near post. He couldn't quite get his foot far enough around the ball, which cannoned back off the woodwork. England had been only a whisker away from their second-ever final.

A minute later it was the Germans' turn, a fast cross by Helmer just eluding Kuntz at the far post. Play was sweeping from end to end now, and for a few moments the ball ricocheted around the German penalty area as if it were on a pin table. It wouldn't fall for England, and there was Möller surging down the centre, Adams retreating in front of him, and a twenty-five-yard drive that had Seaman arching up and back to tip it over. From Möller's corner Kuntz headed home, and English hearts momentarily sunk until it became apparent that the referee had disallowed the goal, apparently for pushing. The offence was hard to spot, and on the following day several German papers complained that a further injustice had been added to Hurst's second goal in 1966. 'Just like thirty years ago,' the *Express* said, 'there was a whiff of a fix.'

The Germans continued to press forward, but Hässler – on as a substitute for Scholl – lost the ball on the left; Sheringham hit a Bobby Charlton-quality long ball to Shearer out on the right, and his first-time volley across the face of goal passed only inches ahead of Gascoigne's out-thrown left leg. It would have been a goal worthy of winning a tournament.

Only eight minutes of extra time had been played and five goals could have been scored in that time. Not surprisingly there was now something of a lull; the first period was almost over when Gascoigne again went close to making contact in the goal area, this time following a cross from McManaman. A minute after the re-start the Germans had a much better opportunity. A one-two with Möller played Ziege well into the penalty area, but as Seaman, Pearce and Southgate all desperately converged on him the German wing-back stabbed the ball wide.

It proved the last clear-cut chance of the match. There were more corners, more shots from distance, but neither goalkeeper was really troubled again. While England were pressing when the final whistle went, a draw had looked the most likely outcome for most of the second period. The two sides had fought each other to a standstill, and once more it would be penalties.

The Germans had not practised them before the game. Vögts had simply given Köpke a list of the English penalty-takers and their favourite corners. England had already come through one such ordeal against Spain, but the memory of 1990 was bound to linger – particularly for Stuart Pearce. He was down to take England's third kick, and when he stepped up to take it the tally was 2–2, Shearer and Platt having scored for England, Hässler and Strunz for Germany.

Pearce also scored, and the roar that reverberated around Wembley might almost have been heard in Turin. Reuter stepped up to take his, and Seaman's fingers were desperately close to making contact. It was the nearest the Germans came to a mistake, the closest England came to the final.

Gascoigne, Ziege, Sheringham and Kuntz all scored. Köpke, who had gone the wrong way for each of the five penalties he had faced, must have been relieved to see Gareth Southgate approaching. Southgate wasn't on his list; he guessed right and saved the defender's weakly struck shot. Möller scored, and England had lost again.

Some put it down to bad luck – penalties are just a lottery, right? – but others weren't so sure. Since 1976 the Germans had been involved in four penalty shoot-outs, all of which they'd won, and had missed only a single penalty. Was this luck? Was it, as Beckenbauer thought, that Germans had 'the best nerves in the world . . . the capacity to concentrate'? Or was there ultimately nothing more reliable than good basic technique?

Sammer and Gascoigne shared a smile during the penalties, and when they were over Eilts could be seen commiserating with the England players. Once again the players of the two nations had been as sporting as anyone could expect, and once again many of England's fans used defeat as an excuse for demonstrating disaffection with their lot in life. As in 1990, foreigners were attacked on the pretext of possibly being German, and mini-riots erupted all over the country. There were two hundred arrests in London and at least two serious knifings.

None of this had much to do with football, and none of it had much to do with Germans. If England had gone out to Spain in the previous round anyone who looked remotely Latin would have been in danger of being beaten up.

In terms of the football, most of the nation basked for several days in another near-thing, another gallant defeat. The German victory in the final confirmed how close England had come, and the soon-to-be-departing Venables was rightly congratulated for moving England forward, for finding at least a hint of that blend of north- and south-European virtues which had served the Germans so well since 1970.

On a more pessimistic note, it was also realised that England's achievement had to be measured against the generally low standard of football on display in Euro '96. There had been no great teams in the tournament and precious few patches of brilliant football. The Germans had proved the best of a poor bunch; the English, on their home turf, one of several teams vying for second spot. Though it wasn't the end of the rainbow it was at least another beginning, another chance to throw off the shackles of the past.

21: schnapp!

Over the next four years English football underwent something of a transformation. At the beginning of the 1996–7 season there was an influx of foreign players who had distinguished themselves in the European Championships, and by the end of the century most teams in the Premiership were fielding teams in which fewer than half of the players were English. In the past, many English Football League teams had included Scotsmen, Welshmen and Irishmen, all of whom had grown up playing a style of football which had been indistinguishable from English football since at least the 1930s. Among the new arrivals of the late 1990s were representatives of every footballing style on earth, and there was no question of their being simply absorbed by the English game. The generally superior technique of the newcomers would at worst allow coaches more tactical leeway, and at best encourage a British-style, high-tempo version of the Continental game.

Whether this hybrid could still be called English football was a moot point. Either way, it brought trophies back to England – two of them, moreover, at the expense of the Germans. Chelsea beat Stuttgart in the 1998 Cup-Winner's Cup final with a team containing three Englishmen and a stunning strike from Italian veteran Gianfranco Zola. A year later in the Nou Camp, Manchester United's winner against Bayern in injury-time was scored by a Norwegian. United had four Englishmen in their team in contrast to Bayern's much higher proportion of Germans.

Under Ferguson, Manchester United had perfected the aforementioned high-tempo British-Continental style. They had a goalkeeper whose dominance extended almost to the halfway-line, central defenders who were much more comfortable on the ball than most of their English counterparts, at least four highly skilled midfield players who were also prepared to work and a posse of mobile strikers who knew where the net was. In Beckham, Giggs and Sheringham, United also had players capable of turning a game with one piece of magic.

Their victory over Bayern in the final was undoubtedly fortunate – Bayern twice hit the woodwork and were a goal up upon entering a mysteriously extended stoppage time – but it was also due reward for Ferguson's determination to play a more ambitious type of football. In the game's aftermath there was much talk in both England and Germany of it representing a triumph for the one country over the other, though such a conclusion was open to question on at least two counts. When seven foreigners and four Englishmen in United shirts played a high-tempo passing game, were they re-defining English football or simply leaving it behind? And when millions of Germans rooted for United out of loathing for Bayern, and millions of Englishmen rooted for Bayern out of loathing for United, what was left of patriotic identification? This had been a victory for the polyglot Premiership and the increasingly international entity known as Manchester United, not a triumph for English football.

What such success implied for the national team was also an open question. In the long run the influx of skills into the Premiership was likely to raise the overall level, which could only benefit English football. In the short run, the presence of so many foreigners was bound to lessen the number of chances young English players had to establish themselves, and the pool of talent from which the England manager drew seemed doomed to shrink.

Both the success of the Premiership and the glut of money which accompanied it were also bound to affect player-behaviour. Modern pressures gave them less time to grow up, instant riches meant that many no longer needed to, and it sometimes seemed as though England was intent on producing players whose enormous talents were matched only by their lack of self-knowledge or self-control. While the problem was probably universal, there was no doubt that the appalling education most young English footballers received often left them less able to handle the pressures than their Continental counterparts.

Both England (now managed by Glenn Hoddle) and Germany qualified for the 1998 World Cup in France, England impressively topping a group which also included Italy. In the finals, they both disappointed. The Germans finished first in a relatively easy group, struggled to beat Mexico in the last sixteen, and were soundly beaten 3–0 by Croatia in the quarter-finals. Their best players were their oldest, which didn't bode well for the future. The English finished second to Romania in their group and went down to Argentina on penalties in the first match of the knock-out phase, David Beckham's moment of petulance cancelling out a spirited performance and Michael Owen's spectacular goal.

The latter was given the instant accolade of a thorny crown. Owen, however, was more often injured than fit over the next two seasons, and on those rare occasions when he did play alongside Alan Shearer in England's attack the partnership noticeably failed to gell. Partly in consequence, England struggled to qualify for Euro 2000, only sneaking in at the last moment when the Swedes beat the Poles in Stockholm. Kevin Keegan had taken over the managership from Hoddle earlier in the year, and his relief at qualifying was soon tempered by news of England's group partners in the finals – Romania, Portugal and . . . Germany. As if that wasn't enough, the two nations came out of the hat together again a few weeks later, this time in a qualification group for the 2002 World Cup in Japan and South Korea. 'KEEGAN LANDS IN DER SCHMIDT', the *Sun* announced before reminding its readers that England hadn't beaten Germany in a competition since 1966. The *Daily Star* thought it was 'HUNCANNY', but also offered up Bobby Charlton's prediction that 'England can beat the Krauts three times'. Though Charlton hadn't actually used those particular words, in the light of the last thirty years his optimism was almost as outrageous.

Or perhaps not. Germany had also struggled to qualify, finally topping a far from formidable group with a highly fortunate home-draw against Turkey. The lack of young homegrown talent in the Bundesliga was highlighted by the continuing presence of the thirty-nine year-old Lothar Matthäus in the national side. Age was taking its toll on Matthäus, as the Dutch forward pairing of Kluivert and van Nistelrooy amply demonstrated in a February friendly. Holland hardly needed to break sweat in the 2–1 win, and the only consolation for coach Ribbeck was a promising debut by the young Hertha Berlin midfielder Sebastian Deisler, who many German critics considered their country's best – some said *only* – hope for the future.

Several members of the squad were clearly unhappy under Ribbeck's tutelage, and Bayern midfielder Jens Jeremies was more vocal than most. He was dropped for the friendly against the Swiss, another lacklustre affair which ended in a draw. In early May, Ribbeck felt obliged to sack assistant Uli Stielike, but the German FA insisted that the national team's former libero be kept on the payroll as a spy, and dispatched him to Wembley to watch England play Brazil. Team captain Oliver Bierhoff now entered the fray, and demanded that the coach recall thirty-four year-old Thomas Hässler and Bayern's two *enfants terribles*, Mario Basler and Stefan Effenberg. Ribbeck admonished Bierhoff, continued to ignore Basler, but did include Hässler in his squad for Euro 2000. Effenberg, still probably Germany's best player, was not invited to reconsider his refusal to play for the national team.

After all this wrangling a last-minute 3–2 victory in a warm-up match against the Czech Republic, in which Bierhoff scored his first goal for nine hours in the national shirt, provided a much-needed boost in morale. Neither Jeremies nor Matthäus, the latter now playing in the US, appeared in this game, and it was hoped that their return for the tournament would improve the team still further.

On the face of it, England were having a better time. The squad, which certainly seemed united under Keegan's enthusiastic direction, took a draw and two wins from pre-tournament friendlies against Brazil, Ukraine and Malta. There was much debate about England's lack of left-sided players and the formation which Keegan would or should employ in the tournament as a consequence. The TV pundits decided that England didn't have the players to make a 3–5–2 formation work, but failed to explain why the same players would make a better fist of playing 4–4–2. In both the Brazil and Ukraine matches the English team had been consistently out-passed, and had only been rescued by Michael Owen's opportunism and David Beckham's astonishing crosses. Much the same script would be acted out in Euro 2000, with less fortunate consequences.

The first match against Portugal began with a deceptive English flourish. In the first twenty minutes, while the English defence struggled to cope with the fluid inter-passing of the Portuguese in midfield, the

Portuguese defence succumbed to two wonderful crosses from Beckham, the first bullet-headed home off the bar by Paul Scholes, the second swept exultantly into the net by Steve McManaman. The Portuguese might have crumbled, but they didn't. They kept flowing forward, mesmerising the English defenders with the swiftness and accuracy of their passing, their complete comfort on the ball. Three glorious goals followed: Figo running straight at Adams and hitting a twenty-five yard thunderbolt past Seaman; a sixteen-pass move which ended with a twisting, diving header from Joao Pinto; an exuberant strike from Nuno Gomes after Rui Costa's raking pass had set the English defenders spinning for the umpteenth time.

After the match there was the usual knee-jerk reaction, the usual resistance to learn from defeat. The English had failed to close down the opposition, the cry went up. They had given them too much space, failed to stop them playing. It was too hard to admit that the Portuguese players had simply *taken* the space by passing and controlling the ball so much better. They had, in the words of their old legend Eusebio, 'showed how to love the ball'. The English had only known how to hit it.

The team now had to win a competitive game against Germany, something they hadn't managed to do in thirty-four years. Fortunately for England, the Germans themselves seemed at an equally low ebb. They took a point from their first game against Romania but their overall performance was utterly unconvincing. In the first half the defence looked a shambles, Matthäus a shadow of the player he had once been. The midfield was uninspired, the attack almost non-existent, and it took a hit-and-hope drive from Scholl to cancel out the goal which sloppy defensive work had gifted to the Romanians. There were glimpses of the old technical efficiency, but few signs of imagination or collective spirit. This was a team running on empty – in one vivid cameo of discord Hässler spent the best part of a minute berating Bierhoff for failing to anticipate his near post cross. If England were ever to beat Germany in a competitive match then this seemed the moment.

In the days leading up to the match the atmosphere inside the two camps was very different. England, though clearly stunned by their experience at the hands of the Portuguese, closed ranks and focused on the forthcoming game. Both Adams and McManaman were ruled out by injuries, so

Martin Keown was brought in to partner Sol Campbell in central defence and Dennis Wise was allotted the problem berth on the left side of midfield. The Neville brothers kept their places at full back, Owen and Shearer theirs upfront. In midfield Ince and Scholes, who had been so comprehensively overrun by the Portuguese, retained their places alongside Beckham.

The Germans, meanwhile, were arguing amongst themselves. There were rumours that a deputation of players – Oliver Kahn, Mehmet Scholl and Jens Nowotny were the names most frequently mentioned – had gone to Ribbeck and demanded the dropping of Matthäus. Ribbeck denied this, but Matthäus seemed less sure of the facts. He said he felt sorry for anyone who couldn't criticise him to his face, and suggested that 'if no individual has the nerve then five can come together'. The squad tried to show a happy collective face at a public training session just across the border in Germany, only for the whole exercise to backfire when captain Bierhoff sustained an injury which sidelined him for the rest of the tournament.

For the game against England, Bierhoff and the ineffective Paulo Rink were replaced up front by Carsten Jancker and Ulf Kirsten, neither of whom promised much in the way of finesse. Sebastian Deisler was brought in on the right side of the usual five-man midfield with instructions to run at the suspect left side of England's defence. Marcus Babbel dropped back to take Thomas Linke's place on the right-hand side of the back three. Liverpool's Dietmar Hamann was drafted into central midfield; Jeremies, Scholl, Ziege Nowotny and Matthäus all retained their places. Hässler was left on the bench. The German press was outwardly confident, but appeared to be relying on habit rather than quality to deliver the expected victory – 'we always beat England' as one *Bild* columnist complacently put it.

There was the usual English hissing of the German national anthem before the game started, but at least the tabloids had been on their best behaviour in the preceding days – there had been no mention of Krauts and mercifully few references to the Second World War. Instead, the obvious weakness of the current German team had induced a touch of English self-pity – would the nation at last be delivered from 'thirty-four years of hurt'?

The initial signs were not good. The first ten minutes were roughly even, but the next ten saw increasing German pressure, and anxious English observers began to wonder whether the rumours of their opponents' decline had been exaggerated. As usual the German midfield players were looking far more comfortable on the ball and enjoying much more of the possession. England, by contrast, were showing their usual inclination to give the ball away and seemed depressingly short of imagination on those rare occasions when they managed to string more than two passes together. On TV Trevor Brooking, once one of England's more thoughtful players, was reduced to praying for 'one decent ball over the top for Michael Owen'.

In the twenty-second minute Jeremies contrived an opening for Scholl, but his scuffed shot from fifteen yards was easily dealt with by Seaman. Four minutes later it was Ziege's turn to have a clear sight of goal from the edge of the penalty area, and again the shot was weak. The Germans continued to play in their usual patient manner, looking confident at the back, passing the ball quickly and accurately through the midfield. The half-hour mark was reached with England yet to mount a single threat to their opponents' goal.

Then, in the thirty-fourth minute, a leaping, twisting Michael Owen turned a hopeful cross from Phil Neville into a great one, heading the ball hard and low to Kahn's left. The German keeper flung himself to tip the ball against the post, and it bounced back across the goalmouth to safety.

The game was still goalless, but it had been turned upside-down. Now the English players were driving forward, and the confidence seemed to be draining from the Germans. Almost immediately, Scholes sent a vicious twenty-five yard volley a few feet over Kahn's bar, and a couple of minutes before half-time the same player might have done better when Beckham's wonderful fifty yard ball found him in space on the left side of the area. When the two teams went in at half-time there was no doubt which held the upper hand.

Given that, it was all the more surprising that the second half began like the first, with the England midfield reluctant to push forward, as if they were afraid that Figo and Rui Costa might suddenly materialise in front of them. Ziege hit a rocket of a free kick just over the angle – the English fire seemed to have dulled as swiftly as it had flared. However, in the fifty-second minute England were awarded a free kick on the

German left, a prime position for Beckham. He whipped the ball in fast and hard, Owen and Nowotny prevented each other from making contact, and Alan Shearer stole in behind everyone to put it past Kahn on the bounce.

This was the end of England as an attacking force, but a combination of strong defence and poor German finishing ensured that one goal would be enough. Campbell and Keown looked much comfortable playing against the English-style Jancker and Kirsten than they had against Portuguese quicksilver, and yet the Germans were still presented with a string of far from difficult chances in the fifteen minutes which followed England's goal. Jancker shot wide on the turn, Scholl put a ground shot past the far post. In the sixty-fourth minute first Kirsten and then Jancker failed to convert gilt-edged chances after Babbel had headed down a Scholl corner.

The last half hour was tense but essentially uneventful. Both sides made changes, neither made chances. When the final whistle blew England had finally beaten the Germans in a competitive match, and the nation duly celebrated.

'HUN-NIL' the *Sunday People* proclaimed, but elsewhere the triumphalism of the English press was more joyful than offensive. It was also mostly restricted to the front and back spreads; on the inside pages the post-match reaction was more subdued, more objective. It felt good to beat the Germans, especially after so long, but was there any real significance to the result? While it was tempting to believe that the English had become genuine contenders, it seemed more realistic to acknowledge that the Germans had simply joined them among the ranks of the also-rans.

It was widely admitted in the England camp that it had been a poor game. Keegan predictably praised the squad for their commitment, endeavour and honesty; Paul Ince, while admitting that the performance had been less than outstanding, claimed with an equal lack of originality that the players had shown 'the bulldog spirit'. Beckham and Scholes were rightly praised for their contributions, but no one was foolish enough to pretend that England had played good football. Erich Ribbeck, his players, and most of the German media thought England had been lucky to win, and so they had if the number of chances created was the most accurate indication of worthiness. In truth it had been the least impressive in a growing line of essentially even games between the two nations.

The strong suspicion of mutual ineptitude was confirmed three days later. Much the same German team was hammered 3–0 by the Portuguese second eleven; England, outclassed by an injury-weakened Rumania, were lucky to escape with only a 3–2 defeat. After thirty-two years of trying, England had finally finished ahead of the Germans in an international tournament, but both were out.

The reaction in England was subdued, even sombre. All the talk of systems and team selections went out of the window, and – for a few days at least – there seemed to be general agreement that the traditional blood and thunder English game could never bring consistent success at the highest level. It was hard to play without the ball, Johan Cruyff patiently explained to BBC viewers, and only good passing sides got the chance to try. A team needed 'eight, nine, ten players who are good on the ball to play a passing game', co-pundit Alan Hansen calculated. The English team that went to Euro 2000 had perhaps four or five. It was as simple as that.

There are two obvious reasons for the peculiar piquancy of the Anglo-German football relationship. One is the legacy of that political and military enmity which afflicted the two nations in the first half of the century, the other lies in a barely conscious recognition of the fact that the two nations are similar in so many ways, yet have fared so differently for so long on the international football stage. The latter reason has been growing less pertinent for several years, and as a new century begins the two nations seem to have achieved an equivalence of mediocrity. The Germans still have the edge where basic technique is concerned, the English have Beckham. Each can now see the other's presence in their World Cup qualifying group as a reason for optimism.

The legacy of the wider conflict has been slowly fading for half a century, and the dawning of a new millennium should add emotional distance to the events of its predecessor. Many of the old prejudices remain – in October 1999 the departing German Ambassador expressed his dismay that this was indeed the case – but that is all they are: there is no real divergence of interest between the English and German peoples, as there clearly was a century ago. When sectional interests collide – as they did, for example, in BMW's jettisoning of Rover in April 2000 – the background hum of prejudice will become slightly more noticeable, but that is all. And when a writer like A.A. Gill (in a July 1999 edition of *The Sunday Times*) decides to abuse the German people *en masse* – 'admit it, we all hate them' – he will merely be displaying the narrowness of his own mind and experience.

A similar congenital defect appears to afflict those responsible for running English football. When Stanley Matthews died early in 2000 those papers were full of glowing tributes, and a young reader could have been forgiven for assuming that the great player had been ever-present in the England side. In fact, he appeared in fewer than half of the internationals played between his first and last caps. Remembering as much might encourage the selection of current and future mavericks; the usual amnesia merely condemns English football to its seemingly endless repetition of the same mistake.

Of course, such players would have to be available for selection. John Cartwright was England's first full-time youth coach under Ron Greenwood, and later technical director at the FA's School of Excellence, a job from which he resigned in disgust. 'There is no naturalness in our young players today,' he told the *Evening Standard* in August 1999, 'no craft. We get by on what we're good at – organisation, plenty of red blood cells and a lot of running and hard work.' Foreign kids were in 'a different class to ours in terms of technique'; the English game had 'no chance of producing great players.' Gazza, he claimed, had 'evolved not because of the system but despite it', and might well be 'the last to do that.'

This doesn't bode well, and the peculiarities of the modern game – too much money, too many games, the poaching of ever-younger players – are more likely to make matters worse than better. It doesn't help that in England we are swimming against the tide of our own history, struggling to rise above our long-nurtured unwillingness to embrace the sort of football which we now glimpse, almost as a revelation, in the polyglot Premiership. The prospects for the biggest clubs and their supporters may be good, but the national team and the long-term health of English football require English defenders who are more than just that, and English forwards with the touch and technique of a Zola, a Bergkamp, a Ginola.

Though England's victory in the 1966 World Cup is a treasured memory, it is the winning which is remembered and not the style or quality of the football. In almost fifty years of watching the game I have occasionally seen British club teams play with the same skill and *élan*, the same sheer joy in excellence which the Hungarians produced in 1953, the Brazilians in 1970, the West Germans in 1972, but I cannot remember ever being similarly inspired by an England team. Perhaps the eleven who humiliated the watching Nazi leaders in 1938 was such a team, but that was a long time ago.

English teams have rarely run short of energy, heart or fighting team spirit, but at the highest level football is primarily a game of skill. Over the last thirty years the Germans have consistently played technically superior football and, more importantly, they have occasionally and memorably demonstrated that the Latin peoples have no monopoly of the beautiful game. It's high time the English followed the example of their old enemy and took up the challenge to match the best where it matters most, in the joyful art of making magic with the ball.

appendix 1: england v. germany/west germany

Friendly, 10 May 1930
(Gruenwald, Berlin)

| Germany | (1) 3 | England | (2) 3 |
| R. Hofmann 3 | | Bradford 2, Jack | |

★ Kress, Schutz, Stubb, Heidkamp, Leinberger, Mantel, Bergmaier, Pöttinger, Kuzorra, R. Hofmann, L. Hofmann
★ Hibbs, Goodall, Blenkinsop, Strange, Webster, Marsden, Crooks, Jack, Watson, Bradford, Rimmer

Friendly, 4 December 1935
(White Hart Lane)

| England | (1) 3 | Germany | (0) 0 |
| Camsell 2, Bastin | | | |

★ Hibbs, Male, Hapgood, Crayston, Barker, Bray, Matthews, Carter, Camsell, Westwood, Bastin
★ Jakob, Haringer, Münzenberg, Janes, Goldbrunner, Gramlich, Lehner, Szepan, Hohmann, Rasselnberg, Fath

Friendly, 14 May 1938
(Olympic Stadium, Berlin)

| Germany | (2) 3 | England | (4) 6 |
| Gellesch, Gauchel, Pesser | | Robinson 2, Matthews, Broome, Bastin, Goulden | |

★Jakob, Janes, Münzenberg, Kupfer, Goldbrunner, Kitzinger, Lehner, Gellesch, Gauchel, Szepan, Pesser

*Woodley, Sproston, Hapgood, Willingham, Young, Welsh, Matthews, Robinson, Broome, Goulden, Bastin

Friendly, 1 December 1954
(Wembley)

England	(1) 3	West Germany	(0) 1
Bentley, Allen, Shackleton		Beck	

* Williams, Staniforth, Byrne, Phillips, Wright, Slater, Matthews, Bentley, Allen, Shackleton, Finney
* Herkenrath, Posipal, Kohlmeyer, Erhardt, Liebrich, Harpers, Kaufhold, Pfeiffer, Seeler, Derwall, Beck

Friendly, 26 May 1956
(Olympic Stadium, Berlin)

West Germany	(0) 1	England	(1) 3
F. Walter		Edwards, Grainger, Haynes	

* Herkenrath, Retter, Juskowiak, Schlienz, Wewers, Mai, Waldner, Morlock (Pfaff), O. Walter, F. Walter, Schäfer
* Matthews, Hall, Byrne, Clayton, Wright, Edwards, Astall, Haynes, Taylor, Wilshaw, Grainger

Friendly, 12 May 1965
(Nuremberg)

West Germany	(0) 0	England	(1) 1
		Paine	

* Tilkowski, Piontek, Höttges, Schulz, Sieloff, Lorenz (Steinmann), Thielen, Krämer, Rodekamp, Overath, Hornig
* Banks, Cohen, Flowers, J. Charlton, Moore, Wilson, Ball, Eastham, Paine, Jones, Temple

Friendly, 23 February 1966
(Wembley)

England	(1) 1	West Germany	(0) 0
Stiles			

* Banks, Cohen, Newton (Wilson), Moore, J. Charlton, Hunter, Stiles, Ball, R. Charlton, Hunt, Hurst

★ Tilkowski, Lutz, Lorenz, Schulz, Weber, Szymaniak, Krämer, Beckenbauer, Held, Netzer, Hornig (Heiss)

World Cup Final, 30 July 1966
(Wembley)

England	(1) 4	West Germany	(1) 2 (aet)
Hurst 3, Peters		Haller, Weber	

★ Banks, Cohen, Wilson, J. Charlton, Moore, Ball, Stiles, R. Charlton, Peters, Hunt, Hurst

★ Tilkowski, Höttges, Schnellinger, Schulz, Weber, Beckenbauer, Haller, Overath, Seeler, Held, Emmerich

Friendly, 1 June 1968
(Hannover)

West Germany	(0) 1	England	(0) 0
Beckenbauer			

★ Wolter, Vögts, Lorenz, L. Müller, Fichtel, Weber, Dörfel, Beckenbauer, Löhr, Overath, Volkert

★ Banks, Newton, Knowles, Moore, Labone, Hunter, Bell, Ball, Summerbee, Hurst, Thompson

World Cup Quarter-final, 14 June 1970
(León)

West Germany	(0) 3	England	(1) 2 (aet)
Beckenbauer, Seeler, Müller		Mullery, Peters	

★ Maier, Vögts, Höttges (Schulz), Beckenbauer, Schnellinger, Fichtel, Libuda (Grabowski), Seeler, G. Müller, Overath, Löhr

★ Bonetti, Newton, Labone, Moore, Cooper, Mullery, Ball, R. Charlton (Bell), Peters (Hunter), Lee, Hurst

European Championship Quarter-final, First Leg, 29 April 1972
(Wembley)

England	(0) 1	West Germany	(1) 3
Lee		Hoeness, Netzer (pen.), Müller	

★ Banks, Madeley, Moore, Hunter, Hughes, Lee, Ball, Bell, Peters,
Chivers, Hurst (Marsh)
★ Maier, Höttges, Breitner, Schwarzenbeck, Beckenbauer, Wimmer,
Grabowski, Hoeness, G. Müller, Netzer, Held

European Championship Quarter-final, Second Leg, 13 May 1972
(Berlin)

West Germany   (0) 0   England   (0) 0
★ Maier, Höttges, Breitner, Schwarzenbeck, Beckenbauer, Wimmer,
Hoeness, Flohe, G. Müller, Netzer, Held
★ Banks, Madeley, Moore, McFarland, Hunter, Hughes, Storey, Ball,
Bell (Peters), Marsh (Summerbee), Chivers

Friendly, 12 March 1975
(Wembley)

England   (1) 2   West Germany   (0) 0
Bell, Macdonald
★ Clemence, Whitworth, Todd, Watson, Gillard, Ball, Bell, Hudson,
Keegan, Macdonald, Channon
★ Maier, Bonhof, Vögts, Körbel, Beckenbauer, Cullmann, Ritshchel,
Flohe, Kostedde (Heynckes), Wimmer (H. Kremers), Hölzenbein.

Friendly, 22 February 1978
(Munich)

West Germany   (0) 2   England   (1) 1
Worm, Bonhof   Pearson
★ Maier, Vögts, H. Zimmermann, Bonhof, Schwarzenbeck, Rüssmann,
Abramczik, Flohe (Burgsmüller), Hölzenbein (Worm), Neumann
(Dietz), Rummenigge
★ Clemence, Neal, Watson, Hughes, Mills, Coppell, Wilkins, Brooking,
Keegan (Francis), Pearson, P. Barnes

World Cup Second-phase Group-match, 29 June 1982
(Madrid)

England   (0) 0   West Germany   (0) 0

★ Shilton, Mills, Butcher, Thompson, Sansom, Coppell, Wilkins, Robson, Rix, Francis (Woodcock), Mariner

★ Schumacher, Kaltz, Stielike, Kh. Förster, Briegel, Dremmler, B. Förster, Breitner, H. Müller (Fischer), Reinders (Littbarski), Rummenigge

Friendly, 13 October 1982
(Wembley)

England   (0) 1   West Germany   (0) 2
Woodcock   Rummenigge 2

★ Shilton, Mabbutt, Butcher, Sansom, Thompson, Devonshire, Wilkins, Hill, Mariner (Woodcock), Regis, (Blissett), Armstrong (Rix)

★ Schumacher, Kaltz, Strack, Kh. Förster (Hieronymous), B. Förster, Meier (Littbarski), Dremmler, Briegel, Matthäus, Rummenigge, Allofs

Friendly, 12 June 1985
(Mexico City)

England   (1) 3   West Germany   (0) 0
Robson, Dixon 2

★ Shilton, Stevens, Sansom, Hoddle, Wright, Butcher, Robson (Bracewell), Reid, Dixon, Lineker (Barnes), Waddle

★ Schumacher, Berthold, Herget, Jakobs, Augenthaler, Brehme, Matthäus, Magath (Thon), Rahn, Littbarski, Mill (Waas)

Friendly, 9 September 1987
(Düsseldorf)

West Germany   (2) 3   England   (1) 1
Littbarski 2, Wuttke   Lineker

★ Immel, Herget, Brehme (Reuter), Kohler, Buchwald, Frontzeck, Littbarski, Thon, Dorfner, Völler (Wuttke), Allofs.

★ Shilton, Anderson, Sansom (Pearce), Hoddle (Webb), Adams, Mabbutt, Reid, Barnes, Beardsley, Lineker, Waddle (Hateley)

World Cup Semi-final, 4 July 1990
(Turin)

England	(0) 1	West Germany	(0) 1
Lineker		Brehme	

(West Germany won 4–3 on penalties)

★ Shilton, Wright, Parker, Butcher (Steven), Walker, Pearce, Gascoigne, Platt, Waddle, Lineker, Beardsley

★ Illgner, Augenthaler, Berthold, Buchwald, Kohler, Brehme, Hässler (Reuter), Matthäus, Thon, Klinsmann, Völler (Riedle)

Friendly, 11 September 1991
(Wembley)

England	(0) 0	Germany	(1) 1
		Riedle	

★ Woods, Dixon, Dorigo, Batty, Parker, Pallister, Platt, Steven (Merson), Smith, Lineker, Salako (Stewart)

★ Illgner, Binz, Effenberg, Kohler, Buchwald, Hässler, Matthäus, Möller, Brehme, Riedle, Doll (Klinsmann)

US Cup, 9 June 1993
(Detroit)

England	(1) 1	Germany	(1) 2
Platt		Effenberg, Klinsmann	

★ Martyn, Barrett, Sinton, Sharpe (Winterburn), Pallister (Keown), Walker, Platt, Ince, Clough (Wright), Merson, Barnes

★ Illgner, Helmer, Buchwald, Schulz, Strunz, Effenberg (Zorc), Matthäus, Möller (Sammer), Ziege, Riedle, Klinsmann

European Championship Semi-final, 26 June 1996
(Wembley)

England	(1) 1	Germany	(1) 1
Shearer		Kuntz	

(Germany won 6–5 on penalties)

★ Seaman, Ince, Pearce, Platt, Adams, Southgate, Anderton, Gascoigne, Shearer, Sheringham, McManaman

★ Köpke, Sammer, Reuter, Babbel, Helmer (Bode), Ziege, Freund (Strunz), Eilts, Scholl (Hässler), Möller, Kuntz

European Championship Group Match, 17 June 2000
(Charleroi, Belgium)

Germany	(0) 0	England	(0) 1
		Shearer	

★ Kahn, Babbel, Matthäus, Nowotny, Deisler (Ballack), Scholl, Hamann, Jeremies (Bode), Ziege, Kirsten (Rink), Jancker.
★ Seaman, G. Neville, Keown, Campbell, P. Neville, Beckham, Scholes (Barmby), Ince, Wise, Shearer, Owen (Gerard)

appendix 2: goalscorers

England

3 Goals
Geoff Hurst

2 Goals
Cliff Bastin
Joe Bradford
George Camsell
Kerry Dixon
Gary Lineker
Martin Peters
Jackie Robinson
Alan Shearer

1 Goal
Ronnie Allen
Colin Bell
Roy Bentley
Frank Broome
Duncan Edwards
Len Goulden
Colin Grainger
Johnny Haynes
David Jack
Francis Lee

West Germany/Germany

3 Goals
Richard Hofmann

2 Goals
Franz Beckenbauer
Pierre Littbarski
Karl-Heinz Rummenigge

1 Goal
Alfred Beck
Rainer Bonhof
Andreas Brehme
Stefan Effenberg
Josef Gauchel
Rudolf Gellesch
Helmut Haller
Uli Hoeness
Jurgen Klinsmann
Stefan Kuntz

Malcolm Macdonald

Stanley Matthews

Alan Mullery

Terry Paine

Stuart Pearson

David Platt

Bryan Robson

Len Shackleton

Nobby Stiles

Tony Woodcock

Günter Netzer

Hans Pesser

Karlheinz Riedle

Uwe Seeler

Fritz Walter

Wolfgang Weber

Ronald Worm

Wolfram Wuttke

appendix 3: national-team managers (1926–2000)

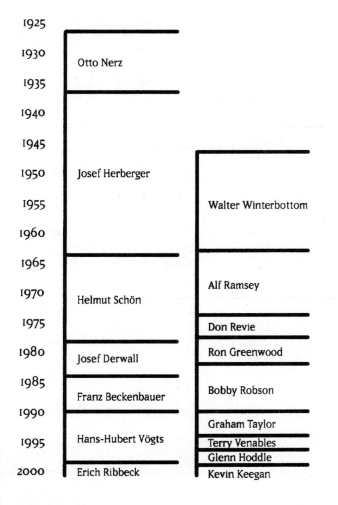

1925		
1930	Otto Nerz	
1935		
1940		
1945		
1950	Josef Herberger	
1955		Walter Winterbottom
1960		
1965		
1970	Helmut Schön	Alf Ramsey
1975		Don Revie
1980	Josef Derwall	Ron Greenwood
1985	Franz Beckenbauer	Bobby Robson
1990		Graham Taylor
1995	Hans-Hubert Vögts	Terry Venables
		Glenn Hoddle
2000	Erich Ribbeck	Kevin Keegan

appendix 4: world cup
performances 1954–98

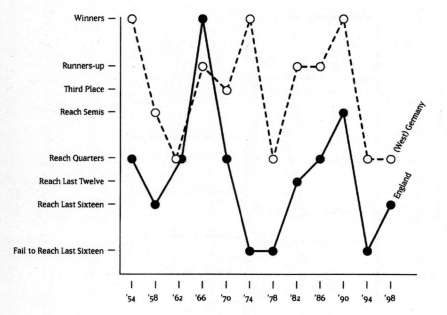

appendix 5: european championship performances 1964–2000

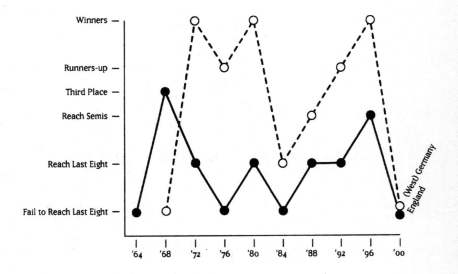

appendix 6: england v. east germany (all friendlies)

29 June 1963
(Leipzig)

East Germany	(1) 1	England	(1) 2
P. Ducke		Hunt, R. Charlton	

* Banks, Armfield, Wilson, Milne, Norman, Moore, Paine, Hunt, Smith, Eastham, R. Charlton

*Fritsche, Urbanczyk, Krampe, Kaiser, Heine, Liebrecht, Nachtigall, Frenzel, Ducke, Nöldner, R. Ducke

25 November 1970
(Wembley)

England	(2) 3	East Germany	(1) 1
Lee, Peters, Clarke		Vogel	

* Shilton, Hughes, Cooper, Mullery, Sadler, Moore, Lee, Ball, Hurst, Clarke, Peters

* Croy, Kurbjuweit, Rock, Sammer, Ganzera, Strempel (Frenzel), Stein, Irmscher, P. Ducke, Kreische, Vogel

29 May 1974
(Leipzig)

East Germany	(0) 1	England	(0) 1
Streich		Channon	

★ Croy, Fritsche, Bransch, Weise, Wätzlich, Pommerenke, Irmscher, Löwe, Streich, Sparwasser, Vogel (Hoffmann)
★ Clemence, Hughes, Lindsay, Todd, Watson, Dobson, Keegan, Channon, Worthington, Bell, Brooking

12 September 1984
(Wembley)

England	(0) 1	East Germany	(1) 0
Robson			

★ Shilton, Duxbury, Sansom, Williams, Wright, Butcher, Robson, Wilkins, Mariner (Hateley), Woodcock (Francis), J. Barnes
★ Müller, Kreer, Dorner, Stahmann, Zotzsche, Troppa, Leibers, teinbach, Streich (Richter), Ernst, Minge

appendix 7: anglo-german meetings in european club competitions (finals and semi-finals)

1964–5	West Ham v. Munich 1860	ECWC (F)	2–0
1965–6	Liverpool v. Borussia Dortmund	ECWC (F)	1–2
	West Ham v. Borussia Dortmund	ECWC (SF)	1–2 (h), 1–3 (a)
1969–70	Manchester City v. Schalke	ECWC (SF)	0–1 (a), 5–1 (h)
1972–3	Liverpool v. Bor. Mönchengladbach	UEFA (F)	3–0 (h), 0–2 (a)
1974–5	Leeds v. Bayern Munich	EC (F)	0–2
1975–6	West Ham v. Eintracht Frankfurt	ECWC (SF)	1–2 (a), 3–1 (h)
1976–7	Liverpool v. Bor. Mönchengladbach	EC (F)	3–1
1977–8	Liverpool v. Bor. Mönchengladbach	EC (SF)	1–2 (a), 3–0 (h)
1978–9	Nottingham Forest v. FC Cologne	EC (SF)	3–3 (h), 1–0 (a)
1979–80	Nottingham Forest v. Hamburg	EC (F)	1–0
1980–1	Ipswich v. FC Cologne	EC (SF)	0–0 (h), 1–1 (a)
1981–2	Aston Villa v. Bayern Munich	EC (F)	1–0
1984–5	Everton v. Bayern Munich	ECWC (SF)	0–0 (a), 3–1 (h)
1996–7	Manchester Utd v. Borussia Dortmund	EC (SF)	0–1 (a), 0–1 (h)
1997–8	Chelsea v. Stuttgart	ECWC (F)	1–0
1998–9	Manchester Utd v. Bayern Munich	ECL (F)	2–1

EC = European Cup
ECL = European Champion's League
ECWC = European Cup-Winners' Cup
F = final
SF = semi-final
UEFA = Union of European Football Associations
(a) = away
(h) = home

appendix 8: record of anglo–west german/german head-to-heads in european club competitions

	1956–57–1969–70	1970–1–1979–80	1980–1–1989–90	1990–1–1999–2000
Bayern Munich		WLWW	LLWLL	LWL
Borussia Dortmund	LLWW			W
Bor. Möchengladbach		LLLLW		W
FC Cologne	LWL	WLLL	L	
Eintracht Frankfurt	WL	LL	L	
Hamburg	W	L	W	
Hannover 96	L			
Kaiserslautern		W	L	WW
Munich 1860	LLL			
Nuremberg	L			
Schalke 04	WL			
Stuttgart	L			LL
Werder Bremen				L
	6W–12L	6W–11L	2W–7L	5W–5L
Arsenal		L		LW
Aston Villa			W	
Birmingham City	W			
Burnley	LWL			
Chelsea	W			W
Coventry City		L		
Everton	W	W	W	
Ipswich Town			W	
Leeds United	W	L		W
Liverpool	WLW	WLWWWW	W	
Manchester City	W	L		
Manchester United	WW			LW
Norwich City				W
Nottingham Forest	W	WW		L
QPR		W		
Sheffield Wednesday	L			L
Southampton			L	
Stoke City		L		
Tottenham Hotspur		W	WLW	L
Watford			W	
West Ham United	WL	W		
Wolverhampton W.	L			
	12W–5L	11W–6L	7W–2L	5W–5L

select bibliography

Football

Banks, Gordon *Banks for England* (1980) Arthur Barker
Bastin, Cliff *Cliff Bastin remembers* (1950) Ettrick Press
Beck, Peter *Scoring for Britain* (1999) Frank Cass
Buchan, Charles *A Lifetime in Football* (1955) Phoenix House
Charlton, Bobby *Forward for England* (1967) Pelham
Clayton, Ronnie *A Slave – to Soccer* (1960) Stanley Paul
Davies, Pete *All Played Out* (1990) Heinemann
Finney, Tom *Finney on Football* (1958) Nicholas Kaye
Fishwick, Nicholas *English Football and Society* (1989) Manchester
    University Press
Giraul, Claude ed. *100 European Cups* (1992) Burlington
Glanville, Brian *The Story of the World Cup* (1997) Faber and Faber
Glanville, Brian *Champions of Europe* (1991) Guinness
Glanville, Brian *Soccer Nemesis* (1955) Secker & Warburg
Greenwood, Ron *Yours Sincerely* (1984) Willow
Hapgood, Eddie *Football Ambassador* (1944) Sporting Handbooks
Haynes, Johnny *Football Today* (1961) Arthur Barker
Hurst, Geoff *The World Game* (1967) Stanley Paul
Hutchinson, Roger *It is now!* (1995) Mainstream
Keegan, Kevin *My Autobiography* (1997) Little, Brown
Kicker magazine, *Fussball Almanach 2000* (1999) Copress Verlag Munchen
Kuper, Simon *Football Against The Enemy* (1996) Phoenix
Matthews, Stanley *Feet First* (1948) Ewen & Dale
Matthews, Stanley *The Way It Was* (2000) Headline

Meisl, Willy *Soccer revolution* (1957) Phoenix Sports Book
Payne, Mike *England: The Complete Post-war Record* (1993) Breedon
Ramsey, Alf *Talking Football* (1952) Stanley Paul
Robinson, John *The European Football Championships 1958–96* (1996)
   Soccer Book
Robson, Bobby *Against the Odds* (1990) Stanley Paul
Rollin, Jack ed. *Rothmans Book of Football Records* (1998) Headline
Rous, Stanley *Football Worlds* (1978) Faber
Rowlands, Alan *Bert Trautmann* (1990) Breedon
Russell, Dave *Football and the English* (1997) Carnegie
Schumacher, Toni *Blowing the Whistle* (1988) Star
Shackleton, Len *Clown Prince of Soccer* (1955) Nicholas Kaye
Trautmann, Bert *Steppes to Wembley* (1956) Hamilton & Co.
Wall, Frederick *Fifty Years of Football* (1935) Cassell & Co.
Walvin, James *The People's Game* (1994) Mainstream
Wangerin, Dave *The Fussball Book* (1990) Perton
Woodcock, Tony *Inside Soccer* (1985) Queen Anne
Wright, Billy *Football is My Passport* (1957) Stanley Paul

Anglo–German relations and stereotypes

Ballance, Dinah *Anglo-German Attitudes* (1992) Goethe Institute
Calder, Angus *The Myth of the Blitz* (1991) Jonathan Cape
Eich, Hermann *The Unloved Germans* (1965) Macdonald
Husemann, Harald *As Others See Us* (1994) P. Lang
Kennedy, Paul *The Rise of Anglo-German Antagonism 1860–1914* (1987)
   Ashfield
Kohn, Hans *The Mind of Germany* (1960) Charles Scribner's Sons
Mander, John *Our German Cousins* (1974) J. Murray
Mommsen, Wolfgang *Two Centuries of Anglo-German Relations* (1984)
German Historical Institute
Paxman, Jeremy *The English* (1998) Michael Joseph
Ziegler, Hans *We Germans and Our British Cousins* (1909) Wilhelm
   Suesserott

index

a note on the author

David Downing is the author of several acclaimed works on twentieth-century history, biographies, and of fiction. His previous book, *Passovotchka: Moscow Dynamo in Britain, 1945* is also published by Bloomsbury. The holder of a Master's degree in international relations, he has travelled extensively, particularly in Eastern Europe and the former Soviet Union. He currently divides his time between Britain and the US.

a note on the type

The text of this book is set in Bembo. The original types for which were cut by Francesco Griffo for the Venetian printer Aldus Manutius, and were first used in 1495 for Cardinal Bembo's *De Aetna*. Claude Garamond (1480–1561) used Bembo as a model and so it became the forerunner of standard European type for the following two centuries. Its modern form was designed, following the original, for Monotype in 1929 and is widely in use today.